THE MĀṆḌŪKYA UPANIṢAD AND THE ĀGAMA ŚĀSTRA

THE MĀṆḌŪKYA UPANIṢAD AND THE ĀGAMA ŚĀSTRA

AN INVESTIGATION INTO THE MEANING OF THE VEDĀNTA

Thomas E. Wood

MOTILAL BANARSIDASS PUBLISHERS
PRIVATE LIMITED • DELHI

First Indian Edition: Delhi, 1992

ISBN: 81-208-0930-0

Also available at:
MOTILAL BANARSIDASS
41 U.A. Bungalow Road, Jawahar Nagar, Delhi 110 007
120 Royapettah High Road, Mylapore, Madras 600 004
16 St. Mark's Road, Bangalore 560 001
Ashok Rajpath, Patna 800 004
Chowk, Varanasi 221 001

PRINTED IN INDIA

BY JAINENDRA PRAKASH JAIN AT SHRI JAINENDRA PRESS, A-45 NARAINA INDUSTRIAL AREA, PHASE I, NEW DELHI 110 0: AND PUBLISHED BY NARENDRA PRAKASH JAIN FOR MOTILAL BANARSIDASS PUBLISHERS PVT. LTD., BUNGALOW ROAD, JAWAHAR NAGAR, DELHI 110 007

TO MY PARENTS

who have been very patient

suṣuptyutkrāntyor bhedena
Because of the difference between sleeping and rising up (from the body).

patyādi śabdebhyaḥ
Because of the words "the Lord" etc.

Brahmasūtra 1.3.42-43

CONTENTS

PART III

APPENDIXES
(transliterated Sanskrit texts)

ABBREVIATIONS

Ait.	Aitareya Upaniṣad
ADP	Advaita-prakaraṇa
ALP	Alāta-śānti-prakaraṇa
ĀP	Āgama-prakaraṇa
ĀŚ	Āgama-śāstra
ĀŚV	Āgama-śāstra-vivaraṇa
BG	Bhagavad-gītā
Bṛhad., BU	Bṛhad-āraṇyakopaniṣad
BS	Brahma-sūtra
BSB	Brahma-sūtra-bhāṣya (Śaṃkara)
BUB	Bṛhad-āraṇyakopaniṣad-bhāṣya (Śaṃkara)
BV	Bṛhad-āraṇyakopaniṣad-bhāṣya-vārttika
BVT	Bṛhad-āraṇyakopaniṣad-bhāṣya-vārttika-ṭīkā
Chānd.	Chāndogya Upaniṣad
CUB	Chāndogyopaniṣad-bhāṣya (Śaṃkara)
ĪU	Īśāvāsya Upaniṣad (Īśopaniṣad)
GK	Gauḍapādīya-kārikās (= ĀŚ)
Kauṣ.	Kauṣītakī Upaniṣad
MAK(P)	Madhyamakālaṅkāra-kārikā-(pañjikā)
Māṇḍ.	Māṇḍūkya Upaniṣad
MHK(V)	Madhyamaka-hṛdaya-kārikā-(vṛtti)
MK	Māṇḍūkya Kārikās (= ĀŚ)
MMK(V)	Mūla-madhyamaka-kārikā-(vṛtti)
MN	Majjhima-nikāya
NKS	Naiṣkarmya-siddhi
NPTU	Nṛsiṃha-pūrva-tāpanīya Upaniṣad
NPV	Nārada-parivrājaka Upaniṣad

NUTU	Nṛsiṃhottara-tāpanīya Upaniṣad
Pra.	Praśna Upaniṣad
RUTU	Rāmottara-tāpanīya Upaniṣad
TS(P)	Tattva-saṃgraha-(pañjikā)
TU, Tait.	Taittirīya Upaniṣad
US	Upadeśa-sāhasrī
VP	Vaitathya-prakaraṇa

INTRODUCTION

The Upaniṣads are the concluding texts of the body of religious literature in India called the Vedas. They are the root texts of the Vedānta, which literally means "the end or culmination of the Vedas."

The Māṇḍūkya Upaniṣad itself is one of the classical (pre-Śaṃkara) Upaniṣads. It is not known when or by whom it was written, but since it predates Śaṃkara it must have been written sometime before the latter part of the 8th century C.E. or even before the 7th century C.E., depending on how one dates Śaṃkara himself.

Despite its exceptional brevity, the Māṇḍūkya is an important Upaniṣad because it is a compendium of the teachings of some of the classical Upaniṣads that predate it. It is also important because it has played a very important role in the history of the Śaṃkara, or nondual (*advaita*), school of the Vedānta. To a large extent, this is due to the close connection that has existed historically between the Māṇḍūkya and another work known as the Āgama-śāstra, also called the "Verses of Gauḍapāda" (*Gauḍapādīya-kārikā*), after the man — about whom we know very little — who is thought to have been its author.

Although it can be shown that the Māṇḍūkya is an independent text, it is not usually *found* as an independent text in the Sanskrit manuscripts themselves. In most cases the Māṇḍūkya is found embedded within twenty-nine memorial verses (*kārikās*) which form a commentary on it — a fact which considerably complicates the task of properly interpreting the Māṇḍūkya itself. To complicate matters further, the Māṇḍūkya and these twenty-nine *kārikās* are often found in the manuscripts as merely the first of four *prakaraṇas* (treatises, chapters) of the aforementioned work, the Āgama-śāstra. When the Māṇḍūkya and the twenty-nine commentarial verses are associated with these other three treatises or chapters (*prakaraṇas*), they are often referred to together as the Āgama-prakaraṇa, i.e. as the Āgamic chapter or treatise of the work called the Āgama-śāstra.

The Śaṃkara school includes Gauḍapāda, the reputed author of the Āgama-śāstra, in its lineage of teachers. According to its traditions, Gauḍapāda was the teacher (*guru*) of a man named Govindapādācārya, who in turn was the *guru* of Śaṃkara. These traditions also assert that the Āgama-śāstra-vivaraṇa — the oldest and most important commentary on the Āgama-śāstra — was written by Ādi Śaṃkara himself.

For the most part, modern scholarship has accepted both parts of this tradition. It has also accepted, by and large, the Śaṃkara school's interpretation of the Māṇḍūkya and the Āgama-śāstra.

According to the Śaṃkara or *advaita* school of the Vedānta, the world is an illusion (*māyā*), and only the nondual absolute (*brahman*) is real. This school draws a sharp distinction, not only between *brahman* and the world, but also between *brahman* and God (*īśvara*). According to Śaṃkara, God is just as real as the world itself is but no more: i.e., God is phenomenally real but ultimately unreal. This school does not reject the theism of the Vedas and the Vedānta, but it holds that *īśvara* belongs only to the purely phenomenal realm (*prapañca*). Consequently, the doctrine of the Śaṃkara school can be said to be a theistic one only at the level of phenomenal or relative truth.

The radical nature of this teaching is nowhere more apparent than when it is applied to the Māṇḍūkya. This Upaniṣad is essentially an epitome or compendium of the teachings of the earlier Upaniṣads, expressed in terms of the doctrine of the four states of the self: waking, dreaming, sleeping and an absolute state of the self which is called simply the fourth (*caturtha*).

Where would God fit into this Upaniṣadic doctrine of the four states of the self? Since the Śaṃkara school holds that God has only a phenomenal reality, it cannot assign God (*īśvara*) to the fourth or absolute state of the self. Instead, it associates *īśvara* with the third (*tṛtīya*) state of the self, i.e. with the state of deep sleep, which is held to be a state of ignorance, or rather the very root of ignorance. (Since the Śaṃkara school's interpretation of the Māṇḍūkya associates the *tṛtīya*, or third state of the self, with *īśvara*, I refer to it as the TI interpretation.) The TI interpretation of the Māṇḍūkya is in sharp contrast with another possible interpretation of the Upaniṣad, which associates *īśvara* with the fourth (*caturtha*) or absolute state of the self (and which I therefore call the IC interpretation of the Māṇḍūkya).

The Śaṃkara school's interpretation of the Māṇḍūkya raises some serious philosophical questions (some of which I address in the last chapter of the present work), but it also raises interpretational and historical problems as well.

One of the problems, as I argue in Chapters 1 and 2 of Part I, is that the Āgama-prakaraṇa (the first part of the Āgama-śāstra) and the Upaniṣads which postdate the Māṇḍūkya do not unequivocally support the TI interpretation of the four states of the self. The same point is made in Chapter 3 about a number of other medieval commentaries and treatises which have something to say, directly or indirectly, about the interpretation of the Māṇḍūkya.

The strongest evidence against the TI interpretation, however, is found in Upaniṣads that *predate* the Māṇḍūkya or were roughly contemporaneous with it. Chapters 4 and 5 show that earlier Upaniṣads clearly favor the IC interpretation of the Māṇḍūkya, and Chapter 6 makes the same point about the Maitrī Upaniṣad, a late classical Upaniṣad which was probably written about the same time as the Māṇḍūkya.

These results raise a number of historical, textual and doctrinal problems connected with the authorship of the Āgama-śāstra and its most important commentary, the Āgama-śāstra-vivaraṇa. The chapters of Part II focus more directly on these problems. My conclusions on these matters are largely opposed to the prevailing scholarly views and the traditions of the Śaṃkara school.

First, I argue that the Āgama-śāstra itself is a quartet of treatises, rather than a single work in four chapters (Chapter 9). Secondly, I argue that the Āgama-śāstra (including the Āgama-prakaraṇa) was probably not written by the *parama-guru* of Śaṃkara (Chapters 7-8, 11-12). Thirdly, I argue that Śaṃkara was not the author of the Āgama-śāstra-vivaraṇa (Chapter 10). Chapter 13 then presents a new theory about the authorship of the Āgama-śāstra, the Āgama-śāstra-vivaraṇa and the history of the TI interpretation of the Māṇḍūkya which I feel is more plausible than the traditional and commonly received view.

I conclude the monograph in Chapter 14 of Part III with a discussion of the philosophy which I believe underlies the Māṇḍūkya. My interpretation of the philosophy of the Māṇḍūkya is based on the IC interpretation of the Upaniṣad. I do not attempt to defend this philosophical doctrine directly, but I do argue that it is a different doctrine — and philosophically a more tenable doctrine —

than the *māyā* doctrine of the Śaṃkara school which has been superimposed on it.

The Appendix contains translations of the Māṇḍūkya and the four *prakaraṇas* of the Āgama-śāstra: the Āgama-prakaraṇa, the Vaitathya-prakaraṇa, the Advaita-prakaraṇa and the Alata-śānti-prakaraṇa. A glossary of some important Sanskrit terms has also been provided.

PART I

I

The Māṇḍūkya is a very short Upaniṣad that consists of a mere twelve sentences (*muntras*). The transliterated Sanskrit of the Upaniṣad as an independent text is given on p. 165 in the Appendix. A translation of the Upaniṣad is given below.

***

1. *Aum*: this syllable is all this. A clear exposition of it is: what was, what is and what will be — all is only *Aum*. And whatever else is beyond is beyond the three times, that also is only *Aum*.

2. All this, indeed, is *brahman*. This Self is *brahman*. This Self itself has four quarters.

3. The waking state (*jāgarita-sthāna*), outwardly cognitive, having seven limbs, having nineteen mouths, enjoying the gross, the universal (*vaiśvānara*): this is the first quarter.

4. The dreaming state (*svapna-sthāna*), inwardly cognitive, having seven limbs, having nineteen mouths, enjoying the refined, the brilliant (*taijasa*): this is the second quarter.

5. Where one, asleep, does not desire any desire whatever, sees no dream whatever, that is deep sleep (*suṣupta*). The sleeping state, which has become one, just a cognition mass, made of bliss, verily an enjoyer of bliss, whose face is thought: *prājña* is the third quarter.

6. This is the lord (*īśvara*) of all; this is the knower of all; this is the inner controller (*antaryāmin*); this is the source of all; indeed the origin as well as the end of all beings.

7. Not inwardly cognitive, not outwardly cognitive, not cognitive both ways, not a cognition mass, not cognitive, not noncognitive, unseen, beyond speech, ungraspable, without any distinctive marks, unthinkable, undesignatable, the essence of the knowledge of the one Self, the cessation of the phenomenal world (*prapañcopaśama*), quiescent, auspicious,

nondual (*advaita*) — such, they think, is the fourth (*caturtha*). He is the Self (*ātman*). He is to be known.

8. This is the Self with regard to the syllable "*Aum*," with regard to the elements (*mātrās*): the quarters are the elements and the elements are the quarters, i.e. the letter *a*, the letter *u*, the letter *m*.

9. *Vaiśvānara* (the universal) is the waking state, the letter *a*, the first element, either from "*āpti*" (obtaining) or from "*ādimattva*" (being first). Verily, he obtains (*āpnoti*) all desires and becomes first (*ādi*) — he who knows this.

10. *Taijasa* (the brilliant) is the dreaming state, the letter *u*, the second element, either from "*utkarṣa*" (exaltation) or from "*ubhayatva*" (intermediateness). Verily, he exalts the stream of knowledge and becomes equal-minded; no one ignorant of *brahman* is born in the family of him who knows this.

11. *Prājña* is the sleeping state, the letter *m*, the third element, either from "*miti*" (measuring) or from "*apīti*" (merging). Verily, he measures this all and he becomes its merging — he who knows this.

12. The fourth (*caturtha*) is what is without an element, what cannot be dealt with or spoken of, the cessation of the phenomenal world (*prapañcopaśama*), auspicious, nondual. Thus *Aum* is the very Self. He enters the Self with the Self — he who knows this.

***

In the first part of the Māṇḍūkya, five *mantras* (3-7) are used to describe four different states of the self. Three of the states are described by one *mantra* each, whereas one of the states is described by two *mantras*. But which one? The first two states of waking and dreaming are straightforward, as they are clearly described by one *mantra* each, i.e. 3 and 4. However, 5-7, and especially 6, are problematic. *Mantra* 7 describes the fourth state and 5 describes the dreaming state, but to which state does 6 belong?

Here there are two possibilities. On the one hand, Māṇḍ. 6 could be linked with Māṇḍ. 5. This reading, which would link *īśvara* with the third (*tṛtīya*) state of the Self, I shall call the TI interpretation. Alternatively, Māṇḍ. 6 could be linked with Māṇḍ. 7. This reading, which links *īśvara* with the fourth (*caturtha*) state of the Self, I shall call the IC interpretation.

Every modern scholar who has discussed these *mantras* in any detail appears to have assumed that *mantra* 6 belongs with *mantra* 5 rather than with 7. Indeed, the severance of the concept of *īśvara* (God) from that of the Absolute is always taken as the most distinctive and historically most important feature of the Māṇḍūkya. Thus, Belvalkar and Ranade say of the Māṇḍūkya:

> It is significant to remember that the Prājña has been called (M.6) the Lord of all, the all-knowing, the inner controller, the source of all, the origin and end of all Being. In fact, the Prājña, to the author of the Māṇḍūkya signifies what philosophy calls God. As contrasted with him, stands the Ātman, which is the Upanishadic equivalent of what philosophy calls the Absolute...It is worth noting that God is sundered here from the Absolute as with a hatchet, and ultimate reality assigned only to the Absolute and not to God, who is described as merely the Absolute gone to sleep; while in the Absolute the whole world (Prapañcha) is described as being annihilated, since the Absolute is one without a second (Advaita), characterized only in negative terms.[1]

Essentially the same idea is found in every modern scholarly work on this Upaniṣad with which I am familiar.[2]

The fact that modern scholars have accepted — or simply taken for granted — the TI interpretation of the Māṇḍūkya has undoubtedly been due, at least in part, to their acceptance of the traditions of the Śaṃkara school of the Vedānta. These traditions trace the TI interpretation of the Māṇḍūkya back to the oldest extant commentary on the Māṇḍūkya. This commentary consists of twenty-nine verses, and forms the first *prakaraṇa* (treatise, chapter) of a work on the Vedānta called the "Āgama-śāstra." According to the present views of the *paṇḍits* of the Śaṃkara school, these verses were written by a man name Gauḍapāda, who is said to have been the *guru* of Śaṃkara's own *guru*, Govinda. Indeed, the verses of the Āgama-śāstra are often referred to as the "Verses of Gauḍapāda" (*Gauḍapādīya-kārikās*).

These traditions raise issues which are of interest both to modern scholars and to the adherents of the other schools of the Vedānta because the Māṇḍūkya is usually found in the Sanskrit manuscripts embedded in these twenty-nine verses. In the texts which present the Māṇḍūkya in this way, the arrangement is invariably as follows:

(1) Māṇḍ. 1-6, followed by *kārikās* 1-9
(2) Māṇḍ. 7, followed by *kārikās* 10-18
(3) Māṇḍ. 8-11, followed by *kārikās* 19-23
(4) Māṇḍ. 12, followed by *kārikās* 24-29.

In other words, *kārikās* 1-9 are a commentary on Māṇḍ. 1-6; *kārikās* 10-18 are a commentary on Māṇḍ. 7; *kārikās* 19-23 are a commentary on Māṇḍ. 8-11; and *kārikās* 24-29 are a commentary on Māṇḍ. 12. The four sets of *kārikās* are on each occasion introduced by the phrase "Here appear the following verses" (*atraite ślokā bhavanti*). The transliterated Sanskrit text is given on pp. 167-169 in the Appendix. A translation of the verses is given below:

***

(*kārikās* 1-9 appear after Māṇḍ. 1-6)
atraite ślokā bhavanti
("Here appear the following verses")

1. *Viśva* (the waking state) is the all-pervading which is outward-cognizing; *taijasa* (the dreaming state) is the inward-cognizing; *prājña* (the sleeping state), likewise, is a mass of cognition. One alone is said to exist three-fold.

2. *Viśva* is in the face, in the right eye. *Taijasa*, however, is inside the mind. And *prājña* is in the space in the heart. It exists in the body in three ways.

3. *Viśva*, indeed, is always the enjoyer of the gross, *taijasa* is the enjoyer of the refined; *prājña*, likewise, is the enjoyer of bliss. Know the three-fold enjoyment.

4. The gross satisfies *viśva*; the refined, again, satisfies *taijasa*; and bliss, likewise, satisfies *prājña*. Know satisfaction to be three-fold.

5. He, again, who knows these two — that which is praised as the object of enjoyment and as the enjoyer in the three states — he, enjoying, is not stained.

6. The origin of all the entities that exist is the well-established conclusion of the Vedānta. The life force (*prāṇa*) gives birth to all; the Lord (*puruṣa*) gives birth to the separate rays of the mind.

7. Other creation-theorists, however, think that creation is the manifested power of the Lord. Creation is imagined by others to be of the same nature as dream and magic (*svapna-māyā*).

8. "Creation is the mere will of the Lord (*prabhu*)," say those who are convinced about creation. The time-theorists think that creation of entities is from time.

9. Others say: "Creation is the object of enjoyment." And others say: "It is the object of play or sport." This is the self-nature (*svabhāva*) of that effulgent being (*deva*). What desire could there be for the one who has attained all desires (*āpta-kāmasya*)?

(*kārikās* 10-18 appear after Māṇḍ. 7)
atraite ślokā bhavanti
("Here appear the following verses")

10. The ordainer (*īśāna*) of the cessation of all suffering, the Lord (*prabhu*), immutable, without a second (*advaita*), the god (*deva*) of all beings : *turya* (the fourth) is traditionally held to be all-pervading.

11. These two — *viśva* and *taijasa* — are considered to be bound by cause and effect. *Prājña*, on the other hand, is bound by cause alone. These two do not exist in *turya*.

12. Neither the Self, nor others, nor truth nor even untruth: *prājña* knows nothing. *Turya* is always all-seeing.

13. Non-perception of duality is common to both *prājña* and *turya*. *Prājña* is bound up with the seed-sleep. But it does not exist in *turya*.

14. The first two (i.e. waking and dreaming) are joined with dream and sleep; *prājña*, on the other hand, is bound with sleep but not with dream. Those with firm conviction see neither sleep nor even dream in *turya*.

15. Dream is for one comprehending otherwise (i.e. falsely); sleep is for one who does not know reality (*tattva*). When these two errors are destroyed, one attains *turīya*.

16. When the individual who is asleep owing to the beginningless illusion awakens, then he awakens to the birthless, sleepless, dreamless nonduality.

17. The phenomenal world (*prapañca*) would no doubt disappear if it existed. This duality is made of magic (*māyā*). Nonduality is the highest truth.

18. If imagination were imagined by anyone it would disappear. This doctrine is for the purpose of instruction. When known, duality does not exist.

(*kārikās* 19-23 appear after Māṇḍ. 11)
atraite ślokā bhavanti
("Here appear the following verses")

19. When the "A-ness" (*a̱tva*) of the waking state (*viśva*) is intended, the common quality of being first (*a̱di*) is patent. And

when the element is spoken, the common quality of being obtained (*āpti*) would be evident.

20. It is evident that when there is knowledge of the "U-ness" (*utva*) of the waking state, exaltation or superiority (*utkarṣa*) is seen. And when the element is spoken, the quality of being intermediate (*ubhayatva*) is evident.

21. In regard to *prājña's* being the letter *m*, the common quality of measurement (*māna*) is evident. When the element is spoken or meditated upon, on the other hand, the common quality of merging (*laya*) is evident.

22. The man of conviction who knows the equal and common quality in each of the three states, he, the wise one, is worthy of the adoration and worship of all beings.

23. The letter *a* leads to the waking state (*viśva*); and the letter *u*, as well, leads to the dreaming state (*taijasa*); the letter *m*, again, leads to the state of deep sleep (*prājña*). There is no goal in what has no element.

(*kārikās* 24-29 appear after Māṇḍ. 12)
atraite ślokā bhavanti
("Here appear the following verses")

24. One should know the *Auṃkāra* quarter by quarter: there is no doubt that the quarters are the elements. Having known *Auṃkāra* quarter by quarter, one should not think of anything whatever.

25. One should fix the mind on *praṇava* (*Aum*); *praṇava* is the fearless *brahman*. There is no fear anywhere for him who is fixed upon *praṇava*.

26. *Praṇava* is, indeed, the lower *brahman*, and it is traditionally regarded as the higher *brahman*. *Praṇava* is unique, without cause, without precedent, without inside, without outside, absolute, immutable.

27. Verily, *praṇava* is the beginning, the middle and likewise the end of everything. Verily, having known *praṇava* thus, one immediately attains to it.

28. One should know *praṇava* indeed as God (*īśvara*) seated in the heart of all. Having thought of the all-pervading *Aum*, the wise one does not grieve.

29. One who has known *Aum*, which is soundless (*amātra*) and of infinite sound, the cessation of duality (*dvaitasyopaśama*), auspicious, is a sage and no other.

***

These verses need to be examined in the light of the aforementioned traditions of the Śaṃkara school. These traditions may be summarized as follows:

(1) The Āgama-prakaraṇa (like the other three *prakaraṇas* of the Āgama-śāstra) was written by Gauḍapāda. Gauḍapāda was the *parama-guru* of Ādi Śaṃkara, and the Āgama-śāstra as a whole is the earliest known work of the Śaṃkara (Māyāvāda or Advaita) school of the Vedānta.

(2) Gauḍapāda advocated what I have called the TI interpretation of the Māṇḍūkya, according to which only the transcendent *turīya* is real. *Īśvara*, on the other hand, is essentially connected with the ignorance of sleep, and is therefore only phenomenally rather than absolutely real.

(3) Finally, it is assumed that in giving this interpretation of the Māṇḍūkya Gauḍapāda did not create a new doctrine, but simply elucidated the plain meaning of the Māṇḍūkya itself.

If one examines the verses carefully, however, one will note problems that immediately throw doubt on the tradition, for the verses do not unequivocally support the TI interpretation of the Māṇḍūkya. Evidence for this contention can be found in (1) ĀP6-9; (2) ĀP 10 and 12; (3) ĀP 24-29; and (4) ĀP 2.

(1) *ĀP 6-9*. ĀP 6 begins with the assertion that the origin of all entities is the well-established conclusion (*viniścaya*) of the Vedānta. ĀP 6c-d - ĀP 8 then list a number of views about this origination: that the origination of the world is from the life-force

(*prāṇa*), from the Lord (*puruṣa*), from the Lord's power (*vibhūti*), from dreams and magic (*svapna-māyā*), from the mere will (*icchā-mātra*) of the Lord, and from time (*kāla*). ĀP 9 then lists the following three views as well: that creation is the object of enjoyment, that it is the object of play or sport (*krīḍā*), and that it is the self-nature (*svabhāva*) of "that effulgent being" (*deva*).

We should, on the commonly accepted view, be able to find clear evidence in these *kārikās* that Gauḍapāda drew a sharp distinction betwen God (*īśvara*) and the fourth, absolute state of the Self (*turīya ātman*). What we find instead, however, is a pretty clear *repudiation* of this illusionistic view.

Note that ĀP 6 begins the discussion with the remark that the origination (i.e. creation) of all things is the well-established conclusion of the Vedānta. It would certainly be odd for a writer to begin a teaching to the effect that *īśvara* and the world are (ultimately) unreal with such a remark. Nor is there any reason to think that the use of the term "*viniścaya*" (well-established) is ironic. In these *kārikās* various descriptions or accounts are given of the nature of *īśvara* as the cause of the phenomenal world. The author appears to be honestly acknowledging the diversity of opinion that existed within the Vedāntic tradition over this matter, but there is nothing in the text which suggests that he regarded such theories as confused or misguided. After all, the *kārikās* are a commentary on Māṇḍ. 6, which simply and straightforwardly asserts the existence of an ultimate cause which is God (*īśvara*), and there is no reason to think that the *kārikā-kāra* denies the reality of what is asserted by the *mantra* on which he is commenting. If there is any irony here at all, it occurs in ĀP 7c-d, where the view that the world is of the nature of dreams and magic is said to be imagined (vikalpita) by its proponents. The term "*vikalpita*" is not used in describing any other view in these four *kārikās*.[3] The other views are described with the rather different terms "*viniścaya*," "*sṛṣṭi-cintaka*," and "*viniścita*." ĀP 9, which surely represents the *kārikā-kāra's* own view (*siddhānta*), is mentioned without any comment whatever.

The oldest and most important commentary on the Āgama-śāstra is the Āgama-śāstra-vivaraṇa. This commentary endorses the TI interpretation of the Māṇḍūkya and is said to have been written by Ādi Śaṃkara himself. An analysis of the Āgama-śāstra-vivaraṇa's commentary on ĀP 7 shows how resistant the ĀP is to the TI interpretation. The ĀŚV takes the second half of the *kārikā* (which says that creation is imagined by some to be of the nature of dreams and magic) to be a criticism of the view which is found in the first half of ĀP 7, which says that creation is the *vibhūti* or manifested power of the Lord. Thus, the ĀŚV compares all the experiences in waking, dream and sleep to the illusions created by a conjurer in the Indian rope-trick, and it says that those who are interested in the highest reality (*turīyākhyaṃ paramārtha-tattvam*) are like the juggler who remains on the ground during the rope-trick, having veiled himself by his own illusion. Then it says: "What is imagined by the creation-theorists is (merely) of the nature of dreams and illusions" (*sṛṣṭi-cintakānām-evaite vikalpā ity-āha svapna-māyā-sarūpeti svapna-sarūpā māyā-sarūpā ceti*).

This interpretation of the *kārikā* is untenable because the first half of the *kārikā* speaks of "*other* creation-theorists who think that creation is due to the will of the Lord," and the second half refers to *others* who think that such creation is illusory, like dreams and magic tricks. So it is quite clear that the second half of the *kārikā* gives a view that *other* theorists hold, and not a view which is held by the *kārikā-kāra* vis-à-vis other proponents. Moreover, the two succeeding *kārikās* cite other views which are held by the "creation theorists," and it would have been wholly inappropriate for the *kārikā-kāra* to introduce his own view in the middle of this list.

Since the view that ĀP 6-9 are based on irony must be rejected, ĀP 9 must be taken as giving the correct view (*siddhānta*), i.e. the view of the *kārikā-kāra*. It is possible that the *siddhānta* is given by the doctrine of self-nature (*svabhāva-vāda*) of ĀP 9c-d only (so that the view that creation is the object of enjoyment or play is also rejected), but it seems more likely that the second half of the *kārikā* simply makes explicit what is implicit in the doctrine that creation is merely the play or sport of *īśvara*, i.e. that there can be no purpose or motive (*prayojana*) in creation, for the Lord is by definition beyond all desires. This is the view of the Brahma-sūtras. BS 2.1.32 and 2.1.33, for example, take the opponent (*pūrvapakṣin*) to argue that *brahman* cannot create, on the grounds that *brahman* cannot have a motive for doing so. The Brahma-sūtra attempts to refute this view by saying that creation is a mere sport to *brahman* (*lokavat tu līlā kaivalyam*).

In view of the above considerations, it is doubtful that any conclusions can be drawn in favor of the TI interpretation from the fact that the ĀP comments on Māṇḍ. 6 and Māṇḍ. 7 in two different sets of verses (i.e. ĀP 6-9 and ĀP 10-18, respectively). ĀP 9, in fact, provides a very elegant transition to Māṇḍ. 7 and to ĀP 10-18. Māṇḍ. 7 emphasizes the transcendent nature of *īśvara*, and it asserts that the source of all things is absolute and nondual. The view that creation is the self-nature or the *līlā* of the Supreme Being does not contradict this teaching: it complements it. *Brahman* can create the world through mere sport or play, and this sport or play is desireless. There is, therefore, no contradiction between the "positive" quality of being the creator and the "negative" quality of being "desireless." ĀP 9, in effect, connects the set of *kārikās* in which it appears with ĀP 10-18. Both sets appear to describe the fourth state of the Self.

(2) *ĀP 10-18* provide the ĀP's commentary on Māṇḍ. 7. If the *kārikā-kāra* supported the TI interpretation of the Māṇḍūkya, and drew a sharp distinction between *īśvara* (Māṇḍ. 6) and *turīya* (Māṇḍ. 7), then we ought to find in ĀP 10-18 that the *kārikā-kāra* describes the *turīya ātman* in purely negative terms, and that he refrains from using any "positive" terms which are applicable to the description of *īśvara*. But this we do not find. This comes out most clearly, perhaps, in ĀP 10, but the same thing is true of ĀP 12.

ĀP 10 says that the fourth (*turya*) is the Lord, the ordainer (*īśāna*), the one without a second, the immutable, the god (*deva*) of all beings, and all-pervading. This verse, which is a commentary on Māṇḍ. 7, quite deliberately combines both "negative" and "positive" descriptions of the fourth state of the self. Some of the descriptions belong with Māṇḍ. 6, e.g., "the ordainer" (*īśāna*), "the Lord" (*prabhu*), and "the god of all beings" (*sarvabhāvānāṃ deva*). Others belong with Māṇḍ. 7: e.g. "the cessation of all suffering" (*nivṛtteḥ sarva-duḥkhānām*), "immutable" (*avyaya*) and "nondual" (*advaita*). These combinations would make no sense if the *kārikā-kāra* had adhered to the TI interpretation of the Māṇḍūkya, but they are exactly what one would expect on the assumption that he adhered to the IC interpretation.

ĀP 12 also supports the IC interpretation of the Māṇḍūkya, for it says that the fourth state of the Self is omniscient. The only natural way of reading this is to link it with Māṇḍ. 6, which says that *īśvara* is omniscient. Consequently, ĀP 12 also supports the IC interpretation.

(3) *ĀP 24-29*. ĀP 24-29 comment on Māṇḍ. 12, which is concerned with the soundless (fourth) part of the mystic syllable *Aum*. If the *kārikā-kāra* favored the *IC* rather than the TI interpretation of the Māṇḍūkya, we would expect him to combine "positive" and "negative" attributes in his commentary on this *mantra*. As in the case of ĀP 10-18, this is what we do find.

For example, ĀP 26 says that *praṇava* (*Aum*) is both the higher and the lower *brahman*, and that it is unique, without cause, without inside, without outside, absolute and immutable. In this passage, the attributes "immutable" and "absolute" belong with Māṇḍ. 7, but the first part of the *kārikā* says that *Aum* is both the higher and the lower *brahman*, and the reference to the lower *brahman* associates the *praṇava* with Māṇḍūkya 6. There is no natural way of reading this statement according to the TI or Māyāvāda interpretations.

ĀP 27 says: "*Praṇava* is the beginning, middle and likewise the end of everything." This, too, clearly links Māṇḍ. 12 (and thereby Māṇḍ. 7) with Māṇḍ. 6, for it is Māṇḍ. 6 that describes *īśvara* as the "beginning and the end of all beings."

ĀP 28 says: "God (*īśvara*) is seated in the heart of all." Note the context here. ĀP 28 is a commentary on Māṇḍ. 12, which is concerned with the soundless (*amātra*) part of the syllable *Aum*, and this, in turn, corresponds to the *turīya ātman* which is described in Māṇḍ. 7. A reference to the *īśvara* who is "seated in the hearts of all" in this verse would therefore have been inappropriate if the *kārikā-kāra* had adhered to the TI interpretation of the Upaniṣad.

Finally, consider ĀP 29, which says that *Aum* is both soundless and of infinite sound and the cessation of duality. This verse also combines predominantly negative attributes (e.g. the term "soundless") with the positive quality of infinity (*anantamātra*).

(4) ĀP 2, which comments on Māṇḍ. 3-5, says:

> *Viśva* is in the face, in the right eye. *Taijasa*, however, is inside the mind. *Prājña* is in the sky in the heart. The Self exists in the body in three ways.

The assertion that the three states of waking, dreaming and sleeping are located *in the body* is implicit in the classical Upaniṣads.

As I shall argue later in chapters 4 and 5, this is in fact one of the strongest reasons for thinking that the Vedāntic tradition never identified the state of sleep either with *īśvara* or with *brahman*.

The IC interpretation of the Māṇḍūkya fits this verse very well, but the TI interpretion does not. For example, the Āgama-śāstra-vivaraṇa, which adheres to the TI interpretation, is forced to construe the term "*vaiśvānara*" in Māṇḍ. 3 to mean the cosmic or universal Virāj. However, there is no support for the view that the normal waking state of the self is identical with the cosmic Virāj in the classical Upaniṣads, for in these Upaniṣads the identification of the Self with the cosmic Virāj is reserved for the *turīya ātman*. In other words, ĀP 2 directly contradicts the ĀŚV's interpretation of Māṇḍ. 3, for ĀP 2 says explicitly that all three of the states of waking, dreaming and sleeping are located *in* the body, and it makes no sense to say that the universal or cosmic Virāj is *in* the body.

Thus, all the *kārikās* which we have considered provide support for the IC rather than the TI interpretation of the Māṇḍūkya. Before we reach the conclusion that the ĀP does not support the Māyāvāda, however, we must take a look at ĀP 17 and 18, which are very peculiar:

17. The phenomenal world (*prapañca*) would no doubt disappear if it existed. This duality is made of magic (*māyā*). Nonduality is the highest truth.

18. If imagination (*vikalpa*) were imagined by anyone it would disappear. This doctrine is for the purpose of instruction. When known, duality does not exist.

These verses *do* appear to support the Māyāvāda. According to these verses, the world does not exist. ĀP 17 uses this assertion, in fact, to show that the world cannot be said to disappear when the delusion of duality vanishes. The first half of this verse has the form "If it were the case that P, then it would be the case that Q," where the propositions P and Q are both false (as for example in the statement "If snow were blue, it would be the same color as the sky"). Just as snow is not blue and is not the same color as the sky, so also, the verse says, the world neither exists nor can be said to disappear.[4] ĀP 18 is, if anything, even more radical than ĀP 17, for it asserts that the world does not even have the ontological status of illusion or imagination (*vikalpa*).

These two verses certainly present problems for the IC interpretation of the Āgama-prakaraṇa. It must also be said, however, that they present problems for *any* interpretation of the ĀP. For example, the Āgama-śāstra is said to be a unitary work by a single author (Gauḍapāda), but ĀP 17 and 18 are very hard to account for on this assumption. ĀP 18 is contradicted by Vaitathya-prakaraṇa (VP) 12, which says: "The shining *ātman* imagines itself by itself through its own *māyā*; it alone cognizes the so-called entities; this is the well-established conclusion of the Vedānta." It is also contradicted by Vaitathya-prakaraṇa 13, which says: "The Lord (*prabhu*) diversifies other entities existing in the mind; outward-minded, he diversifies the well-defined things also. Thus does the Lord imagine." Similarly, ĀP 17 is contradicted by VP 18, which says: "As imagination (*vikalpa*) disappears when the rope is well-ascertained and there is the nonduality of the rope, so also when the *ātman* is well-ascertained."

The gravest problem with ĀP 17 and 18, however, is not textual: it is philosophical. How can the doctrine that the world is unreal account for the fact that we perceive the world, or, at the very least, that we perceive *something*? It will not do to say in reply that what we see is an illusion (*māyā*), for this explains nothing. How can something that is *totally* unreal be seen? As Descartes observed, even if you are dreaming the world, it must still be real *as a dream*.

It is interesting to compare ĀP 17 and 18 with ĀP 7. ĀP 7 has always puzzled scholars who favor the Śaṃkara school of the Vedānta, for, as we have seen, this *kārikā* clearly fails to endorse the *svapna-māyā* view of creation. Now the Māyāvādin might try to interpret ĀP 7 in the light of ĀP 17 and 18.[5] If one did this, one would get the result that the idea that the world is an illusion or a dream is not illusionistic enough, for the truth is that the world does not exist even as an imagination or as an illusion. Consequently, the doctrine of *māyā* becomes a *māyāvic* view, held by those who are still in the grip of *māyā*!

However, ĀP 7 will not support this interpretation. Note that ĀP 7 is a commentary on Māṇḍ. 6, which asserts that there *is* an *īśvara* or lord of all, a point which is underscored by ĀP 6, which asserts that the origin of the world from *īśvara* is a well-established conclusion of the Vedānta. In other words, using the present *kārikā* to interpret ĀP 7 could explain how the *svapna-māyā* view found its way into a list of creationist views (all of which are ultimately rejected), only at the cost of undermining the teaching about the origination of the world so completely that ĀP 6-10 could no longer be regarded as a commentary on Māṇḍ. 6. That this is not what the *kārikā-kāra* meant is shown very clearly by all of the evidence I have adduced in (1)-(4) above. Furthermore, this interpretation is totally implausible philosophically, for it provides, as I have just argued, no way of explaining even the *appearance* of the world.

ĀP 17 and 18 are, on any interpretation, anomalous. They certainly do not support the IC interpretation, but they create insuperable problems for any other interpretation as well. I think that ĀP 17-18 make it impossible to give a consistent interpretation of the ĀP, and I am therefore inclined to regard even the ĀP as a composite work.[6] Apart from these two verses, however, the ĀP does teach a consistent and coherent doctrine, and the consistent part of the teachings clearly favor the IC rather than the TI interpretation of the Māṇḍūkya.[7]

Since only ĀP 17 and 18 support the TI interpretation of the Māṇḍūkya, the ĀP does not, on the whole, support the illusionistic (*māyā-vāda*) interpretation of the Vedānta. This very fact raises problems for the traditions of the Śaṃkara school, which maintains that the author of the Āgama-prakaraṇa was Gauḍapāda, the earliest founder of the Śaṃkara school and the *parama-guru* of Ādi Śaṃkara. To defend this tradition, one would have to explain the fact that the great majority of the verses of the Āgama-prakaraṇa do *not* support the TI interpretation.

The situation is made even more confusing by the fact that the Māṇḍūkya and its twenty-nine commentarial verses are very frequently found as merely the first of four *prakaraṇas* (chapters, treatises) of the aforementioned work, the Āgama-śāstra. This fact raises additional interpretational and historical problems, for these *prakaraṇas*, taken as a whole, *do* give an unequivocal statement of the Māyāvāda interpretation of the Vedānta.

The second, third and fourth *prakaraṇas* of the Āgama-śāstra are known as the Vaitathya-prakaraṇa (VP), the Advaita-prakaraṇa (ADP) and the Alāta-śānti-prakaraṇa (ALP). These contain 38, 48 and 100 verses, respectively, and are given below. (The transliterated Sanskrit texts are given on pp. 171-189 in the Appendix.) Note that these *prakaraṇas*, unlike the Āgama-prakaraṇa, are in no sense direct commentaries (*bhāṣyas*) on the Māṇḍūkya.

***

VAITATHYA-PRAKARAṆA

1. Verily, the wise declare the unreality of all entities in dream, because of their location within, and because of their being enclosed.

2. Besides, one does not, having gone to places in dream, actually see things there, because of the shortness of time involved. Moreover, when awakened, no one is ever found to be in those places.

3. The absence of chariots etc. in dream is taught in the *śruti* from the standpoint of logic. They say that dream's unreality is established and revealed by that.

4. It is traditionally taught that, because of their interior location, entities in the waking state are thus unreal. As it is there, so it is in dream: the difference is in the state of being enclosed.

5. Verily, the wise say that the dream and waking states are one, on the basis of well-established reasoning concerning the sameness of the entities in the two states.

6. That which does not exist in the beginning and the end is such in the present also. Though on a par with things unreal, things are seen as if they were not unreal.

7. Their utility is contradicted in dream; therefore, because of their having a beginning and an end they are indeed traditionally known as unreal and nothing else.

8. Thus, indeed, the fixed characteristics of the dwellers in heaven is their *karma* (*apūrva*). This person, having gone

there, sees these entities, just as a well-informed person sees things here.

9. Even in the dream state, again, what is imagined by the mind within verily does not exist; what is apprehended by the mind outside does exist. The unreality of both these is seen.

10. Even in the waking state, again, what is imagined by the mind within verily does not exist; what is apprehended by the mind outside does exist. The unreality of both these is reasonable.

11. If there is unreality of the entities in *both* of these states, who cognizes the entities; who, indeed, imagines them?

12. The shining *ātman* imagines itself by itself through its own illusion. It alone cognizes the entities: this is the well-established conclusion of the Vedānta.

13. The Lord (*prabhu*) diversifies other well-defined entities existing in the mind; outward-minded, He diversifies the well-defined things also. Thus does the Lord imagine.

14. Those things that exist mentally as long as the thought lasts and the things likewise that exist objectively — all these are only imaginations. There is no other reason for the distinction.

15. Those things which are unmanifest within, and those that are clear without: all these are only imagined. The distinction, again, is in the difference of the sense-organs.

16. First the individual self (*jīva*) is imagined, then, verily, the entities external and internal. As the knowledge is, so is the memory.

17. As a rope not definitely ascertained in the dark is imagined to be things like a snake, a line of water, etc., so also is the Self imagined.

18. As imagination disappears when the rope is well-ascertained and there is the nonduality "This is only a rope," so also when the Self is well-ascertained.

19. The Self is imagined to be the life-force (*prāṇa*) and all these innumerable entities. This is the illusion of that shining one (i.e. the Self) by which it itself is deluded.

20. Those who know the life-force (*prāṇa*) say it is *prāṇa*; those who know the elements say it is the elements. The knowers of the qualities say it is the qualities; and the knowers of the categories say it is the categories.

21. Those who know the the quarters say it is the quarters; those who know the objects say it is the objects. Those who know the the worlds say it is the worlds, and those who know the gods say it is the gods.

22. Those who know the Vedas say it is the Vedas, and those who know the sacrifice say it is the sacrifice. Those who know the enjoyer say it is the enjoyer, and those who know the objects of enjoyment say it is the objects of enjoyment.

23. Those who know the subtle say it is the subtle, and those who know the gross say it is the gross. Those who know form say it is form, and those who know the formless say it is the formless.

24. Those who know time say it is time, and those who know the four quarters of space say it is the four quarters of space. Those who know the philosophical theories say it is the philosophical theories, and those who know the worlds say it is the worlds.

25. Those who know mind say it is mind, and those who know the discriminative faculty say it is the discriminative faculty. Those who know thought say it is thought, and those who know right and wrong say it is right and wrong.

26. Some say that the Self consists of twenty-five principles and others say that it consists of twenty-six; some say that it has thirty-one principles, and others say the principles are endless.

27. Those who know the worlds say it is the worlds, and those who know the stages of religious life say it is the stages. Grammarians say it is masculine, feminine and neuter, and others say it is the higher and lower *brahman*.

28. Those who know creation say it is creation, and those who know dissolution say it is dissolution. Those who know subsistence say it is subsistence; and all these here again always (are imagined as the Self).

29. Whatever entity is presented to someone, he indeed sees that entity. That entity having become him, protects him; absorption in that encompasses him.

30. This Self is regarded as different owing only to these non-different objects. Whoever knows this truly may imagine the Self to be anything at all without any hesitation.

31. As dream and magic (*svapna-māyā*) are seen, and as an illusory city in the sky, so is this universe seen by those who are well-versed in the Vedānta.

32. There is no destruction, nor again origination; no one who is bound and no spiritual aspirant. There is no one longing for liberation, nor indeed any one who is liberated. This is the highest truth.

33. Furthermore, this Self is imagined to be the nonexisting entities themselves by the nondual (*advaya*). The entities are also imagined by the nondual Self. Therefore nonduality is auspicious.

34. This world is not manifold at all, either by the nature of the Self or by its own nature. Nothing whatever is different or non-different. The knowers of the truth (*tattva*) know this.

35. Those who have reached the other shore of the Vedas, the wise ones devoid of desire, fear and anger, see that which is free from imagination, the cessation of the phenomenal world (*prapañca*), the nondual.

36. Therefore, having known this, one should fix one's memory on nonduality. Having attained the nondual, one should act like an insensate person.

37. Without praise, without making salutation, and quite without the utterance of *svadhā* (i.e. the performance of *śrāddha* rites for the ancestors), and having one's support anywhere and everywhere, one should be an ascetic, dependent on the circumstances of chance.

38. Having seen the reality (*tattva*) within as well as the reality without, becoming one with the reality, delighting in it, one should not deviate from the reality.

ADVAITA-PRAKARAṆA

1. Religious duty (*dharma*) associated with devotion arises when *brahman* is born. Before birth everything is unborn (*aja*). Therefore religious duty is traditionally regarded as pitiable.

2. Hence I shall speak of that which is not pitiable, which is without origination (*ajāti*), which has gone to sameness. Thus those things which are apparently being born on all sides are not born at all.

3. For the Self, like space, arises as individual selves (*jīvas*) like the pot-spaces. The aggregates are like the jars etc. This is the illustration of birth (*jāti*).

4. Just as when the pots etc. are dissolved, the pot-spaces etc. are completely merged into space, so the individual selves (*jīvas*) are merged here in the Self (*ātman*).

5. Just as the pot-spaces are not polluted with dust and smoke etc. when one pot-space is, so likewise the *jīvas* with respect to happiness etc.

6. And though form, function and name indeed differ here and there, there is no difference in space. Similarly, this is the definite conclusion with regard to the *jīvas*.

7. Just as the pot-space is not a modification or a part of space, so the *jīva* is never a modification or a part of the *ātman*.

8. As the sky becomes soiled with impurities to children, so also the *ātman* becomes soiled with impurities to the wise.

9. In death and verily in birth, in going and coming also, in existing in all bodies, the *ātman* is like space.

10. All aggregates are projected, dream-like, by the Self's illusion. For whether superior or all the same, there is no proper ground for them.

11. The sheaths (*kośas*) which are the essence etc. are described in the Taittirīyaka (i.e. TU II. 1-6). Their Self is the supreme *jīva* which is like the sky, as is there made clear.

12. The supreme *brahman* is clearly established in each of the pairs in the *madhu-jñāna* (i.e. in BU II. 5), just as space is clearly established in the earth and also in the stomach.

13. The identity without distinction of the *jīva* and the *ātman* is praised, and diversity is condemned. For only thus is all that tenable.

14. The separateness which is declared of the *jīva* and the *ātman* before origination is figurative, referring to the future. Its primary sense is certainly not reasonable.

15. The creation which has been expounded by means of the examples of earth, metal, sparks (of fire) etc. is only a means of introducing the subject. There is no difference whatsoever.

16. There are three stages of life, having low, intermediate, and superior views. This worship is taught for them out of compassion.

17. The dualists are firmly fixed in their own views. They contradict each other. This doctrine of nonduality does not contradict them.

18. Nonduality is indeed the highest truth. Duality (i.e. the lower or relative truth) is said to be different from it. For the dualists, duality is both (i.e. the absolute and the relative truth). Nonduality does not conflict with the dualist doctrine.

19. Nonduality becomes different only through illusion, for the unborn (*aja*) does not become different in any other way. For if it became differentiated in reality it would go the way of death.

20. The disputants wish to prove the birth of an unborn entity (*bhāva*). But an entity which is unborn is immortal. How could it undergo death?

21. The immortal does not become mortal, and likewise the mortal does not become immortal. There can be no change in nature (*prakṛti*) in any way whatever.

22. He for whom an entity (*bhāva*), immortal by nature, goes to death — how will his immortal entity, since it is a mere product, remain changeless?

23. The *śruti* is the same in regard to creation from the existent or from the nonexistent. But that which is ascertained and supported by reason is the true meaning, and not the other.

24. The *śruti* teaches: "There is no diversity here etc.," and also "Indra by means of illusion etc." Being birthless, he indeed is born through illusion in various ways.

25. And by the denial of birth, becoming is denied. In the *śruti* passage "Who again would give birth to it?," the cause of birth is denied.

26. The *śruti* passage "He is not this, not this" denies what is explained. Therefore because all things are ungraspable they are declared to be birthless (*aja*).

27. For the birth of the existent (*sat*) is reasonable through illusion, not however in reality. Indeed, to him for whom birth is real, the born is born!

28. The birth of the nonexistent is not reasonable through illusion or in reality, either. The son of a barren woman is not born either through illusion or in reality.

29. Just as in dream the mind vibrates through illusion with the appearance of duality, so also in the waking state the mind vibrates through illusion with the appearance of duality.

30. There is no doubt that in dream the mind which is without a second has the appearance of duality. And similarly in the waking state there is no doubt that the mind which is without a second has the appearance of duality.

31. This duality in whatever form, both the moving and the unmoving, is mind-perceived. For when the mind ceases to be mind, the duality is not perceived at all.

32. When, as a result of the realization of the truth of the Self, the mind does not imagine, it goes to the state of being non-mind; in the absence of anything to grasp, it is non-grasping.

33. They assert the knowledge free from imagination, birthless, not different from what is known. *Brahman* is that which is known, birthless, eternal. The birthless knows the birthless.

34. The state of the mind of the wise man — controlled and free from modifications — is to be known. Sleep is different and not like it.

35. For in deep sleep the mind goes under; when the mind is completely controlled, it does not do so. That alone is *brahman*, free from fear, possessing the light of knowledge all around.

36. It is unborn, without sleep, without dream, without name, without form, ever shining, omniscient. There is no practicing whatsoever.

37. It is *samādhi*, entirely beyond speech, risen above all thought, completely calm, ever shining, unmoving and fearless.

38. There is no apprehension or abandonment where thought does not exist. Then knowledge is established in the Self, is unborn, and goes to the state of sameness.

39. This, verily, is the "non-touch yoga" (*asparśa-yoga*) by name; all *yogins* find its realization difficult. For the *yogins* are afraid of it, seeing fear in the fearless.

40. For all *yogins*, fearlessness, destruction of misery, complete awakening and eternal peace itself depend on the control of the mind.

41. Without unrelenting, undismayed effort, the control of the mind would be like the emptying of the sea with the point of a blade of *kuśa* grass, one drop at a time.

42. With the proper means, one should control the mind, dispersed among desire and enjoyments, and also completely tranquil in merging. As is desire, so is the merging.

43. Keeping constantly in mind that everything is suffering, one should withdraw from the enjoyment of desires. Keeping constantly in mind the birthless, one indeed does not even see that which is born.

44. One should awaken the mind in the merged state; again, make it tranquil when it is distracted. One should know it to be full of desire. When it is in a state of equilibrium, one should not disturb it.

45. One should not enjoy happiness there; one should be unattached through wisdom (*prajñā*). One should make the mind one-pointed through diligence when, steadied, it wants to move out.

46. When the mind does not go under, and when again it is not distracted, then that, motionless and without appearances, becomes *brahman*.

47. They say it rests in itself, is calm, is *nirvāṇic*, indescribable, the highest bliss, omniscient, and is birthless with the birthless that is known.

48. No *jīva* whatsoever is born. There is no becoming for it. This is the highest truth where nothing whatever is born.

ALĀTA-ŚĀNTI-PRAKARAṆA

1. I pay homage to the best of bipeds, who, through knowledge like the sky, and not different from what is known, has fully realized the *dharmas* resembling the sky.

2. The *yoga* called "non-touch" (*asparśa-yoga*) is pleasant to all beings, beneficial, free from dispute, without contradiction, and traditionally taught. I bow down to it.

3. Disputing amongst themselves, some disputants wish to establish the birth of the existent, other wise ones wish to establish the birth of that which is nonexistent.

4. There is no birth whatever of the existent; the nonexistent also is not born. Those dualists thus disputing amongst themselves assuredly proclaim birthlessness (*ajāti*).

5. We endorse the birthlessness proclaimed by them. We do not dispute with them. Know that which is free from dispute.

6. The disputants wish to establish the birth of the entity (*dharma*) which is birthless only. For how can a birthless, deathless entity undergo death?

7. The deathless does not become mortal, and the mortal does not become deathless. There can be no change in nature (*prakṛti*) in any way whatsoever.

8. He for whom an entity (*dharma*), deathless by nature, undergoes death — how will his deathless entity, since it is a product, remain changeless?

9. Nature (*prakṛti*) is to be known as that which is self-established, self-existent, innate, and not artificial. It does not give up its self-nature (*svabhāva*).

10. All *dharmas* are intrinsically free from old age and death. By thinking of birth and death those wishing to establish birth and death fall.

11. Indeed, for whomever the cause is the effect, his cause is born. Being born, how can it be birthless? Being modified, how can it be eternal?

12. If the effect is non-different from the cause, then it is birthless. Since the effect is born, how can the cause be eternal?

13. There is certainly no illustration for the person who holds that the effect is born from the unborn. And if it is maintained that there is birth from the already born, there is the fallacy of infinite regress.

14. How can they, for whom the effect is the antecedent of the cause, and the cause the antecedent of the effect, describe the beginninglessness of both the cause and the effect?

15. For those who maintain that the antecedent of the cause is the effect and that the antecedent of the effect is the cause, birth would be like the birth of the father from the son.

16. The order in the origination of cause and effect needs to be determined by you, since in simultaneous origination there would be the absence of relationship, like the horns of a cow.

17. Your cause, being produced from the effect, would not be established. Being unestablished, how will the cause produce the effect?

18. If the establishment of the cause is from the effect, and the establishment of the effect is from the cause, which one is produced first? Which one's establishment is dependent?

19. Your incapacity to answer, the absence of full knowledge, or, again, the violation of the sequence of cause and effect: thus indeed absolute birthlessness has been proclaimed by the *buddhas* (enlightened ones).

20. The illustration of the seed and its sprout is itself something that is to be proved. Surely no reason that is like the *sādhya* (the proposition to be proved) can be used in establishing the *sādhya*.

21. The lack of full knowledge about what is anterior and what is posterior in the causal sequence is the full illuminator of birthlessness. For, since an entity is born, why is its antecedent not grasped?

22. No thing whatsoever is born, either from itself or from another. No thing whatsoever — existent, nonexistent, or existent and nonexistent — is born.

23. From the very nature of things, the cause, since it is beginningless, is not born, and the effect is not born either. If something has no beginning, one should not say that it does.

24. (Some say): the percept (*prajñapti*) has a cause (*nimitta*), otherwise there would be the disappearance of duality. And because there is experience of impurity (*saṃkleśa*), the existence of cause and percept is thought to be "dependent" (*paratantra*).

25. (However, the view that) the percept (*prajñapti*) has a cause is maintained from the viewpoint of reasoning. That the cause is not a cause is maintained from the viewpoint of reality.

26. The mind does not touch an object, nor does it touch the appearance of an object, either. Since the object is nonexistent, the appearance of the object is nonexistent also.

27. The mind never touches any object (or cause) in the three periods of time. Being objectless (causeless), how could error arise in it?

28. Therefore, neither the mind nor what is perceived by the mind is born. Those who see its birth truly see a footprint in the sky.

29. Since it is the unborn that is said to be born, birthlessness is its very nature (*prakṛti*). There can be no change in nature in any way whatever.

30. Moreover, *saṃsāra* would not have an end, nor would it be beginningless. And liberation (*mokṣa*), having a beginning, would not be endless.

31. That which does not exist at the beginning and at the end is such in the present also. Though they are on a par with things that are unreal, they are seen as if they were not unreal.

32. Their utility is contradicted in dream; therefore, because they have a beginning and an end they are traditionally known as entirely unreal.

33. All entities (*dharmas*) in dream are false because they are seen within the body. How can there be perception of real entities in this enclosed space?

34. It is not reasonable that, having gone there, there is actual perception in dream, because there is no fixed rule of time for the act of going. Moreover, when awakened, no one is ever found to be in that place (i.e. the one dreamt).

35. When one awakens, friends and others with whom one has deliberated in dream are not to be found; likewise, when one awakens, nothing whatever of what one has grasped is to be seen.

36. The body seen in dream is unreal, since another, different one is seen when one is dreaming. As in the case with the body, so all the things seen by the mind in dream are unreal.

37. Since dream is experienced as wakefulness is (*jāgarita-vat*), dream is considered to have that (i.e. the waking state) as its cause. But since it has that as its cause, its truth is considered to be the waking state alone.

38. Since origination (*utpāda*) is not established, it is declared that everything is unborn. There is no origination whatsoever of the nonexistent from the existent.

39. Having seen an unreal thing in the waking state (*jāgarita*) and being absorbed in it, one sees it in dream. And having seen an unreal thing in dream, one does not see it when one awakes.

40. The nonexistent (*asat*) does not have the nonexistent as its cause; likewise the existent (*sat*) does not have the nonexistent as its cause. And the existent does not have the exis-

tent as its cause. How can the nonexistent have the existent as it cause?

41. Just as one may, in the waking state, contact unthinkable things as if they were real through error, so in dream one sees things (*dharmas*) through error only.

42. The *buddhas* teach the doctrine of birth (*jāti*) to those who are ever afraid of the doctrine of birthlessness — who, on the basis of perception and common practice, maintain that things exist.

43. Those who are afraid of the doctrine of non-birth and who go astray owing to perception are not affected by the evil of *jāti* (i.e. the doctrine that things are born.) The evil will be of no great account.

44. Just as an illusory elephant is said to exist on the basis of perception and common practice, so a thing is said to exist on the basis of perception and common practice.

45. Consciousness (*vijñāna*), which has the appearance of birth, of motion, and of being a thing, is in reality unborn, unmoving, quiescent, nondual (*advaya*), and lacks the character of being a thing.

46. Thus mind is not born; thus *dharmas* are traditionally taught to be unborn. Those alone who know this do not fall into error.

47. Just as the fire-brand when it is in motion has the appearance of being straight, crooked and so on, so consciousness (*vijñāna*) when it is in motion has the appearance of being the perceiver and perceived.

48. Just as a fire-brand when it does not move has no appearance and is unborn, so consciousness (*vijñāna*) when it does not move has no appearance and is unborn.

49. The appearances do not arise from anything else when the fire-brand is moving. They are nowhere else than the flaming stick when it is not moving; nor do they enter it then.

50. They do not go out from the fire-brand for they have no substance (*dravya*). In respect to consciousness also it must be the same, for as appearance there is no difference.

51. The appearances do not arise from anything else when consciousness is moving. They are nowhere else than consciousness when it is not moving; nor do they enter it then.

52. They do not go out from consciousness for they have no substance. Because the relationship of cause and effect is lacking, they are always unthinkable.

53. A substance can be the cause of a substance, and what is other than a substance can be the cause of what is other than a substance. It is impossible to maintain that the *dharmas* have the nature of substantiality or have any other existence than that of a substance.

54. The *dharmas* are not mind-born, and neither is the mind *dharma*-born. Thus the wise enter the birthlessness of cause and effect.

55. As long as there is the preoccupation with cause and effect, so long is there the arising (*udbhava*) of cause and effect. When the preoccupation with cause and effect is destroyed, there is no arising of cause and effect.

56. As long as there is the preoccupation with cause and effect, so long does *saṃsāra* continue. When the preoccupation with cause and effect is destroyed, *saṃsāra* is no longer possible.

57. According to the relative truth (*saṃvṛti*) everything is born; hence nothing is eternal (*śāśvata*). In reality, however, everything is unborn; hence nothing is annihilated (*uccheda*).

58. Those *dharmas* (*ye dharmāḥ*) which are said to be born are in reality not born. Their birth is like an illusion, and that illusion itself does not exist.

59. Like a seed made of illusion, a sprout equally illusory is born. The sprout is neither eternal nor subject to annihilation (*uccheda*). The same thing applies to the *dharmas*.

60. The term "eternal/non-eternal" does not apply when all *dharmas* are unborn. Where words fail, there discrimination is not expressed (*nocyate*).

61. As the mind having the appearance of duality moves in dream illusorily, so the mind having the appearance of duality moves illusorily in the waking state (*jāgrat*).

62. Without a doubt the mind in sleep is nondual (*advaya*) and has the appearance of duality. Thus, without a doubt the mind in the waking state is nondual and has the appearance of duality.

63. All the living beings (*jīvas*) — egg-born or sweat-born — which the dreamer moving about in dream ever sees that are located in the ten directions of space —

64. They, since they are seen by the mind of the dreamer, do not exist apart from it. This (i.e. the world of living beings), since it is seen by that alone (i.e. the mind) is said to be just the mind of the dreamer.

65. All the living beings — egg-born or sweat-born — which the waking person moving about in the waking state ever sees that are located in the ten directions of space —

66. They, since they are seen by the mind of the waking person, do not exist apart from it. This (i.e. the world of living beings), since it is seen by that alone (i.e. the mind), is said to be the waking mind.

67. They both are perceived by the other. Then does the mind exist? It isn't said (*nocyate*). Both (i.e. mind and the object of the mind) being devoid of characteristics (*lakṣaṇāśūnya*) are grasped by the mind alone.

68. Just as a living being being made of dream (*svapna-māyā*) is born and also dies, so all these living beings in the waking state both are and are not.

69. Just as a living being made of illusion is born and also dies, so all these living beings in the waking state both are and are not.

70. Just as a living being made of supernatural power (*nirmitaka*) is born and also dies, so all these living beings in the waking state both are and are not.

71. No living being whatsoever is born: there is no becoming for it. This is that highest truth where nothing whatsoever is born.

72. This duality which consists of the perceived and the perceiver is merely the vibration of the mind. The mind is therefore proclaimed to be without an object, eternally unrelated to anything.

73. What exists according to imagined relative truth (*kalpita-saṃvṛti*) does not exist according to absolute truth. What would exist according to the dependent relative truth (*paratantrābhisaṃvṛti*) does not exist in the absolute truth.

74. That which is unborn according to the imagined relative truth (*kalpita-saṃvṛti*) is, according to the absolute truth, not even unborn. But it is born according to the relative truth which is a "dependent appearance" (*paratantrābhiniṣpatti*).

75. There is persistent preoccupation with the nonexistent; but duality does not really exist. Only by realizing the nonexistence of duality he (i.e. the one who realizes this) is not born, being free from causation.

76. When one does not get causes, superior, intermediate or inferior, then the mind is not born. When it is without a cause, how can there be an effect?

77. The mind has no cause: consequently, everything is unborn (*anutpatti*), the same, and nondual (*advaya*). Everything is unborn: consequently, everything is only mind-perceived.

78. When one realizes the true causelessness, and not obtaining a separate cause, one attains the state free from suffering, desire and fear.

79. When the mind is pre-occupied with the nonexistent it turns toward that which is similar. Only by realizing the nonexistence of a thing it turns away, unrelated to anything.

80. Then the state of the mind that is without modification and turned away from any object is unmoving. That is the field of activity (*viṣaya*) of the *buddhas*: the same, unborn, and nondual (*advaya*).

81. Birthless, sleepless, dreamless, it is self-effulgent. Indeed, the fundamental reality of the *dharmas* (*dharmo dhātu* = *dharmadhātu*) is always illumined of its very nature.

82. That Lord (*bhagavān*) is always covered easily and uncovered with difficulty by the grasping of some *dharma* or other.

83. "Is," "is not," "is and is not," or again "neither is nor is not": the immature person thus covers the Lord over with notions of the moving, the steady, both, and the nonexistence of both.

84. These are the four alternatives (*koṭyaś catasra*) by the grasping of which the Lord is ever covered over. The Lord is untouched by these. He who sees this is all-seeing.

85. When one attains the all-knowing, perfect, nondual, *brāhmaṇic* state which has no beginning, middle and end, what may one desire beyond it?

86. This, indeed, is the discipline (*vinaya*) of the wise, naturally quiescent, and controlled because it has the property of being naturally controlled. Thus the wise one should attain tranquillity.

87. That which has both an object and perception is held to be the "dualistic mundane" (*dvayaṃ laukika*). That which has no object but has perception is held to be the "pure mundane" (*śuddhaṃ laukika*).

88. That which has no object and no perception is traditionally held to be the "super-mundane" (*lokottara*). Knowledge, the thing to be known by knowledge, and the thing to be known by the mind (*vijñāna*) are always praised by the *buddhas*.

89. When knowledge and the three-fold thing to be known are known spontaneously and by stages, there is omniscience everywhere on all sides for the wise one.

90. That which is to be abandoned, that which is to be known, that which is to be attained, and that which is to be matured are to be understood according to the first vehicle (*agrayāṇataḥ* = *agrayānataḥ*). It is traditionally taught that there is perception of these in the three, apart from the thing to be known by *vijñāna*.

91. All the *dharmas* are to be known as beginningless, by nature like the sky. There is no difference in them whatsoever.

92. All *dharmas* are well ascertained to be enlightened from the very beginning (*ādi-buddha*). One who becomes imperturbable in this way becomes fit for the state of deathlessness.

93. By their very nature (*prakṛti*), all *dharmas* are quiescent from the very beginning, unoriginated (*anutpanna*), completely unmodified, the same and non-different. The ultimate reality is birthless, uniform and free from fear (*viśārada*).

94. There is, however, no fearlessness (*vaiśāradya*) at all for those who always move about in the realm of differences. Those who hold the doctrine of separateness are prone to difference. Therefore they are regarded as pitiable.

95. But whoever is fully convinced of the birthless, the uniform, is possessed of great knowledge in the world. But the ordinary people of the world do not fathom it.

96. It is held that the birthless knowledge (*jñāna*) does not pass over to the birthless *dharmas*. Since knowledge does not pass over to the *dharmas*, it is praised as unrelated to any object.

97. There is never unrelatedness for one who has the misapprehension that something *dharmic*, even one the measure of an atom, is born.

98. All *dharmas* are without covering, pure by nature, enlightened from the very beginning (*ādi-buddha*), and thus liberated (*mukta*). Those who lead others on the path to salvation (i.e. the *buddhas*), it is said, know this.

99. The knowledge of the *buddha* who teaches the way (*tāyin*) does not cross over to the *dharmas*. Thus, all *dharmas are* knowledge. This was not spoken by the Buddha.

100. Having awakened to the state hard to see, very profound, birthless, uniform, free from fear (*viśārada*), not diverse, we honor it to the best of our ability.

***

There has been a great deal of scholarly controversy about the relations among the Māṇḍūkya, the *kārikās* of the Āgama-prakaraṇa, and the *kārikās* of the last three *prakaraṇas* of the Āgama-śāstra. There have been at least five different views on this matter:

(1) The Māṇḍūkya is an independent work. Furthermore, it is an Upaniṣad and therefore *śruti*, and the twenty-nine *kārikās* are a

direct commentary on it. The 186 verses of the other three *kārikās* are a continuation and extension of the ideas expressed in this commentary, and in this respect may be regarded as a kind of indirect commentary on the Māṇḍūkya. The author of all 215 verses was Gauḍapāda.

This is the view of the contemporary *paṇḍits* of the Śaṃkara school, and it is the prevailing view of modern scholars in the West and in India.

(2) The Māṇḍūkya and the twenty-nine *kārikās* of the Āgama-prakaraṇa constitute a single work, and *both* are *śruti*. On this view, the Māṇḍūkya consists of twelve prose *mantras* and twenty-nine *kārikās*.[8]

B. N. K. Sharma has shown that this was the view held by late writers of the Śaṃkara school in the 14th to 18th centuries like Madhusūdana Sarasvatī, Appaya Dīkṣita, Vidyāraṇya, Advaitānanda and Kṛṣṇānanda Sarasvatī.[9] This is also the view of the Viśiṣṭādvaita (qualified nondualist) and Dvaita (dualist) schools of the Vedānta. Unlike the aforementioned writers of the Śaṃkara school, however, the Dvaitins and Viśiṣṭādvaitins do not regard the last three *prakaraṇas* as authoritative; indeed, so far as I know, the founders and early classical writers of these two schools never even *mention* the last three *prakaraṇas* of the Āgama-śāstra. This is hardly surprising, since these *prakaraṇas* teach, in a very uncompromising way, the Māyāvāda interpretation of the Vedānta which the Dvaitins and the Viśiṣṭādvaitins reject.

(3) The Māṇḍūkya, the twenty-nine verses, and the other three *prakaraṇas* of the Āgama-śāstra comprise a single work, and all of it is *śruti*. Thus, there are some MSS of the Āgama-śāstra in which the last three *prakaraṇas* are also regarded as *śruti*, and are referred to as "Advaita-prakaraṇa Upaniṣad," "Alāta-śānti-prakaraṇa Upaniṣad" etc.[10] There may even have been a tradition to this effect in the later period of the Śaṃkara school, for (as we shall see later in chapter 9), there is a late writer of this school called Nārāyaṇāśramin who refers to such a tradition.

(4) The Māṇḍūkya and the four *prakaraṇas* of the Āgama-śāstra were not written as separate works. The view that the Māṇḍūkya has a special status, and that it counts as *śruti*, was a later development, and occurred in the Śaṃkara school when the origins and nature of the text had been forgotten — or deliberately ignored

— through the passage of time. This view was advocated by Paul Deussen in 1906 and by A. Venkatasubbiah in a series of articles which he published in the early 1930s.[11]

(5) The Māṇḍūkya and the Āgama-prakaraṇa are separate works, and the ĀP (together with the other three *prakaraṇas* of the Āgama-śāstra) are the *primary* works. The twelve prose sentences of the Māṇḍūkya are a commentary on the twenty-nine *kārikās* of the Āgama-prakaraṇa. This view was advocated by V. Bhattacharya.[12]

I do not think that *any* one of these five views is wholly correct. However, a start can be made in sorting out all these possibilities by noting that we can be reasonably certain that in Śaṃkara's time the twelve prose *mantras* had attained the status of *śruti* whereas the twenty-nine *kārikās* had not.

On the one hand, it is virtually certain that the Māṇḍūkya was known in Śaṃkara's time as an Upaniṣad (i.e. as *śruti*), for Sureśvara (fl. 760 C.E.), an immediate disciple of Śaṃkara-bhagavat-pāda, cites Māṇḍ. 6 in his Vārttika on Śaṃkara's Bṛhad-āraṇyakopaniṣad-bhāṣya, and refers to it as *śruti*.[13] We may conclude that theories (4) and (5) above are untenable, for Sureśvara would not have referred to a work by Gauḍapāda or any other human author as *śruti*.

On the other hand, theories (2) and (3) are rendered untenable by the fact that Sureśvara and Śaṃkara, in works which are surely authentic, refer to some of the *kārikās* of Gauḍapāda, and when they do, they do *not* refer to them as *śruti*. The following are some examples:

(1) Śaṃkara in Brahma-sūtra-bhāṣya 2.1.9 cites ĀP 16 and introduces it with the words "Here it is said by the teacher who knows the tradition of the Vedānta" (*atroktaṃ vedāntārtha-saṃpradāya-vidbhir ācāryaiḥ*); and in Brahma-sūtra-bhāṣya 1.4.14 he introduces his citation of Advaita-prakaraṇa 15 with the words "Thus it is said by the knower (or knowers) of the tradition" (*tathā ca saṃpradāya-vido vadanti*). In the Vedic tradition, *śruti* is held to be without a human author (*apauruṣeya*), so Śaṃkara would not have referred to a passage which he regarded as *śruti* in this way.

(2) Maṇḍanamiśra, Śaṃkara's senior contemporary, quotes ĀP 11 in his Brahma-siddhi, but does not mention it as *śruti*.

(3) Furthermore, Sureśvara, in his Naiṣkarmya-siddhi IV, 41-44, cites ĀP 11 and ĀP 15 and attributes them to Gauḍapāda.

In the next chapter I discuss some of the later Upaniṣads that have something to say, directly or indirectly, about the interpretation of the Māṇḍūkya. These Upaniṣads show that, although it was not universally accepted, the TI interpretation of the Māṇḍūkya and of the four states of the Self did exist when these Upaniṣads were written. The discussion in chapters 5 and 6, on the other hand, will show that the Upaniṣads that *predate* the Māṇḍūkya unequivocally support the IC interpretation of the Māṇḍūkya.

Since the TI interpretation cannot be supported by the earlier Upaniṣads, whereas it can be supported by the later Upaniṣads, it is tempting to suppose that the TI interpretation was introduced by Gauḍapāda, Śaṃkara, or his immediate followers. However, we have already seen a major difficulty in ascribing the TI interpretation of the Māṇḍūkya to Gauḍapāda, and additional difficulties will be presented in later chapters. Furthermore, there are pressing reasons for not ascribing the introduction of the TI interpretation of the Māṇḍūkya to Śaṃkara either.[14] These questions concerning the history of the TI interpretation of the Māṇḍūkya and the authorship of the Āgama-śāstra and the Āgama-śāstra-vivaraṇa are discussed in more detail in the chapters of Part II.

II

The "later Upaniṣads" are a very heterogeneous collection of texts. Many of them are concerned with occult physiology and the details of *haṭha-yoga*; some are sectarian in character and attempt to glorify either Viṣṇu or Śiva in terms of traditional Vedāntic doctrine; some teach salvation through the use of *mantras*; and nearly all of them have been heavily influenced by the ascetic tradition of homeless wanderers (*avadhūtas, paramahaṃsas, parivrājakas*). It is quite possible that these homeless ascetics of India tended to be eclectic doctrinally; in any case, clear signs of Sāṃkhya and Buddhist influence can be found in the later Upaniṣads.

Because of the Buddhist influence in particular, these Upaniṣads are one of the logical places to look for textual support for the TI interpretation of the Māṇḍūkya. In fact, it *is* possible to find passages in these texts which support the Māyāvāda (i.e. TI) interpretation. Equally important, however, are passages in these texts which support the IC interpretation of the Māṇḍūkya.

The field to be covered here is a very large one, and cannot be treated exhaustively in this work.[1] I shall, however, briefly mention (1) Nārada-parivrājaka (NPV) 8, which gives perhaps the clearest support to the TI interpretation of the Māṇḍūkya; (2) the Nṛsiṃhottara-tāpanīyopaniṣad (NUTU), which is somewhat ambivalent between TI and IC doctrines; and (3) two passages from later Upaniṣads which clearly support the IC interpretation of the Māṇḍūkya: Śāṇḍilya 2 and Subāla 5. I shall also consider the Nṛsiṃha-pūrva-tāpanīya (NPTU) and Rāmottara-tāpanīya (RUTU) Upaniṣads. These are particularly interesting, for they cite the first seven *mantras* of the Māṇḍūkya, and group these into subsets in a way that clearly favors the IC interpretation of the Māṇḍūkya.

(1) Nārada-parivrājaka 8 is a good example of a later Upaniṣadic passage that supports the Māyāvāda interpretation of the four states of the Self.

Nārada-parivrājaka 8 does not cite the Māṇḍūkya directly or exactly, but it clearly refers to it, and it describes the waking and dreaming states of the Self in much the same way as the Māṇḍūkya. This passage unequivocally associates all the terms of Māṇḍ. 6 with the state of deep sleep which is described in Māṇḍ. 5. The TI interpretation is also implicit in the fact that the Upaniṣad says that the lord of all (*sarveśvara*), the omniscient one (*sarvajña*), the inner ruler (*antaryāmin*) and the source of all (*yoniḥ sarvasya*) is unreal (*māyāvic*). Furthermore, the description which Nārada-parivrājaka 8 gives of the fourth state of the Self does not include any descriptions related to the *īśvara* of Māṇḍ. 6.

(2) Nṛsiṃhottara-tāpanīyopaniṣad (NUTU) 1 also associates Māṇḍ. 6 with Māṇḍ. 5., for, though it does not cite the Māṇḍūkya verbatim, it explicitly adds the term "*īśvara*" to the Māṇḍūkya's description of the third (i.e. sleeping) state of the self, and it also says that *īśvara* is "devoured by" the "fourth" (*īśvara-grāsas-turīya-turīyaḥ*).

However, there is also evidence in this Upaniṣad that its author (or authors) were not entirely comfortable with associating *īśvara* with the state of sleep. For in NUTU 2 it is also said that the *turīya* which "devours" *īśvara* is itself the self-ruler (*svarāj*) and the self-*īśvara* (*svayam-īśvara*). In the light of NUTU 2, the passage from NUTU 1 which I have just cited may mean, not that *īśvara per se* is unreal, but only that *īśvara* is not different from the Self. Such a view would be quite compatible with the IC interpretation of the Māṇḍūkya.

(3) Unlike NPV 8 and NUTU 1, Śāṇḍilyopaniṣad 2 unequivocally supports the IC interpretation of the Māṇḍūkya.

In this passage, *brahman* is said to be without hands or feet, without body, ungraspable (*agrāhya*), indefinable, one and nondual (*ekam-advitīya*), like space, actionless, mere being (*sanmātra*), auspicious, calm and deathless. These qualities correspond to Māṇḍ. 7. Then, without any interruption, the Śāṇḍilya proceeds to describe this *brahman* as the one god (*eka-deva*), the prime cause of all things which is the power of the Self (*ātma-śakti-pradhāna*), omniscient (*sarvajña*), the lord of all (*sarveśvara*), the innermost self of all beings (*sarva-bhūtāntarātman*), the source of beings (*bhūta-yoni*), and as that which emanates the universe, makes it shine, and enjoys it. These qualities correspond to Māṇḍ. 6.

(4) A very similar passage is found at the end of Subālopaniṣad 5. This passage begins by saying that the Self is omniscient (*sarvajña*), the lord of all (*sarveśvara*), the ruler of all (*sarvādhipati*), the inner ruler (*antaryāmin*), and the source of all (*yoniḥ sarvasya*), exactly as does Māṇḍ. 6. However, as in the

Māṇḍūkya, this *īśvara* is regarded as *absolute*, for the Subāla goes on to say:

> It is one: duality does not exist...It is not inwardly conscious (*nāntaḥprajña*), not outwardly conscious (*na bahiḥprajña*), not conscious both ways (*nobhayataḥprajña*), not a mass of consciousness (*na prajñānaghana*), not consciousness (*na prajña*), not unconsciousness (*nāprajña*).

As in Śāṇḍilya 2, there is nothing in this passage to suggest that these "positive" and "negative" descriptions refer to two different things.

(5) Nṛsiṃha-pūrva-tāpanīya (NPTU) 4 and Rāma-uttara-tāpanīya (RUTU) 3 are particularly interesting because they cite the first seven *mantras* of the Māṇḍūkya verbatim. To judge from the printed texts which I have consulted — those by J. L. Shastri (1970) and Wasudev Pansikar (1913) — the manuscipts of these Upaniṣads appear to favor the IC interpretation of the Māṇḍūkya.[2]

(a) The *Rāma-uttara-tāpanīya*. J. L. Shastri's edition of the RUTU clearly places Māṇḍ. 6 and 7 together (pp. 401-402). This edition has a single vertical bar sign (i.e. a minor break) placed after "all is only *Aum*" (*sarvam oṃkāra eva*), "that also is only *Aum*" (*tad apy oṃkāra eva*), "all this, indeed is *brahman*" (*hy etad brahma*), "that is deep sleep" (*tat suṣuptam*), "the origin as well as the end of all beings" (*prabhavāpyayau hi bhūtānām*), and "such, they think, is the fourth" (*caturthaṃ manyante*). It also has a double vertical bar sign (presumably a major break) after "this is the first quarter" (*prathamaḥ pādaḥ*), "this is the second quarter" (*dvitīyaḥ pādaḥ*) and "this (*prājña*) is the third quarter" (*tṛtīyah pādaḥ*). After that (except for the minor breaks after "*hi bhūtānām*" and "*caturthaṃ manyante*") the text runs continuously to the end of the Māṇḍūkya and even beyond it into the text of the RUTU itself.

The double vertical bar sign placement, in particular, gives a very sensible organization to the first seven *mantras* of the Māṇḍūkya, because a major break is placed — if we assume that one can be read into the text after the "*sa vijñeyaḥ*" which concludes Māṇḍ. 7 — after each sentence of the Māṇḍūkya which enumerates a quarter of the self, i.e. "first *pāda*," "second *pāda*," etc. Note that this grouping places Māṇḍ. 6 with Māṇḍ. 7, and not with Māṇḍ. 5.

The reading of RUTU 3 given by Pansikar in his edition (pp. 700-701) is substantially the same as Shastri's. It has a single vertical bar sign (presumably a minor break) placed after "all is only *Aum*" (*sarvam oṃkāra eva*), "that also is only *Aum*" (*tad apy oṃkāra eva*), "all this, indeed is *brahman*" (*hy etad brahma*), "that is deep sleep," (*tat suṣuptam*) "the origin as well as the end of all beings" (*prabhavāpyayau hi bhūtānām*), and "such, they think, is the fourth" (*caturthaṃ manyante*). It also has a double vertical bar sign (presumably a major break) after "this is the first quarter" (*prathamaḥ pādaḥ*), "this is the second quarter" (*dvitīyaḥ pādaḥ*) and "this (*prājña*) is the third quarter" (*tṛtīyaḥ pādaḥ*). Like the J. L. Shastri edition, the Pansikar edition has a minor break (i.e. single vertical bar sign) between the conclusion of Māṇḍ. 6 and the beginning of Māṇḍ. 7. However, the major grouping — which is presumably given by two vertical bar signs — clearly links Māṇḍ. 6 with Māṇḍ. 7 rather than Māṇḍ. 5.

(b) The *Nṛsiṃha-pūrva-tāpanīya*. J. L. Shastri's edition of the NPTU gives the text of the Māṇḍūkya (p. 223) without any grouping of the *mantras* at all, and this does not shed any light on the issue one way or the other. Pansikar's edition of the NPTU, however, unmistakably associates Māṇḍ. 6 with Māṇḍ. 7 rather than with Māṇḍ. 5. In the Pansikar edition (pp. 380-381) the *mantras* are grouped into sets by means of a single vertical bar sign, and bar signs are placed after "this is the first quarter" (*prathamaḥ pādaḥ*), "this is the second quarter" (*dvitīyaḥ pādaḥ*), and "this is the third quarter" (*tṛtīyaḥ pādaḥ*), and the entire citation is closed with a double bar sign after "*sa vijñeyaḥ*."[3] Pansikar's reading of the NPTU is important, for it confirms both his reading of the RUTU and J. L. Shastri's reading of the RUTU. All three of these agree in placing Māṇḍ. 6 and Māṇḍ. 7 together — at least in terms of the major groupings.[4]

The present discussion has been based on available printed editions rather than on actual manuscripts, which are, for the most part, available only in India and in Er and. It would be an interesting task to examine these manuscripts to see if they provide any further evidence for or against what I have called the TI and IC interpretations of the Māṇḍūkya.[5] No doubt there is a basis in the manuscripts themselves for the differences in the printed texts of the Upaniṣads which I have noted above, and a careful comparison of the available manuscripts could eventually throw some light on the interpretation of the Māṇḍūkya. Undoubtedly, the most interesting manuscripts to examine would be those that give the texts of the NPTU and the RUTU (and therefore Māṇḍ. 1-7) without any interruptions of text by later commentators.

In any case, the printed texts of the Upaniṣads which I have discussed in sections (1)-(5) in this chapter do not provide much support for the TI interpretation of the Māṇḍūkya. In spite of the fact that these are later Upaniṣads, they tend to favor the IC interpretation as much as — or more than — the Māyāvāda interpretation.

III

In this chapter I compare four medieval treatises. The first two works which I consider are the Āgama-śāstra-vivaraṇa (which is traditionally attributed to Ādi Śaṃkara) and the Brahma-siddhi of Maṇḍanamiśra; both of these works endorse the TI interpretation of the Vedāntic doctrine of the four states of the Self. In sections 3 and 4 I contrast these two works with Kūranārāyaṇa's commentary on the Māṇḍūkya and with a late commentary on the Nṛsiṃha-pūrva-tāpanīyopaniṣad which has been erroneously ascribed to Ādi Śaṃkara. These two later works are significant because they show that even at a rather late date in Indian history the Māṇḍūkya was interpreted by some writers according to the IC interpretation.

(1) Maṇḍanamiśra (fl. 690 C.E.), an early figure of the Advaita Vedānta, was an elder contemporary of Śaṃkara-bhagavat-pāda. According to the traditions of the Śaṃkara school, he belonged originally to the Pūrva Mīmāṃsā, and became known as Sureśvara after he was converted to the Advaita by Śaṃkara. Professors Mysore Hiriyanna and S. Kuppuswami Sastri, however, have thrown considerable doubt on the Maṇḍana-Sureśvara equation.[1] According to these scholars, Maṇḍanamiśra was always an independent thinker, whereas Sureśvara appears to have followed Śaṃkarācārya more faithfully. Consequently, on some fundamental points the works attributed to Maṇḍanamiśra diverge from those attributed to Sureśvara.

There is a passage in Maṇḍanamiśra's Brahma-siddhi which cites from the *śruti* the terms "*sarvajña*" and "*sarveśvara*."[2] The discussion in the Brahma-siddhi that provides the context for this citation is very interesting, for in it Maṇḍanamiśra argues that according to the highest truth *sarvajñatva* and *sarveśvaratva* cannot apply to *brahman* itself (*brahma-rūpa*). In this early passage, therefore, Maṇḍanamiśra sets forth the basic idea behind the TI interpretation of the Māṇḍūkya.

The passage in question occurs in the *niyoga-kāṇḍa* of the Brahma-siddhi. In the *niyoga-kāṇḍa*, Maṇḍana argues against the Prabhākara school of the Pūrva Mīmāṃsā, which held that the teachings of the Upaniṣads do not give knowledge of *brahman* or the Self, but are instead injunctions (*vidhi*) of a certain kind. One of the suggestions made by the *pūrvapakṣin* is that the Upaniṣads should be interpreted as *enjoining* the attainment of the knowledge of the nondual Self, on the grounds that this kind of knowledge is a *means* of attaining liberation (*mokṣa*). Maṇḍanamiśra's view, however, was that knowledge just *is* liberation; it is therefore an end in itself and the sole concern of the Upaniṣadic teachings. In order to refute the *pūrvapakṣin*, Maṇḍana tries to show that all the possible definitions of liberation which regard knowledge as one thing and liberation as another are untenable.

One of the definitions taken up for discussion is that liberation is the attainment of supreme lordship (*aiśvarya*, *īśvaratva*). Maṇḍana's preferred interpretation of the texts that refer to the attainment of *īśvaratva* is that this state is merely the consequence of the knowledge of *brahman* with qualities (*saguṇa-vidyā-vipāka*). This, he says, is an inferior knowledge that pertains to the realm of qualities and differences. This is the knowledge that is referred to, he says, in passages from the Chāndogya like "The self is onefold, threefold etc." "He obtains all worlds and desires," and "He becomes autonomous."[3] But the knowledge of *brahman* as it really is, according to Maṇḍana, is the knowledge of *brahman* as being devoid of qualities (*nirupādhi-brahma-vidyā*). The *aiśvarya* that is the result of the *saguṇa-vidyā*, therefore, even if it puts an end to rebirths (*apunar-āvṛtti*), is not the state of liberation (*mokṣa*).

Maṇḍana also mentions another opinion (*anye tu manyante*), which is that the texts which speak of *aiśvarya* refer to the manifested form of *brahman* (*āvirbhūta-brahma-rūpa*) rather than to *brahman* as it is in itself (*brahma-rūpa*).[4] According to this interpretation, the individual who attains *aiśvarya* does merge in *brahman*, but not *brahman* as it truly is, but only the manifested form of *brahman* (*āvirbhūta-brahma-rūpa*). According to the proponents of this interpretation, this *āvirbhūta-brahma-rūpa* is the *sarveśvara* and *sarvāntaryāmin* of the Upaniṣadic texts — i.e., it is the very nature of the Self of all beings (*sarvātmatva*) and it consists of the bliss (*ānandamaya*) of the gods and all other beings. This, it is alleged, is what the Chāndogya means when it says "He obtains all the worlds and all desires" and "He becomes autonomous."[5]

But wouldn't the view that the liberated self becomes the Self of all (*sarvātma*) entail that the liberated Self attains all sorrows and delusions as well as all desires? According to the proponents of the present interpretation, this is not a valid objection because sorrows and delusions pertain to the superimposition of nescience (*avidyā-adhyastā*) and not to the true nature of the manifested *brahman*, whereas knowledge (*jñāna*), omnipotence (*aiśvarya*) and bliss (*ānanda*) do belong to the nature of *brahman* (but only to the manifested *brahman*). Thus it is said in the *śruti*: "*Brahman* is mind and bliss," "There is no other seer," "On a particle of this bliss other creatures live," "This is the lord of all," "Verily, at the command of that imperishable, O Gārgī" etc.[6] Hence the correct view is that *īśvaratva*, bliss, etc. belong to the manifested *brahma-rūpa*, whereas grief etc. are the result of the superimposition of nescience.

Why, Maṇḍana asks, do the proponents of this interpretation hold that *aiśvarya* etc. belong only to the manifested *brahma-svarūpa* (*te katham-āvirbhūta-brahma-svarūpam-āskandeyuḥ*)? The reason, he says, is that there can be no doubt that there is nothing to be known and no mind (*vijñāna*) or *aiśvarya* in the *brahma-svarūpa* itself, for it is devoid of all things pertaining to the phenomenal world (*prapañca-śūnya*). Hence, he says, when the *śruti* says "*sarvajña*" and "*sarveśvara*" it must be understood in this way alone (*tatra sarvajña sarveśvara ity-api śrutī samādheye eva*). Omniscience etc. is not really the essence of the matter (*naitat sāram*), for there can be no relation of difference or duality between *brahman* and something that is made (*kṛta*) or known (*jñeya*) or governed from the outside (*īśitavya*) by *brahman*.

What, then, is the ultimate meaning of the Upaniṣadic passages which speak of *īśvara*? Maṇḍanamiśra gives two different answers to this question. One of his answers is that *brahman* is said to have these qualities because it is the pure consciousness (*caitanya*) or light (*prakāśa*) in which the whole phenomenal world is illuminated. Thus the *śruti* says: "The whole world is illumined with his light" and "There is no other seer."[7] Just as Agni's power of burning (*agner-daha-śakti*) does not depend on anything outside of Agni, so the power of the Lord (*īśāna-śakti*) is intrinsic to it. This, it is said, is the omniscience of which the *śruti* speaks. Alternatively, if the *śruti* does not refer to this conception of omniscience, it must refer to the godhood (*īśvaratva*) of the various Vedic deities. Thus, when the *śruti* says "This is the lord of all" and "This is the world guardian,"[8] it may also refer to the *aiśvarya* of Brahma, Indra, Yama etc.

Finally, Maṇḍanamiśra mentions yet another interpretation (*anye tv-āhuḥ*) of the concept of *īśvaratva*, which is that all descriptions of *brahman* which involve name and form (*nāma-rūpa*) are intended only for the purposes of meditation (*ādhyāna*); as such, they are concerned only with the manifested *brahman*, and not directly with liberation (*mokṣa*).

It is quite likely that Maṇḍanamiśra's citation of "*sarvajña*" and "*sarveśvara*" in this passage refers to Māṇḍ. 6. It is true that these terms are found elsewhere in the Upaniṣads, but they are linked together very prominently in the Māṇḍūkya. Furthermore, in arguing that these two terms do not apply to the highest state of *mokṣa*, Maṇḍanamiśra contends that the essence of *brahman* (*brahma-svarūpa*) is devoid of the things of the phenomenal world (*prapañca-śūnya*). It is quite likely that this refers to the term "*prapañcopaśama*" which is found in Māṇḍ. 7.

Thus, this may be the oldest passage in the extant Vedāntic literature in which an attempt is made to separate the concept of *īśvara* from the concept of *brahman*.[9] It is, therefore, of particular interest that Maṇḍanamiśra does not feel entitled to assume the correctness of this interpretation, but has to argue for it. Notice that he says: "The terms '*sarvajña*' and '*sarveśvara*' must be understood in this way alone" (*tatra sarvajña sarveśvara ity-api śrutī samādheye eva*). The term "*samādheya*" may mean (1) to be put in order or set right, (2) to be directed or informed or instructed, or (3) to be granted or admitted.[10] Maṇḍanamiśra's use of the term in this passage comes very close to the first meaning. He argues, in effect, that these terms cannot be taken literally or at their face value. Although they might seem at first sight to refer to the highest state, they in fact refer to an inferior state.

Maṇḍanamiśra's sensitivity to this point is understandable, for the straightforward way of understanding the Māṇḍūkya is to take Māṇḍ. 6 and 7 as complementary descriptions of the fourth state (*pāda*) of the self. Maṇḍanamiśra's attempts to explain this away are not convincing.

Maṇḍanamiśra is on solid ground textually when he argues that there is nothing apart from *brahman*, and that there is therefore no external thing to be known or governed by *brahman*. He is also on solid ground textually when he contends that *brahman* in itself is essentially consciousness (*caitanya*). However, he also appears to hold the view that *īśvara* and the power of *īśvara* (*īśāna-śakti*) are concepts that apply only to the (ultimately unreal) *manifested brahman* (*āvirbhūta-brahma-rūpa*). Here his views appear to diverge from the standpoint of the classical Upaniṣads, including the Māṇḍūkya, for the classical Upaniṣads (as I shall argue at some length later in this work) maintain that the *caitanya-śakti* that manifests the world is a real power of *brahman*, rather than something that belongs only to an illusory, lower aspect of *brahman*. In the classical Upaniṣadic tradition, in other words, the world is a real manifestation of *brahman* in the sense that it is a real transformation of an absolute consciousness, which manifests it and also transcends it.

A good example of the textual weakness of Maṇḍanamiśra's interpretation of the terms "*sarvajña*" and "*sarveśvara*" is Kaṭhopaniṣad 5.15, which he himself cites. This passage says: "In its light all other things shine" (*tasya bhāsā sarvam-idaṃ vibhāti*). But what is this light which illumines the whole world? The preceding passage of the Kaṭha says:

> 'This is it!' (*tad etad iti*): this, they think, is the highest, indescribable bliss. How, then, may I understand 'this'? Does it shine of itself or in reflection?

What does the Kaṭha mean by "this" (*tat*)? The answer is plainly given in the preceding two verses:

> The inner self (*sarva-bhūtāntar-ātman*) of all things, the one controller, who makes his one form manifold: the wise who perceive him as abiding in the Self, they, and no others, have eternal happiness.
>
> The one eternal amongst transient things, the conscious one amongst what is unconscious, the one amongst the many, who grants desires: the wise who perceive him as standing in the Self, they, and no others, have eternal peace.

In other words, the light (*bhāsā*) in which all things shine is identical with the *īśvara* and *antaryāmin* of Māṇḍ. 6. Furthermore, since there is nothing in the Kaṭha to suggest the distinction that Maṇḍana draws between the *brahma-svarūpa* and *īśvara*, the Kaṭha, like the other classical Upaniṣads, holds that the light in which all things shine is simply *brahman*. For Maṇḍana, however, these must be different things, on the grounds that the concept of *īśvara* applies only to the lower — and ultimately illusory — plane.

Maṇḍana's second interpretation is also untenable. The term *sarveśvara* cannot be applied to the Vedic deities like Brahmā, Indra, Agni etc., for logically there cannot be more than one lord of all (*sarveśvara*). Maṇḍanamiśra cites the Chāndogya in this connection, but there is nothing in the Chāndogya which directly links the concept of *svarāj* with the concept of the lord of all (*sarveśvara*) or with the concept of omniscience (*sarvajña*), for the Chāndogya speaks of a *multiplicity* of finite (though liberated) souls.

It is true that the Chāndogya says that the individual in the state of liberation from the body attains all his desires, but it never says or even implies that such an individual is omniscient (*sarvajña*) or that it is omnipotent (*sarveśvara*). Consequently, Chānd. 8.12 is not directly relevant to the interpretation of Māṇḍ. 6. As we shall see in chapter 5, the Māṇḍūkya is clearly based on Bṛhad. 4.2.1-4.4.25 and not on the Chāndogya, and in the Bṛhad-āraṇyakopaniṣad the liberated soul is said to merge in the nondual self or *brahma*n that is the "lord and ruler of all." Furthermore, in the Bṛhad-āraṇyaka this *sarveśvara* is also the *turīya ātman* of Māṇḍ. 7.

(2) The ĀŚV is a commentary on the four *prakaraṇas* of the Āgama-śāstra, and it is traditionally ascribed to Ādi Śaṃkarācārya.

The ĀŚV introduces its discussion of Māṇḍ. 7 with the remark: "The fourth quarter, the stage which has now been reached, will now be described" (*caturthaḥ pādaḥ krama-prāpto vaktavya iti āha*), which implies that the preceding *mantra* — Māṇḍ. 6 — describes the sleeping state rather than the *turīya*. The ĀŚV then proceeds in its commentary on Māṇḍ. 7 to draw a very sharp distinction between the fourth state of the Self, which is to be defined only through negative attributes, and the *īśvara* of Māṇḍ. 6. The ĀŚV's commentary at this point spells out quite clearly the implications of the TI interpretation of the Māṇḍūkya, so I will give an outline of the commentary here.

According to the ĀŚV, the first three quarters of the Self comprise the unreal and illusory aspects of the Self, like the illusion of the snake and the rope. This aspect, it says, has the same nature as the seed and the sprout, i.e. it is bound up with the notion of causality. Thus, it is not *īśvara* as such that produces the world-appearance, for what we call *īśvara* is just the *ātman* which is conjoined with the illusory adjunct (*upādhi*) of the life-force (*prāṇa*). The pure *ātman* is not a cause at all. Furthermore, the pure Self is attained only by negating the characteristics of the three states, just as the true nature of the rope is ascertained by negating the illusory snake.

The ĀŚV cites a number of Upaniṣadic passages in its commentary on Māṇḍ. 7, but none of these citations *directly* supports the TI interpretation of the Upaniṣad. In fact, the only passage which can be taken as supporting the separation of Māṇḍ. 7 from Māṇḍ. 6 is its citation of Chānd. 6.8.2, which appears in its commentary on Māṇḍ. 6. Chānd. 6.8.2 says:

> Just as a bird fastened with a string, after flying in this direction and that without finding an abode elsewhere, settles down on its fastening — even so, my dear, the mind (*manas*), after flying in this direction and in that without finding an abode elsewhere, rests down upon breath (*prāṇa*); for the mind, my dear, has breath as its fastening.

Presumably, the idea behind the citation of Chānd. 6.8.2 is that in sleep the *ātman* is associated with *prāṇa* in a condition of ignorance, and that the universe arises from this *prāṇa* in the Self's state of ignorance. However, there is nothing in Chānd. 6.8.2 which supports this cosmological or metaphysical view. This passage in the Chāndogya simply means that in the state of sleep the mind is associated with the *prāṇa*, which continues to function and keep the body alive when the person is withdrawn from the everyday world in sleep and dreams. Chānd. 6.8.2 itself says nothing about *brahman* or *īśvara* at all, and the ĀŚV's association of this particular passage with these concepts is quite unjustified. Hence the ĀŚV really presents no textual support for its contention that it is not the Self or *brahman* as such, but only the Self in conjunction with the illusory adjunct of the *prāṇa*, which is responsible for the world-appearance.

The ĀŚV is the oldest and most authoritative work which advocates the TI interpretation of the Māṇḍūkya; it is, in fact, the *ur*-text or root-text for that kind of interpretation of the Upaniṣad. The paucity and weakness of the textual support which the ĀŚV cites in defense of its separation of Māṇḍ. 6 from Māṇḍ. 7 is therefore very significant. If one compares the ĀŚV's commentary on Māṇḍ. 6 and 7 with the standards of textual citation which can be found in other early Vedāntist works, like the Brahma-sūtras and the Brahma-sūtra-bhāṣyas, the weakness of the ĀŚV's commentary becomes even clearer. Such a comparison makes it very hard to believe that the TI interpretation was the prevailing interpretation of the Māṇḍūkya in the classical period.

(3) There exists a commentary on the Māṇḍūkya and the Āgama-prakaraṇa by Kūranārāyaṇa.[11] His date is uncertain, but as he is a follower of Rāmānuja (fl. 1120 C.E.) he cannot be dated before the 12th century. Kūranārāyaṇa's commentary is interesting for our purposes because it endorses, despite its rather late date, the IC rather than the TI interpretation of the Māṇḍūkya.

Kūranārāyaṇa concludes his commentary on Māṇḍ 3 with the words "Thus the first form of the Self is described" (*prathamaṃ rūpam-ity-arthaḥ*), and he concludes his commentary on Māṇḍ 4 with the words "Thus the second form of the Self is described" (*dvitīyaṃ rūpam-ity-arthaḥ*). His commentary on Māṇḍ 5 then describes the *taijasa* that which is characterized by ignorance but which is blissful and great (*yatra deśe supto 'jñāna-vṛtaḥ sukha-rūpaṃ bhagavantam*), and there is nothing in his commentary on this *mantra* which connects the *taijasa* with the *sarveśvara* that is the subject of Māṇḍ 6. Furthermore, he concludes his commentary on Māṇḍ 5 with the same words that he uses to conclude his commentaries on the previous two *mantras*: "Thus the third state of the Self; the third aspect" (*ātmanas-tṛtīyaḥ pādaḥ / tṛtīyaṃ rūpam*). Then he introduces Māṇḍ. 6 and *ślokas* 1-9 of the Āgama-prakaraṇa (which he regards as part of the Māṇḍūkyopaniṣad) with the following words:

> Having thus described the three-fold forms of the Self, the fourth *pāda* of the Self will be described with the words 'not inwardly cognitive' etc. [i.e. by Māṇḍ 7]. The intermediary passages (*madhye*) concerning the aspect of the *vaiśvānara* etc. referred to the places and functions of the Self. Now the greatness of the four forms will be described with respect to the fourth state of the Self.[12]

Immediately after this he cites Māṇḍ 6. Kūranārāyaṇa, therefore, clearly endorses the IC interpretation of the Māṇḍūkya.

Kūranārāyaṇa's endorsement of the IC interpretation of the Māṇḍūkya is also clear from some of his comments on *ślokas* 1-9. For example, in his commentary on ĀP 6 he connects the notion of the origin of all beings with the Self of four forms (*sarvabhāvānāṃ sarva-vastunāṃ yathāyogam-utpatti-hetuś-caturūpātmeti yojyam*), and he associates the *puruṣa* of Māṇḍ 6d with Hari (Viṣṇu) of the four aspects (*caturūpātmā hariḥ*). He also rejects both the *pariṇāmavāda* and *brahma-vivartavāda* doctrines in favor of the view that the world is the product of the mere will of the Lord, which is performed out of mere play or sport.

It is true that Kūranārāyaṇa concludes his discussion of AP 1-9 with the words "Now the description of the three-fold aspects is complete" (*iti śabdo rūpa-traya-nirūpaṇa-samāptau*) and that he introduces Māṇḍ 7 with the words "Now with respect to the fourth *pāda* of the Self" (*caturtha-pādam-ātmana āha*), but that is because he is convinced that the Upaniṣad (which he takes to include the *ślokas* as well as the *mantras*) is in four sections (*khaṇḍa*). Therefore, when he begins the second section he feels it appropriate to remark that the first three aspects of the Self have been fully described (whereas the fourth has been only partially described), and to *repeat* what he had said earlier, i.e. that Māṇḍ 7 (*nāntaḥprajñam-ity-ādi*) refers to the fourth state of the Self. In any case, one cannot conclude from his aforementioned remarks that Kūranārāyaṇa endorsed the TI interpretation of the Upaniṣad, for he clearly ends the discussion of the third state of the Self with Māṇḍ 5, and includes Māṇḍ 6 in his discussion of the fourth state of the Self.

(4) There is a commentary on the Nṛsiṃha-tāpanīyopaniṣad which has been erroneously ascribed to Ādi Śaṃkara. This is undoubtedly a work of the Śaṃkara school of a rather late date, and it is particularly interesting for that very reason, for there is evidence in it that there was a rather late tradition within the Śaṃkara school which supported the IC rather than the TI interpretation of the Māṇḍūkya.

In his commentary on Nṛsiṃha-pūrva-tāpanīya 4, where the Upaniṣad cites (without attribution) the *mantras* of the Māṇḍūkya, the unknown author of the commentary interrupts the text after

Māṇḍ. 6 (i.e. ... *prabhavāpyayau hi bhūtānām*) with a commentary on Māṇḍ. 2-6. At one point in his commentary he says:

> Though the reading is for the most part the same in both places (i.e. in both the Tāpanīya and the Māṇḍūkya), some differences are also to be seen. In the context of explaining the fourth (*turīya*) *mātra*, the reading in the Māṇḍūkya is '*eṣo 'ntaryāmy-eṣa īśāna eṣa prabhur-iti.*' But in the Tāpanīya, the reading is '*eṣo 'ntaryāmy-esa yonir-iti,*' leaving out the two words '*īśāna*' and '*prabhu.*'[13]

This passage is very interesting for two reasons. First, the passage says that the words "*īśāna*" and "*prabhu*" are found in Māṇḍ. 6, though the texts of the Māṇḍūkya which are extant today do not have these terms. There are two possible explanations for this discrepancy. It is possible — though unlikely, I think —that there was a variant reading of the Māṇḍūkya even in a rather late period of the history of the Vedānta which contained these terms. It is more likely, however, that this statement is an error — and one, moreover, that provides additional evidence that the Nṛsiṃha-tāpanīya-bhāṣya is not by Ādi Śaṃkara. This point was made by T. M. P. Mahadevan, who also noted that there may have been a confusion operating in the commentator's mind between the Māṇḍūkya and the Āgama-prakaraṇa, for ĀP 10 *does* contain the words "*īśāna*" and "*prabhu.*"[14]

The passage, however, is even more interesting because the commentator says explicitly that Māṇḍ. 6 is a description of the *fourth* state of the self. This is, of course, the IC interpretation of of the Māṇḍūkya.

Although the Nṛsiṃha-tāpanīya-bhāṣya is undoubtedly apocryphal, it provides further evidence that the Māṇḍūkya was originally interpreted according to the IC interpretation. Indeed, its testimony is particularly significant, for it is undoubtedly a writing that belongs to a comparatively late period of the *Śaṃkara* school of the Vedānta.

IV

One of the most obvious objections to the TI interpretation is that, prima facie, it makes no *sense* to associate the state of deep sleep (which is described in Māṇḍ. 5) with the omnisicient lord of all (which is described in Māṇḍ. 6), for we ordinarily think of the state of deep sleep as a state of ignorance or unconsciousness. In fact, there are passages in the classical Upaniṣads which show that the Vedāntic tradition regarded the state of sleep in just this way. Chāndogya 8.11 and 8.12 are particularly explicit on this point.

Chānd. 8.11 and 8.12 form the conclusion of an extended passage of the Chāndogya which begins with Chānd. 8.7. In Chānd. 8.7, Prajāpati begins to instruct Indra about the Self which is "free from evil, ageless and deathless." At first, Indra identifies this ageless and deathless Self with the physical body (Chānd. 8.8-8.9) and then with the Self in the dreaming state (Chānd. 8.10). Eventually, however, Indra himself rejects both of these views.

Then, in Chānd. 8.11, we find Indra entertaining the hypothesis that the Self which is "free from evil, ageless and deathless" is the Self which sleeps:

> Now, when one is sound asleep, composed (*samasta*), serene (*saṃprasanna*) and knows no dream, that is the *ātman*, that is the immortal, the fearless, that is *brahman*.

However, Indra himself comes to reject this view. Thus, the Upaniṣad says:

> Then, even before reaching the gods, he (Indra) saw this danger: 'Assuredly, indeed, this one (in the state of deep sleep) does not exactly know himself (*ātmānam*) with the thought "I am he," nor indeed the things here. He becomes one who has gone to destruction (*vināśa*). I see nothing enjoyable in this.'

This passage rejects the idea that the state of deep sleep is one in which the Self is "free from evil, ageless and deathless" so categorically that it is unlikely that any later Upaniṣad like the Māṇḍūkya could have contradicted it.

Chānd. 8.12 provides further evidence against the identification of God (*īśvara*) with the sleeping state of the Self, because this passage identifies the sleeping state with an *embodied* state of the Self, whereas the "ageless and deathless " Self is not in the body at all. Thus 8.12 says:

> This body is mortal. It belongs to death. But it is the support of that deathless, bodiless Self. Verily, the embodied Self (*saśarīra*) is held by pleasure and pain. Verily, there is no freedom from pleasure and pain for one who is embodied. Verily, pleasure and pain do not touch one who is bodiless.

Then the passage says that it is only when the "serene one" (*saṃprasāda*) rises up from the body at death that it "reaches the highest light" (*paraṃ-jyoti*) and appears with its own form (*svarūpa*). It is important to note here the use of the term "*saṃprasāda*," for this term is virtually identical with the term "*saṃprasanna*," which Chānd. 8.11 uses to describe the sleeping state of the Self. Thus, the Chāndogya uses the term "*saṃprasanna*" or "*saṃprasāda*" to designate two things: (1) the state of deep sleep, wherein one knows nothing, either within or without and (2) the state which is a prelude to death. In neither sense can this state be regarded as the "ageless and deathless" Self. According to the Chāndogya, the "ageless and deathless" Self is attained only at the time of death, when one is released from the body.

This interpretation of the Chāndogya's teaching on the subject of sleep is confirmed by Chānd. 8.6 as well. In Chānd. 8.6 the terms "composed" (*samasta*) and "serene" (*saṃprasanna*) are used to describe the Self in the state of deep sleep (Chānd. 8.6.3) and the Self in the state of weakness which precedes death (Chānd. 8.6.4). According to the Chāndogya, the *saṃprasanna ātman* is located in the channels of the heart. The Upaniṣad says that at death the Self departs from these channels of the heart to the head, and from there passes along the rays of the sun to immortality (Chānd. 8.6.1 and 8.6.6).

One other passage of the Chāndogya must be considered in order to complete the analysis of the Chāndogya's teachings about the state of deep sleep: Uddālaka Āruṇi's instructions to his son Śvetaketu in Chānd. 6.8. Chānd. 6.8.1 has frequently been interpreted by scholars to mean that in the state of deep sleep the Self attains "Being," which is the Chāndogya's favorite term for the Absolute.[1] This interpretation, it seems to me, is untenable. All that 6.8.1 says is that in the state of deep sleep the person has become "full," "complete," "perfected" or "serene" (*saṃpanna*), and that he has "gone to his own" (*svam apīta*). The term "*saṃpanna*," as we have already seen, is used in Chānd. 8.11 and 8.12 in a way which clearly precludes its meaning "being" (*sat*). Furthermore, Chānd. 6.8.2 goes on to say that in the state of deep sleep the mind rests upon the breath (*prāṇa*), and this is clearly not regarded as the ultimate or highest state, for Chānd. 6.8.6 says:

> When a person here is dying, my dear, his voice goes into his mind; *his mind, into his breath* (*prāṇa*); his breath, into heat (*tejas*); the heat, into the highest divinity (*parasyām devatāyām*). That which is the finest essence: all this has that as its Self. That is reality (*satya*). That is *ātman*. You are that (*tat tvam asi*), Śvetaketu.

In this passage the breath — which has previously been associated with the state of deep sleep — is said to be two stages removed from the state in which the person is identified with the Absolute.

In summary, Chānd. 6.8, 8.6 and 8.11-12 present a teaching on the sleeping state which is internally consistent and also incompatible with the TI interpretation of the Māṇḍūkya. For it would appear to make no sense to associate the state in which one "does not know himself" and in which one has "gone to destruction" with the omniscient, omnipotent *īśvara* which is described in Māṇḍ. 6. The Chāndogyopaniṣad shows very clearly that the Vedāntists of the early Upaniṣadic tradition were no more inclined than we are to associate the concept of *īśvara* with the state of deep sleep. According to the Chāndogya, the state of deep sleep is simply one of the three states of the *embodied* Self, and not a particularly desirable one at that.

V

The Bṛhad-āraṇyakopaniṣad (BU) has a special importance for the Māṇḍūkya, as previous writers on the subject have already noted.[1] This is especially true of BU 4.2.1-4.4.25. This extended passage is, in a sense, the "root text" of the Māṇḍūkya, for the Māṇḍūkya's teachings about the four states (*pādas*) of the Self are undoubtedly derived from it. An analysis of this important passage will show that the *īśvara* of Māṇḍ. 6 must be identified with the fourth state of the Self which is described in Māṇḍ. 7, and not with the state of deep sleep.

BU 4.2.1-4.4.25 consists of a dialogue (or series of dialogues) between Yājñavalkya and King Janaka, the main subject of which is: "What happens to the Self at death?"[2] Yājñavalkya's answer to his own question is given in BU 4.3.35-4.4.25, but it is preceded by some preliminary teachings which are largely concerned with the states of dreaming and sleeping. The teachings of the Bṛhad-āraṇyaka on the state of sleep are very similar to those of the Chāndogya, and, like those of the Chāndogya, are incompatible with the TI interpretation of the Māṇḍūkya. Here I shall note briefly the essential points of Yājñavalkya's teachings on the subject of sleeping and dreaming, and then outline his teachings on the subject of what happens to the soul at death.

BU 4.2.3 speaks of the "space of the heart" (*hṛdaya-ākāśa*), the channels (*hita*) of the heart, and of the "path which leads upward from the heart" — all of which is reminiscent of Chānd. 8.6. Unlike Chānd 8.6, however, BU 4.2.3 does not explicitly identify the channels of the heart as the location of the sleeping Self. Nevertheless, it is clear that the author of the *Māṇḍūkya* regarded BU 4.2.3 as associating the sleeping Self with the heart, for Māṇḍ. 4, which is concerned with the dreaming state, refers to the Self which is "an eater of more refined food (*pravivikta-bhuj*) than is the bodily Self," and BU 4.2.3 associates this *pravivikta-bhuj* with the heart.

It is also clear from BU 4.2.4 that the Upaniṣad does not regard the sleeping state as the highest state of the Self. For BU 4.2.4, after saying that in the state of deep sleep the Self becomes identified with the *prāṇas* ("The eastern breaths are his eastern quarter; the southern breaths are his southern quarter" etc.), denies that this state is the real state of the Self. The Self, it says, is "not this, not that" (*neti neti*), and is unseizable (*agṛhya*), indestructible (*aśīrya*) and is unrelated to anything (*asaṅga*). According to the Bṛhad-āraṇyaka, such terms apply only to the fourth state of the Self.

Although the Bṛhad-āraṇyaka does not actually enumerate the four different states of the Self in exactly the same way the Māṇḍūkya does, the four states of the Māṇḍūkya are *implicit* in the Bṛhad-āraṇyaka, as follows:

(1) BU 4.3.7 and 4.3.9 refer to the *svapna-sthāna*. This is described as an intermediate state between being in "this world" and being in "that world" (i.e. the postmortem state). It includes both the dreaming state (which is described in Māṇḍ. 4) and the sleeping state (which is described in Māṇḍ. 5).

(2) The BU also recognizes the waking state, which it refers to as *buddhānta* (BU 4.3.18, 4.3.34). This is also the state which is implied in BU 4.3.7's description of "being in this world."

(3) The dreamless, sleeping state is referred to in BU 4.3.19. In fact, the Māṇḍūkya's description of this state as the one where one "desires no desires and sees no dreams" (*yatra na kaṃcana kāmam kāmayate na kaṃcana svapnaṃ paśyati*) is taken verbatim from this passage of the Bṛhad-āraṇyaka.

(4) BU 4.3.35-4.4.25 describe the "state of being in the other world," i.e. the *disembodied* state of the Self. As we shall see shortly, the postmortem state (at least for the individual who has transcended all desires before he dies) is the same as the fourth state of the Self (*caturtha, turīya*) which is described in Māṇḍ. 6 and 7.

In other words, all four states of the Māṇḍūkya are clearly described in the Bṛhad-āraṇyaka. The only difference is that the Māṇḍūkya clearly differentiates the dreaming (*svapna*) from the dreamless (*suṣupta*) states, whereas the distinction between these two states is not always clear in the BU. The Bṛhad-āraṇyaka conflates these two states in BU 4.3.7-4.3.34; and, as a result, it enumerates clearly only three states. However, it clearly *describes* four of them. If one makes explicit the distinction between the dreaming state and the dreamless state, as the Māṇḍūkya does, then (a) the *svapna-sthāna* of BU 4.3.7 becomes the second (dreaming) and third (dreamless) states of Māṇḍ. 4 and 5, and (b) the post-mortem state becomes the fourth state (Māṇḍ. 6 and 7).

The description of the after death state is given by the Bṛhad-āraṇyaka in 4.3.35-4.4.25. Some parts of this description closely resemble the description of the after death state in the Chāndogya. Thus, like the Chāndogya, the Bṛhad-āraṇyaka speaks of a state of weakness which precedes death, and, like the Chāndogya, it says that in this state the person retires to the channels of the heart. Here, the Bṛhad-āraṇyaka says, the person "becomes unified" (*ekī-bhavati*).[3] Then at death, the "point of his heart becomes lit up" and by that light the "Self departs, either by the eye, or by the head or by other bodily parts." All of this is very similar to the description of death and the dying process in Chānd. 8.12.

Then BU 4.4.3-4.3.6 describes the process of rebirth. BU 4.4.3 begins by comparing the dying person who relinquishes the body to a caterpillar that has come to the end of a blade of grass. Then it is said (BU 4.4.4) that, like the caterpillar, the dying person creates new forms for itself, like that of the fathers, gods, Prajāpati, or Brahmā, or of other beings. It can do this, BU 4.4.5 says, because the Self is *brahman* (*ayam ātmā brahma*),[4] and because it is "made of knowledge, of mind, of breath, of seeing" etc. — in fact, made of everything (*sarva-maya*). Accordingly, the forms one attains and the experiences one has are determined by one's desires and conduct (BU 4.4.5-4.4.6). BU 4.4.6 concludes this teaching by citing the following verse:

> Where one's mind is attached — the subtle Self (*liṅgaṃ manas*)
> Goes together with action, being attached to it alone.
> Obtaining the end of his action,
> Whatever he does in this world,
> He comes again from that world
> To this world of action.

BU 4.4.6 and 4.4.7 then introduce some important ideas which *cannot* be found in the parallel passage of the Chāndogya (Chānd. 8.12).

BU 4.4.6 says (in effect) that the preceding description of the process of rebirth and the process whereby the dying Self creates new forms for itself applies only to the man who still has desires. In the case of the man who has no desires, whose desire is satisfied (*āpta-kāma*), whose desire is the Self, the process is different: being *brahman*, such a man goes to *brahman*. Then BU 4.4.7-4.4.21 cites some verses, of which the following are particularly interesting:

When are liberated all
The desires that lodge in one's heart,
Then a mortal becomes immortal.
Therein he reaches *brahman*!

He who has found and has awakened to the Self
That has entered this conglomerate abode
He is the maker of everything (*viśvakṛt*), for he is the creator of all (*sarvasya kartā*);
The world is his: indeed, he is the world itself (*sa u loka eva*).

By the mind alone is it to be perceived.
There is in it no diversity.
He gets death after death
Who perceives here, as it were, diversity.

As a unity only is to be looked upon –
This indemonstrable, immeasurable and eternal being.
This Self is spotless, beyond space,unborn (*aja*), great, and eternal (*dhruva*).

This is significantly different from the parallel passage regarding the fourth state of the Self in Chānd. 8.12.[5] For one thing, this passage does not ascribe any individual form to the person who has merged into *brahman*. Indeed, any such ascription would appear to be precluded by the fact that the passages emphasize that this state is a state of nonduality. Furthermore, this state is described as one of divinity as well as freedom: as BU 4.4.13 says, the Self in *this* state is the maker of everything — indeed, the world itself. In this passage, then, the qualities of *īśvara* which are described in Māṇḍ. 6 and the qualities of the transcendent, nondual *ātman* which are described in Māṇḍ. 7 are combined in a *single* description of the liberated soul that has merged in *brahman*.

BU 4.4.22-4.4.25 concludes Yājñavalkya's description of what happens to the Self at death. This passage alone is sufficient proof that the TI interpretation of the Māṇḍūkya cannot be reconciled with the early Upaniṣadic teachings about the four states of the

Self. For BU 4.4.22 speaks of the great, unborn Self, who is located in the space within the heart, and who is the lord of all (*sarveśvara*), the overlord of beings (*bhūtādhipati*) and the protector of beings (*bhūta-pāla*). He is the one who is sought by those who perform the Vedic sacrifices, engage in penance, become ascetics and leave their homes and wander forth as mendicants. This Self is beyond desires. At the same time, the Upaniṣad also describes this state purely negatively. The Self is not "not this, not that," and it is unseizable, indestructible and not attached. Thus BU 4.4.22-4.4.25, like Māṇḍ. 6 and 7, also combine "positive" and "negative" attributes in a single description of the fourth state of the Self.

Before we leave the Bṛhad-āraṇyaka, we should also look at BU 3.7 and 3.8. These passages provide important additional evidence that the Bṛhad-āraṇyaka regarded the concept of *īśvara* and purely negative descriptions of the absolute as complementary descriptions of the *same* thing.

BU 3.7, for example, identifies *brahman* with both the *ātman* and the inner controller (*antaryāmin*). This *antaryāmin*, who is said to dwell in the waters, fire, atmosphere etc., is also said to to be the "unseen (*adṛṣṭa*) seer, the unheard hearer, the unthought thinker and the ununderstood understander." Here the term "*antaryāmin*" corresponds to the same term in Māṇḍ. 6, while the description of the "unseen hearer" etc. corresponds to the purely negative descriptions of the fourth state of the Self in Māṇḍ. 7.

BU 3.8 is concerned with the concept of the "imperishable" (*akṣara*), which is described in terms of both negative attributes (like those of Māṇḍ. 7) and in terms of attributes which belong with Māṇḍ. 6. Thus, BU 3.8.8 says that the *akṣara* is what is not coarse, not fine, not short, not long, not glowing, not adhesive, not shadow, not darkness, not air, not space, unrelated to anything (*asaṅga*), without taste, without smell, without eye, without ear, without voice, without mind, without brilliance, without breath, without mouth, without measure (*amātra*), without inside (*anantara*), and without outside (*abāhya*). At the same time, however, BU 3.8.9 says that it is at the command of this imperishable (*akṣara*) that the sun and moon stand apart, that the moments, hours, days etc. stand apart, and that "some rivers flow from the snowy mountains to the east and others to the west." In this passage of the Bṛhad-āraṇyaka, 3.8.9 is clearly the counterpart of Māṇḍ. 6, and 3.8.8 is the counterpart to Māṇḍ. 7. Both passages are presented as complementary descriptions of the same thing.

It is, of course, well known that Śaṃkara in his Bṛhadāraṇyakopaniṣad-bhāṣya (BUB) gives a very different interpretation of these important passages. According to BUB 3.8.12, the imperishable Self (*akṣara*) is different from the *antaryāmin*, for the *antaryāmin* is the Self as it is conditioned by the limited adjuncts (*upādhis*) of the power of eternal and unlimited knowledge, whereas the imperishable (*akṣara*) or the supreme Self (*paramātman*) is the Self which is free from these illusory adjuncts.

Śaṃkara's interpretation involves reading quite a lot into the text which is not there. BU 3.8.8 simply describes the *akṣara* with a series of negative attributes, and BU 3.8.9 then commences with the statement, "Verily, O Gārgī, at the command of that imperishable the sun and moon" etc. The BU clearly intends to identify the *akṣara* with the inner controller (*antaryāmin*) of all things, as do *mantras* 6 and 7 of the Māṇḍūkya.

VI

The Maitrī, like the Māṇḍūkya, is a late — though still classical — Upaniṣad. Since we do not know the dates when these two Upaniṣads were written, we do not know if the Maitrī influenced the Māṇḍūkya, or whether the influence (if any) was the other way around. However, even if the Maitrī was not one of the sources for the Māṇḍūkya, it undoubtedly furnishes valuable information about the Vedāntic thinking of the period when the Māṇḍūkya was probably written.

As we have just seen, the oldest Upaniṣad, the Bṛhad-āraṇyaka, regards *īśvara* and the negatively described transcendent *ātman* as two different descriptions of the same thing. Maitrī 7.1-7.7 show unmistakably that when the Maitrī was written the same teaching was still upheld in the Upaniṣadic tradition. The parts of this passage which are particularly relevant for the interpretation of the Māṇḍūkya are given below:

Maitrī 7.1:

He is unthinkable, formless, unfathomable, hidden, blameless, compact, impenetrable, devoid of qualities (*nirguṇa*), pure, brilliant, enjoying qualities (*guṇabhuj*), awesome, unproduced, the lord who is a *yogin* (*yogīśvara*), omniscient, munificent, immeasurable, without beginning or end, illustrious, unborn (*aja*), intelligent, indescribable, the creator of all (*sarvasṛj*), the self of all (*sarvasyātman*), the enjoyer of all (*sarvabhuj*), the lord of all (*sarvasyeśāna*), the inmost being of everything (*sarvasyāntarāntara*).

Maitrī 7.2:

He is tranquil, soundless, fearless, sorrowless, blissful, satisfied, steadfast, unmoving, immortal, enduring...

Maitrī 7.3:

He is without beginning or end, unmeasured, unlimited, not to be moved by another, independent, devoid of marks, formless, of endless power (*ananta-śakti*), the creator (*dhātṛ*), the enlightener.

Maitrī 7.4:

He is pure within, clean, void (*śūnya*), tranquil, breathless, selfless (*nirātman*), endless (*ananta*).

Maitrī 7.5:

...him who is called *praṇava* (*Aum*), a leader, brilliant, beyond sleep, ageless, deathless, sorrowless.

Maitrī 7.6:

He who is wise, the ordainer, within all (*sarvāntara*), imperishable (*akṣara*), pure, clean, shining, patient, tranquil.

Maitrī 7.7:

He, indeed, is the Self within the heart, very subtle, kindled like fire, assuming all forms (*viśva-rūpa*). This whole world is his food. On him creatures here are woven. He is the Self which is free from evil, ageless, deathless, sorrowless, free from uncertainty, free from fetters, whose conception is the real, whose desire is the real. He is the supreme lord (*parameśvara*), he is the ruler of beings (*bhūtādhipati*), he is the protector of beings (*bhūta-pāla*). He is the separating bridge. This self, assuredly, is Īśāna, Śambhu, Bhava, Rudra, Prajāpati, Viśvasṛj, Hiraṇyagarbha, Satya, Prāṇa, Spirit, the Punisher, the Unshaken, Viṣṇu, Nārāyaṇa. He who is in the fire, and he who is here in the heart, and he who is yonder in the sun: he is one. To you who are all this, the all-formed (*viśva-rūpa*), hidden in the real ether, be adoration.

Here, both "positive" and "negative" descriptions are used in a single description of the highest Self. Since the Māṇḍūkya and the Maitrī were probably written about the same time (i.e. in the late classical period), this is a further indication that the Māṇḍūkya must have been interpreted originally according to the IC rather than the TI interpretation.

PART II

VII

It has been shown in chapters 4-6 that the Māṇḍūkya was undoubtedly interpreted in the classical, pre-Śaṃkara period according to the IC rather than the TI interpretation. This raises the question: When and how did the *TI* interpretation enter the tradition of the Vedānta?

An initially attractive hypothesis is that it did so with the author of the Āgama-prakaraṇa, the oldest commentary on the Māṇḍūkya, who is generally thought to have been Gauḍapāda, the *parama-guru* of Ādi Śaṃkara. However, the discussion in chapter 1 has cast doubt on the view that the author of the Āgama-prakaraṇa upheld the TI interpretation of the Māṇḍūkya. If we want to determine how and when the TI interpretation of the Māṇḍūkya entered the Vedāntic tradition, therefore, we must look, not to the Āgama-prakaraṇa, but to the Vaitathya-prakaraṇa (VP), the Advaita-prakaraṇa (ADP) and the Alāta-śānti-prakaraṇa (ALP) of the Āgama-śāstra, for these *prakaraṇas*, taken as a whole, do teach in a very clear and unequivocal way the doctrine that the world is nothing but the false imagination of the mind, and it is on the doctrine of the unreality of the world that the TI interpretation of the Māṇḍūkya is based.

In this chapter I shall confine my attention to the ALP, which is the most puzzling and interesting of these *prakaraṇas*. I cannot cover all of the issues raised by this *prakaraṇa* here; however, I will attempt to reach some definite conclusions about the attitude which the author of this treatise takes towards Buddhism, for it is this issue, it turns out, that is crucial to the question of when and how the TI interpretation of the Māṇḍūkya entered the Vedāntic tradition.

The Alāta-śānti-prakaraṇa has fascinated scholars for a long time.[1] It is a peculiar work, for the terminology of the *prakaraṇa* is thoroughly Buddhist, yet the work appears as the fourth chapter of a larger work called the "Āgama-śāstra," the first three chapters of which are clearly treatises on the Vedānta. Furthermore, there is a dedicatory verse (*maṅgalācaraṇa*) at the beginning of the work which can only be to Gautama Buddha.[2]

On the face of it, there would appear to be three possible explanations for the above facts:

(1) The ALP is, in fact, a Buddhist text, and it was written by a Buddhist. This is so despite the fact that the first three *prakaraṇas* of the Āgama-śāstra (ĀŚ) are treatises on the Vedānta. This seems to have been the view held by S. N. Dasgupta, V. Bhattacharya, T. R. V. Murti and S. Mayeda.[3]

(2) The ALP is a purely Vedāntic treatise which uses Buddhist terminology for an ulterior purpose — perhaps to proselytize Buddhists or persons sympathetic to Buddhism to the Vedānta system. The result is that the ALP resembles the Buddhist system in many respects, but it is in fact critical of Buddhist views.

ALP 99 is particularly important for this interpretation of the ALP. According to this view, when Gauḍapāda says "This was not taught by the Buddha" (*naitad buddhena bhāṣitam*), he simply means that his doctrines are not those of the Buddha.

This interpretation of the ALP has been defended by a number of scholars, including T. M. P. Mahadevan and R. D. Karmarkar.[4]

(3) A third possibility is that the ALP is a purely Vedāntic treatise, but that it is *not* critical of the Buddha. The terminology is Buddhist, but that is only because the author wanted to show that, in the final analysis, the teachings of the Buddha are in fact Vedāntic teachings.

It is clear that the ALP attempts to effect some kind of *rapprochement* between Buddhism and the Vedānta. The real question is: what is the nature of the resulting doctrine, and does it do justice to the wordviews of both systems?

If, as I believe, Buddhism and the Vedānta represent very different and largely irreconcilable worldviews, some compromises would have had to be made in order to achieve any kind of *rapprochement*. According to the Upaniṣads, the world is real and is the manifestation of *brahman*, in the sense that *brahman* is both the material and the efficient cause of the world.[5] In Buddhism, on the other hand, the world is explained purely phenomenally, according to the principle of dependent co-origination (*pratītya-samutpāda*). There is no possibility within orthodox Buddhism of explaining the world in terms of a transcendent Absolute which lies outside of or beyond this purely phenomenal chain of cause and effect. It is true that some of the very radical Mahāyānists (Mādhyamika Śūnyavādins) held that all *dharmas* were, from the level of absolute reality, non-existent and void (*śūnya*), and that the chain of cause and effect was therefore ultimately unreal.[6] Nevertheless, all Buddhists were in agreement that either (1) the world was unreal from the level of ultimate reality (*atyantābhāva*, *atyanta-śūnya*) or (2) that it was real and could be explained, even at the ultimate level, entirely in terms of the purely phenomenal chain of cause and effect (*pratītya-samutpāda*). Both formulations are fundamentally incompatible with the Upaniṣadic doctrines.

Although a full reconciliation of the Vedānta and Buddhism was manifestly impossible, it is clear that the author of the ALP attempted a synthesis between the two systems. Essentially, what he did to bridge the differences between the two systems of thought was to deny the reality of the world (as the Mahāyānists did) while also asserting the existence of a nondual, all-pervading reality which is identical with pure consciousness.

The result, it must be said, is neither good Buddhism nor good Vedānta. It is not good Vedānta, because there is no way that the Upaniṣads can be interpreted to mean that the world is unreal. According to the Upaniṣads, the world is real because it *is brahman*, whereas according to the ALP (and the VP and ADP as well), it is unreal because it is *not brahman*. On the other hand, the resulting doctrine is not good Buddhism because no orthodox Buddhist could have upheld the doctrine of an Absolute which is unchanging, pure consciousness. Such a view was anathematized very early in the history of the Buddhism.[7]

I shall not review here all of the evidence which can be found in the ALP to support the contention that it teaches what, in Buddhist terms, is an eternalist (*śāśvata*), and therefore false and pernicious doctrine. I shall limit myself to discussing some particularly clear and interesting examples.

Let us begin with ALP 7-9, which says:

> The deathless does not become mortal, and the mortal does not become deathless. There will be no change (literally, 'becoming other') in nature in any way whatever.(ALP 7)

> He for whom an entity (*dharma*), deathless by nature, undergoes death, how will his deathless entity, since it is a product (*kṛtaka*), remain changeless (*niścala*)?(ALP 8)

> Nature (*prakṛti*) is to be known as that which is self-established (*sāṃsiddhikī*), self-existent (*svābhāvikī*), innate (*sahajā*), not artificial (*akṛtā*), and as something which does not give up its self-nature.(ALP 9)[8]

As V. Bhattacharya pointed out,[9] these verses irresistibly call to mind passages in Nāgārjuna's Mūla-madhyamaka-kārikās (MMK). The second sentence of ALP 7, in fact, has exactly the same meaning and virtually the same wording as MMK XV.8 (*prakṛter-anyathābhāvo na hi jātūpapadyate*). But what are we to infer from this fact? It does not mean, as Bhattacharya implied, that the author of the ALP was teaching Nāgārjunian doctrines. Quite the contrary: the ALP is teaching a doctrine that directly *contradicts* the one held by Nāgārjuna.

According to Nāgārjuna — who in this respect is quite faithful to fundamental Buddhist principles — everything is impermanent (*anitya*). In fact, according to Nāgārjuna, it is precisely this essential characteristic of all *dharmas* which explains (1) why everything is suffering and how the cycle of suffering can arise (the first and second of the four-fold noble truths of Buddhism) and (2) how it is possible to put an end to the cycle of suffering (the third and fourth of the four-fold noble truths). Nāgārjuna intends the statement that there can be no change in a nature (*prakṛter-anyathābhāvo na hi jātūpapadyate*) to be taken as a refutation of the view of the opponent (*pūrvapakṣin*), who holds that things have a self-nature (*svabhāva*, *prakṛti*). Against this eternalist doctrine, Nāgārjuna upholds the view that all *dharmas* lack a self-nature and have no real, independent existence apart from their causes and conditions (*sarva-dharma-śūnyatā*).

In the ALP, on the other hand, this *svabhāva-vāda* or *prakṛti-vāda* is taken to be the correct view (*siddhānta*). It is easy to miss this point because the ALP fully accepts the validity of Nāgārjuna's destructive arguments as long as they are directed against the independent, self-existent reality of things (*bhāvas*) or *dharmas*. However, the ALP, unlike Nāgārjuna, maintains that there is a non-*dharmic* reality which is unborn, unchanging and eternal. According to the ALP, this underlying reality is mind or consciousness (*vijñāna*, *citta*), and it is the *only* thing that exists. All the *dharmas* (as Nāgārjuna has shown) are illusory. But *mind* or consciousness is real, and it is deathless, immutable, self-established, self-existent, innate, and never gives up its self-nature.

According to the Buddhists, this is an "eternalist" (*śāśvata*) view, and it is precisely the kind of view that Nāgārjuna was arguing *against*. Nāgārjuna does so throughout the MMK, and it is the specific target of his attack in the *svabhāva-parīkṣā* (or "chapter on self-nature") where the statement *prakṛter-anyathābhāvo* etc. is found. Nāgārjuna uses it there as an essential part of a reductio ad absurdum argument, which essentially goes as follows: (1) If things had a self-nature, then there could be no change in things whatever; (2) But this is wrong, for the view that things never change is preposterous; (3) Hence things do not have any self-nature. In other words, the view that Nāgārjuna takes as the absurdum of his argument is taken by the ALP as the *siddhānta*.[10]

This one example shows quite clearly that the first interpretation of the ALP outlined above must be rejected. The ALP was undoubtedly not written by a Buddhist author and it is not a Buddhist text. No alert, orthodox Buddhist could ever have accepted the ALP's interpretation of *prakṛter-anyathābhāvo na hi jātūpapadyate* from MMK XV.8, for in this passage the author of the ALP is trying to turn Nāgārjuna on his head.

What are we to say about the second interpretation? Scholars who have advocated this interpretation have insisted that the Buddhist terminology of the ALP must not be taken at face value. I think that this is essentially correct. However, their view has also been that Gauḍapāda's real intention was to criticize the views of the Buddha, or, at the very least, to show where they fell short of the true teaching, and this view seems to me to be incorrect. I think that it cannot be reasonably doubted that the author of the ALP, whoever he was, wrote the ALP in order to identify the Buddha's views with his own. We probably will never know what his motive was in doing so, and his substantialist and eternalist interpretation of Buddhism must undoubtedly be rejected; nevertheless, it is impossible to doubt that such was his underlying purpose in writing the ALP. There is incontrovertible evidence for this in the dedicatory verse (*maṅgalācaraṇa*) which begins the ALP, for this verse cannot possibly refer to anyone but Gautama Buddha.

The Āgama-śāstra-vivaraṇa takes the term "*dvipadāṃ varam*" in this verse to mean *puruṣottama*, a common term in the Vedic tradition which can also mean, like "*dvipadāṃ varam*," "best of men." On this basis, the ĀŚV contends that the verse refers to Nārāyaṇa. Upaniṣadbrahmayogin, a late writer of the Śaṃkara school, says that the phrase refers to Śuka, an *avatāra* of Nārāyaṇa.[11] Both of these interpretations are very implausible. "*Dvipadāṃ varam*" is a very common epithet of the Buddha in Buddhist works, and the view that all *dharmas* are like the sky (*ākāśa-kalpa*) and that there is no difference between knowledge (*jñāna*) and what is known (*jñeya*) is taught frequently in the Mahāyāna *sūtras*. On the other hand, there is no basis for attributing such views to the *ṛṣi* and *avatāra* Nārāyaṇa or to Śukadeva rather than to Gautama Buddha. Furthermore, the *maṅgalācaraṇa* introduces a work which is filled with specifically Buddhist terminology. To assume that the author of the *maṅgalācaraṇa* intended it to praise anyone other than Gautama Buddha is to imply that its author was being deliberately and flagrantly misleading.

The view that the *maṅgalācaraṇa* eulogizes Gautama Buddha, and that the author of the ALP regarded his doctrines and those of the Buddha as identical, is not contradicted by ALP 99. This *kārikā* comes at the conclusion of the *prakaraṇa*. It says:

> The knowledge (*jñāna*) of the *buddha* who teaches the way (*tāyin*) does not cross over to the *dharmas*. Thus, all *dharmas* are knowledge. This was not spoken by the Buddha (*naitad buddhena bhāṣitam*).

The proponents of the second interpretation (which is the traditional one) maintain that the phrase "*naitad buddhena bhāṣitam*" simply means that the author's views were not those of the Buddha. But when the verse is placed in context it is clear that it does not mean this. The statement that knowledge does not pass over to the *dharmas* is also found in ALP 96, from which it is concluded that knowledge is unrelated (*asaṅga*) to anything. ALP 97 then connects the proposition that knowledge is unrelated to anything with the view that all *dharmas* are unborn, which is a fundamental Mahāyāna doctrine. ALP 98 then says that all *dharmas* are without covering (*alabdhāvaraṇa*), pure by nature (*prakṛti-nirmala*), enlightened from the very beginning (*ādi-buddha*), and thus liberated (*mukta*). Then ALP 98 concludes: "Those who lead others on the path (*nāyakas*), it is said, know this (*budhyanta*)." (The term "*nāyaka*" is frequently used in Buddhist texts to refer to the Buddha.) What ALP 98 says, therefore, is that all the foregoing teachings, including the teaching that knowledge does not cross over to the *dharmas*, is taught by the Buddhas. Taken in conjunction with the preceding verse (ALP 98), it is clear that ALP 99 simply means that the *buddhas know* that knowledge does not cross over to the *dharmas*, that *dharmas* are unborn, that they are without covering etc., but that they do not *say* this.[12]

According to the ALP, the reason why the Buddhas do not teach this truth (although they know it) is that it is beyond the reach of words. The fundamental nature of the *dharmas* (*dharmatā*) can be realized through an intuitive realization on the part of the individual (*svasaṃvedana*), but strictly speaking it cannot be taught. This doctrine was probably held by all of the Buddhist schools, but it was particularly emphasized by the Mahāyāna. There are many passages in the Mahāyāna literature where it is said that from the day of his enlightenment, the Buddha never (really) uttered a single word etc.[13] Hence ALP 99 does not contradict the plain meaning of the *maṅgalācaraṇa* at the beginning of the *prakaraṇa*.

It should be noted, however, that even here the *kārikā-kāra* is giving a very non-Buddhist interpretation to the silence of the Buddha. According to the ALP, there is an absolute, eternal and unchanging reality which is identical with pure consciousness (*citta*, *vijñāna*), and, like the *brahman* of the Upaniṣads, it is beyond the reach of speech and mind. (In fact, as we shall see shortly, it *is* *brahman*, even though it is not called "*brahman*" in the ALP.) This doctrine, as I have already pointed out, is a Buddhist heresy. The heresy is not immediately apparent because the ALP deliberately eschews the use of any Vedāntic terminology, and therefore does not designate this Absolute by Vedāntic terms like "*ātman*" or "*brahman*." However, the heresy becomes apparent when we look carefully at what the ALP says about mind or consciousness (*citta*, *manas*, *vijñāna*).

The basic doctrine of the ALP is that the whole phenomenal universe (*prapañca*) arises from the vibration (*spandana*) and imagination (*vikalpa*) of the mind, and that, as such, the world is unreal, like dreams and magic (*svapna-māyā*).[14] But what about the mind itself? Does it continue to exist after the illusion of a phenomenal world existing outside of the mind is dispelled? According to Buddhist doctrine (even Vijñānavāda doctrine), the answer to this question must be "No." In Buddhism, mind (*citta*, *vijñāna*) is simply one of the five *skandhas*. As such, it is simply part of the chain of causation (*pratītya-samutpāda*). Mind cannot be an Absolute in Buddhism. Since it is a *skandha*, is compounded (*saṃskṛta*), and is involved in the cycle of suffering, it is extinguished in *nirvāṇa*.[15] Consequently, if the ALP were teaching a Buddhist doctrine, it would have to teach either (1) that the mind never exists, which was the view of the Śūnyavāda Mādhyamikas, or (2) that it exists — specifically, that it has an "other dependent" or *paratantra* existence — but that it ceases to exist in *nirvāṇa*, which was the view of all of the other Buddhist schools. It is clear that neither of these Buddhist views is taught in the *prakaraṇas* of the Āgama-śāstra.

Let us consider first two *kārikās* from the Advaita-prakaraṇa. ADP 32-33 says:

> When, as a result of the realization of the truth of the *ātman*, (the mind) does not imagine, it goes to the state of being non-mind (*amanas*); in the absence of anything to grasp, it is is non-grasping.
>
> They (the wise ones) assert the *jñāna* free from imagination, birthless, not different from what is known. *Brahman* is that which is known, birthless, eternal. The birthless is known by the birthless.

Despite the fact that ADP 32 says that the mind becomes non-mind (*amanas*) when it ceases to imagine, ADP 32 cannot be taken to mean that mind *as such* ceases to exist when imagination ceases, on pain of inconsistency. The only way that ADP 32 and 33 can be interpreted together, and contradiction can be avoided, is to assume that the *kārikā-kāra* is using the word "mind" in two senses: (1) as the imagination of the mind, or what the mind imagines; and (2) what does the imagining. When ADP 32 says that the mind becomes non-mind, it must be taken to mean that when false imagination ceases, mind in the former sense disappears, but that mind in the latter sense — i.e. what does the imagining — does not. According to ADP 33, when the mind becomes non-grasping, no longer imagines, and is no longer caught up in illusion, it becomes *brahman*, the Absolute, which is not different from what is known, and which is birthless and eternal. As I have already pointed out, this kind of doctrine is a Buddhist heresy. Yet it is the same doctrine as the one taught in the Alāta-śānti-prakaraṇa. The only difference is that the ALP deliberately refrains from using the Vedāntist terms "*ātman*" and "*brahman*." Since the terminology of the ALP is thoroughly Buddhist, the identity of doctrine is not immediately apparent. Once this terminology is clearly understood, however, the identity of doctrine is obvious.

There was a well-known dispute between the two Mahāyānist schools — the Vijñānavādins and Mādhyamikas — over the nature of the mind. According to the Vijñānavādins, the mind really does arise and perish dependently according to the chain of causation. This was denied by the Mādhyamikas, who held that the mind did not have even a dependent (*paratantra*) reality. On this issue of causality, the ALP clearly takes sides against the Vijñānavādins in favor of the Mādhyamikas. This appears clearly in ALP 24 and 25. ALP 24 gives the view of the opponent (*pūrvapakṣin*), and ALP 25 gives the *kārikā-kara's* own view (*siddhānta*):

> (Some say:) the percept (*prajñapti*) has a cause (*nimitta*) — otherwise there would be the disappearance of duality (*dvaya*). And because there is the experience of impurity, the doctrine of 'dependent existence' (*paratantra*) is upheld.
>
> (But) the doctrine that the percept (*prajñapti*) has a cause is maintained (only) from the viewpoint of reasoning. That the cause is not a cause is maintained from the standpoint of reality (*bhūta*).

Similarly, ALP 73cd says:

> What would exist (*syāt*) according to the dependent relative truth (*paratantrābhisaṃvṛti*) does not exist according to the absolute truth (*paramārtha*).

However, this rejection of the reality of the *paratantra* in favor of the sole reality of the *paramārtha* has a very different meaning in the ALP from its meaning in Śūnyavāda writings. In rejecting the reality of the dependent reality, the Śūnyavādins had held that everything was totally void and non-existent (*atyanta-śūnyatā*, *atyantābhāva*), including mind or consciousness (*vijñāna*). But in rejecting the "dependent reality," the ALP embraces the doctrine of an eternal and unchanging absolute, which is essentially mind. This view is expressed very clearly in ALP 72:

> This duality which consists of the perceived and the perceiver is merely the vibration of the mind (*citta-spanditam eva*). The mind is therefore declared to be without an object (*nirviṣaya*), eternally unrelated to anything (*nityam-asaṅga*).

In other words, what ceases to exist when the true nature of the mind is seen is only the vibration or imagination of the mind, not the mind itself. The conclusion which the ALP reaches, therefore, is not that the mind does not exist (which is a Śūnyavāda doctrine), but that the mind in its true nature is unborn, unchanging and eternal. This teaching appears very explicitly in ALP 45, 48 and 80:

> Consciousness (*vijñāna*), which has the appearance (*ābhāsa*) of birth, of motion, and of a thing (*vastu*), is (in reality) unborn, unmoving, quiescent, nondual, and lacks the character of a thing.
>
> Just as a fire-brand when it does not move has no appearance and is unborn, so consciousness (*vijñāna*) when it does not move has no appearance and is unborn.
>
> Then the state (of mind) is attained that is without modification (*nivṛtta*), is turned away (*apravṛtta*) (from any object), and is unmoving (*niścala*). That is the field of activity (*viṣaya*) of the *buddhas*, which is everywhere the same, unborn, and nondual (*advaya*).

In the light of its teachings on the nature of mind, it is clear that the ALP's interpretation of the silence of the Buddha in ALP 99 is heretical from the Buddhist point of view, because it invokes the concept of a pure and unchanging consciousness which is eternal. According to ALP 99, the Buddha knows something which cannot be spoken. He has attained the state in which the mind is free from thought, perception and imagination, which is unrelated to anything, and which is all-pervading and eternal. Even if others seemed to hear the Buddha speak, in reality he said nothing. He had merged in the eternal, unchanging and immutable reality which is called the "field of activity" of the Buddhas. This, according to the ALP, is nothing but the *ātman-brahman* of the Upaniṣads (interpreted according to the Māyāvāda).

VIII

The foregoing considerations force us to reject the hypothesis that the ALP is a Vedāntic text which criticizes the Buddha, or which teaches doctrines which it regards as different from those of Buddhism (hypothesis 2). However, they also force us to reject the hypothesis that the ALP is a Buddhist text (hypothesis 1), for the doctrines taught there violate fundamental teachings of orthodox Buddhism, and present interpretations of Buddhist texts (e.g. the Mūla-madhayamaka-kārikās of Nāgārjuna) which could not possibly have been accepted by any orthodox Buddhist. Hence we are led to accept the third hypothesis I outlined at the beginning of the previous chapter. According to this view, the ALP is a Vedāntic treatise, and it is not critical of the Buddha. The ALP contends, in effect, that what the Māyāvāda Vedānta openly teaches is what the Buddha knew, but did not speak. The Buddha was a crypto-Vedāntist.

In chapter 1 I argued that a careful analysis of the Āgama-prakaraṇa raises problems for the traditional interpretation of the ĀP. Now, as a result of the discussion in the last chapter, we can see that there are also problems with the traditional interpretation of the ALP.

The problem is that the traditions of the Śaṃkara school present us with a set of assertions which is totally implausible in the light of the interpretation of the ALP at which we have arrived. Consider first the following four assertions:

1. Gauḍapāda wrote all four *prakaraṇas* of the Āgama-śāstra, including the ALP.

2. Gauḍapāda was the *parama-guru* of Ādi Śaṃkara. Specifically, the tradition tells us, Śaṃkara was the immediate disciple (*śiṣya*) of Govinda (or Govinda-bhagavat-pāda), and Govinda was the immediate disciple of Gauḍapāda. If we follow the usual rule of allowing thirty years for each teacher in a school's line of succession of teachers (*saṃpradāya*), Śaṃkara was only about sixty years removed from Gauḍapāda.

3. Ādi Śaṃkara was the author of the ĀŚV. The fourth chapter of this work is a commentary on the Alāta-śānti-prakaraṇa of his *parama-guru*. According to the ĀŚV's interpretation, the ALP asserts that the Buddha's doctrines are in some ways close to those of

the Vedānta, but that in actual fact they are not the same. The *maṅgalācaraṇa* at the beginning of the work is not to Gautama Buddha. The epithet "*dvipadāṃ varam*" (best of bipeds) of the *maṅgalācaraṇa* simply means "*puruṣottama*," a common epithet of Nārāyaṇa in the Hindu tradition. The *maṅgalācaraṇa* at the beginning of the ALP, therefore, does not praise Gautama Buddha: it praises Nārāyaṇa.

4. Ādi Śaṃkara was a relentless opponent of the Buddhists. In works which are certainly his (e.g. the Bṛhad-āraṇyakopaniṣad-bhāṣya and the Brahma-sūtra-bhāṣya), he criticizes the Buddhists in very strong terms, and even calls them "nihilists" (*vaināśikas*). According to the traditions of the Śaṃkara school, in fact, it was precisely the great founder of their school who saved the Vedic tradition from being overwhelmed by the Buddhist nihilists. In his short life Śaṃkara campaigned ceaselessly against them, and eventually saved the day by defeating the leading Buddhist philosophers and scholastics of his time on the debating fields of India.

In the light of the considerations of the last chapter, these four assertions of the Śaṃkara school must also be reconciled with the following proposition as well:

5. The interpretation of the ALP which is found in the ĀŚV is untenable. The Alāta-śānti-prakaraṇa praises the Buddha in its opening verse, and then proceeds to present the Buddha's doctrine as the true doctrine. There is no difference between the Buddha's doctrines and the author's own interpretation of the Vedānta (Māyāvāda Vedānta). In effect, the Buddha's doctrines are just Māyāvāda Vedānta presented under the guise of an idiosyncratic terminology.

These five propositions have a very pronounced tendency to repel each other. Obviously, we must give up at least one of the foregoing propositions. It is quite implausible that Govinda was directly taught by Gauḍapāda, that Śaṃkara was directly taught by Govinda, and that Śaṃkara held a view of the Buddha which was at odds with the view held by his *parama-guru*, Gauḍapāda.

The implausibility of this claim, it seems to me, is the real reason why the traditional interpretation of the ALP (as represented in the Āgama-śāstra-vivaraṇa) continues to be held by some scholars, in spite of the overwhelming evidence which can be found against it in the text itself.[1] For the traditional interpretation of the ALP is crucial to most of the traditions of the Śaṃkara school about Śaṃkara's relations to Gauḍapāda and to its interpretations of the Āgama-prakaraṇa and the Māṇḍūkya. Remove this one cornerstone, and the whole thing begins to collapse.

To see why a rejection of the traditional interpretation of the ALP is fatal to most of the Śaṃkara school's traditions on these matters, let us try to reconstruct the historical events on the assumption that all five of the preceding assertions are true simultaneously. The scenario would go something like this:

> Śaṃkara's *parama-guru* was Gauḍapāda. Gauḍapāda admired the Buddha and thought that his doctrines were true and essentially the same as those of the Māyāvāda of the Vedānta. But Śaṃkara could not bring himself to believe this. (Even if he did believe it once, he ceased to believe it.) He was, therefore, presented with a major problem. The question of the doctrinal differences between the Vedānta and Buddhism was a major issue of the day, and on this important issue Śaṃkara held (or came to hold) a view which diverged from that of his *parama-guru* (and even, conceivably, from that of his immediate *guru*, Govinda). To make matters worse, his *parama-guru* had written a work called the Alāta-śānti-prakaraṇa, in which he had praised the Buddha and identified the Buddha's views with his own.
>
> Śaṃkara dealt with this problem in the following way. He sat down and wrote a commentary (the ĀŚV) in which he took the ALP and twisted its obvious meaning. The *maṅgalācaraṇa*, he argued, is to Nārāyaṇa. The Buddhist doctrines are similar to those of the Vedānta, but are not identical with it. Where they diverge from the Vedānta, they are incorrect. Buddha's views were not the same as Gauḍapāda's, and Gauḍapāda had never said (or implied) that they were.

That this scenario makes no sense is obvious. Who could it have fooled? People in Śaṃkara's own *saṃpradāya*? But Śaṃkara, according to the traditional accounts, was only about sixty years removed from Gauḍapāda. When he wrote the ĀŚV, therefore, people in his own lineage could not have been taken in by the fraud.

What if we give up the hypothesis that Gauḍapāda was the *parama-guru* of Ādi Śaṃkara? Abandoning this hypothesis does not help, for people *outside* his *saṃpradāya* would not have accepted the ĀŚV's interpretation of the Alāta-śānti-prakaraṇa either. Could *anyone* in India in Śaṃkara's time or before have believed that the *maṅgalācaraṇa* of the ALP was not written in praise of the Buddha?[2] It is one thing to say something and another thing to get people to believe it. The *prakaraṇa* begins with a *maṅgalācaraṇa* to the "best of bipeds" (clearly the Buddha) and is filled with patently Buddhist terminology from beginning to end. People in Śaṃkara's time or before would not have assumed that the author of the Alāta-śānti-prakaraṇa was indulging in a private language game. Hence they could not have taken the ĀŚV's interpretation of the ALP seriously.

Furthermore, dropping the assumption that Gauḍapāda was the *parama-guru* of Śaṃkara makes other parts of the traditional account look even more untenable. For if we accept that Gauḍapāda *was* the *parama-guru* of Ādi Śaṃkara we can at least supply a motivation for Śaṃkara's writing of the ĀŚV. According to this account, Śaṃkara was confronted with a text, and he did the best with it that he could, given that the text he had to interpret presented an interpretation of Buddhism which he did not hold or had come to reject.

But if Śaṃkara was not connected with the author of the Alāta-śānti-prakaraṇa through a direct lineage, it is hard to understand why Śaṃkara wrote the ĀŚV at all. There is every reason to think that the Śaṃkara who wrote the Brahma-sūtra-bhāṣya and the Bṛhad-āraṇyakopaniṣad-bhāṣya would not have wanted to touch the ALP with a long stick. The Śaṃkara that we know from these works (and from the legends about him as well) was an unrelenting critic of the Buddhists, whom he calls "nihilists" (*vaināśikas*). Moreover, Ādi Śaṃkara must have had enough trouble defending himself against the charge of crypto-Buddhist unorthodoxy without having had anything to do with a work which begins with the words: "I bow to the best of bipeds who has fully realized (*saṃbuddha*) the *dharmas* which are like the sky (*gaganopama*)" etc.[3]

The foregoing considerations provide very strong grounds for rejecting the tradition that the author of the ALP was Śaṃkara's *parama-guru*. Clearly, we must abandon at least this element of the traditions of the Śaṃkara school. However, as I will show in the following chapters, other elements of this tradition must be abandoned as well.

In the following chapters, I shall argue that Ādi Śaṃkara was not the author of the Āgama-śāstra-vivaraṇa. I shall also argue that it is unlikely that Gauḍapāda wrote all four *prakaraṇas* of the Āgama-śāstra. I shall also argue that it may be doubted whether he advocated the TI interpretation of the Māṇḍūkya, and that there are *other* compelling reasons (besides the ones mentioned in this chapter) for thinking that Gauḍapāda was not the *parama-guru* of Ādi Śaṃkara. In short, I will eventually argue that almost every element of the traditional account regarding Gauḍapāda, the Āgama-śāstra and the Āgama-śāstra-vivaraṇa is either doubtful or untenable.

IX

If the Āgama-śāstra-vivaraṇa were a genuine work of Śaṃkara's, it would be the only example known to us where Śaṃkara chose to write a commentary on a Vedānta-śāstra (i.e. a philosophical treatise on the Vedānta) as opposed to a commentary on one of the *prasthāna-traya* (i.e. the Upaniṣads, the Brahma-sūtras, and the Bhagavad-gītā). This alone should make us somewhat hesitant to regard the ĀŚV as an authentic work. An even more decisive consideration, however, is that the work on which the ĀŚV comments is not, strictly speaking, *a work at all*. The *bhāṣya-kāra* (whoever he was) actually tells us that this is the case at the very outset.[1]

The Vivaraṇa begins with a Vedic invocation to the gods and two benedictory verses. After this, one naturally expects to find the introductory words of the treatise (*prakaraṇa*) that is being *commented on*, which would then be followed by the words of the commentary. What we find instead is that the next passage is by the *bhāṣya-kāra* himself. He begins his work with the following words:

> *Om-ity-etad-akṣaram-idaṃ sarvaṃ tasyopavyākhyānam / vedāntārtha-sāra-saṃgraha-bhūtam-idaṃ prakaraṇa-catuṣṭayam-om-ity-etad-akṣaram-ity-ādy-ārabhyate.*

That is to say, the *bhāṣya-kāra* begins by citing the first words of the Māṇḍūkya: "*Om ity etad akṣaram idaṃ sarvaṃ tasyopavyākhyānam.*" Then he says: "This work, a quartet of treatises (*prakaraṇa-catuṣṭaya*), is one which gives the essence of the meaning of the Vedānta, (and it) commences with the words *Om ity etad akṣaram etc.*"

It is significant that the *bhāṣya-kāra* says that the work is a *prakaraṇa-catuṣṭaya* (i.e. a quartet of treatises). A "quartet of treatises," or a "four-fold collection of treatises," is not the same thing as a "treatise in four parts" or a "four-chaptered treatise". A *prakaraṇa-catuṣṭaya* is not, strictly speaking, a work at all, but a collection of different works which are strung together for a particular purpose.[2]

That the Vivaraṇa is a commentary on a quartet of different treatises is confirmed by the next sentence. It says:

> For that very reason (*ata eva*) there is no separate statement of the relation (*saṃbandha*), subject-matter (*abhidheya*) and purpose (*prayojana*) of the treatise.

Treatises (*prakaraṇas*) were expected to contain in their introductions a statement of the reason why the treatise is being written, a statement of the subject matter of the treatise, and a statement of the relation between the treatise and the subject matter. The *bhāṣya-kāra* says in this sentence that there is no such thing in this case "for that very reason" (*ata eva*). But what is the reason? Here there are only two possibilities. Either there is no such statement because the work is an "epitome of the essence of the meaning of the Vedānta," or there is no such statement because the work is a "quartet of treatises" (*prakaraṇa-catuṣṭaya*). The first meaning must be rejected, for (as the following sentence will emphasize) all treatises on the Vedānta *do* contain such statements. The second meaning, however, fits perfectly. Hence what the *bhāṣya-kāra* means by this sentence is simply that there is no statement of purpose etc. — as is the case with a real treatise (*prakaraṇa*) — because he is not commenting on a single work at all, but rather a quartet of treatises.

Since he is simply stringing together four different treatises, the *bhāṣya-kāra* has to supply the statement of purpose etc. himself. This is what he tell us in the following sentence:

> However, there *should be* (*bhavitum arhanti*) a statement of the *saṃbandha*, *abhidheya* and *prayojana*, as is usual in the Vedānta (*yāny-eva tu vedānte saṃbandhābhidheya-prayojanāni tāny-eveha bhavitum-arhanti*). Thus, in a desire to explain a treatise, is the following brief statement.

The *bhāṣya-kāra* then proceeds to give, in effect, a statement of the relation, subject matter and purpose for *each* of the four *prakaraṇas*. Thus, we know that the work called the "Āgama-śāstra" was not originally a work at all. It was *constructed* out of separate works by the *bhāṣya-kāra*.[3]

The fact that the ĀŚV's Introduction actually *says* that it is a commentary on four different works seems to have been overlooked by the later scholiasts of the Śaṃkara school and by modern scholarship as well. It is true that V. Bhattacharya and A. Venkatasubbiah were prepared to reject certain elements of the tradition about these four *prakaraṇas*, but even they seem to have missed the real significance of the *bhāṣya-kāra's* use of the term "*prakaraṇa-catuṣṭaya.*"

V. Bhattacharya, for example, recognized that the Āgama-śāstra was not a single work in four chapters, but rather a collection of four separate treatises, and in his book on the Āgama-śāstra he presented compelling reasons for thinking that this was so.[4] Surprisingly, however, Bhattacharya failed to note the fact that the *bhāṣya-kāra* tells us himself that the work is a composite one. According to Bhattacharya, "Śaṃkara, the commentator, with his followers, holds that the four Books are the different parts of the same work entitled Āgamaśāstra."[5]

It is true that the Śaṃkara school now regards the four parts of the Āgama-śāstra as a single work. However, the *bhāṣya-kāra* who wrote the ĀŚV does not seem to have believed this. In fact, he goes out of his way, it seems to me, to tell us that this is *not* the case.

In a paper which was published in 1935, A. Venkatasubbiah said:

> ...the collection of verses now known as *Gauḍapāda-kārikā* and divided into four sections called *Āgama-prakaraṇa*, *Vaitathya-prakaraṇa*, *Advaita-prakaraṇa*, and *Alāta-śānti-prakaraṇa*, bore originally the name of Āgama-śāstra.

After citing the sentences of the Introduction which we have just considered, Venkatasubbiah then said:

> In this passage, it will be observed, Śaṃkara says that he is going to comment on a quartet of prakaraṇas. This statement is incompatible with the belief that the Āgama-śāstra consisted of the four prakaraṇas in question; for if such had been the case, Śaṃkara would have without doubt said that he was going to comment on the book Āgama-śāstra.[6]

It is interesting to see Venkatasubbiah noting the fact that in his Introduction to the ĀŚV the *bhāṣya-kāra* says that he is going to comment on a *quartet of prakaraṇas*. Venkatasubbhiah in this paper came very close to recognizing the significance of the fact that the *bhāṣya-kāra* does not cite any title for the work on which he was going to comment. However, since Subbiah was convinced that there *was* a single work called the Āgama-śāstra, he drew the wrong conclusions from his observations.

What Subbiah concluded was that there were *more* than four *prakaraṇas* to the original work entitled "Āgama-śāstra." This inference was unwarranted. The *bhāṣya-kāra* surely doesn't mean: "I am commenting on a quartet of *prakaraṇas* out of a 4+x-chaptered work called the Āgama-śāstra." For one thing, he never calls the work on which he is commenting the "Āgama-śāstra"; indeed, he never names it at all, which would be very hard to explain if there had been a pre-existing work which had ever had a title. Furthermore, if there had been a single work consisting of a greater number of chapters, *that* work should have contained an introduction containing a statement of *saṃbandha*, *abhidheya* and *prayojana* which the *bhāṣya-kāra* would then have cited. Finally, if the *bhāṣya-kāra* had meant that he was writing a commentary on a selection of four *prakaraṇas* out of an *x*-chaptered work, presumably he would have said so. What he does say — and what is fully intelligible in the light of what follows — is simply that he is going to comment on a *prakaraṇa-catuṣṭaya* which will begin with the words "*Om ity etad*" etc.

In his 1933 paper, Venkatasubbiah noted that if one assumes that the Āgama-śāstra *is* a single work one is led to a surprising result. He began with two premisses: (1) Śaṃkara was indeed the *bhāṣya-kāra*, and (2) there was a single work, the "Āgama-śāstra" by Gauḍapāda, on which Śaṃkara wrote his commentary. Subbiah argued in his paper that these two assumptions led to certain surprising consequences. In particular, Subbiah argued very cogently on the basis of these two assumptions (both of which I think are false), that Śaṃkara himself believed that Gauḍapāda was the author of the Māṇḍūkya.

His reasoning was as follows. The *bhāṣya-kāra* (i.e. Śaṃkara) says at the beginning of his commentary that the work on which he is going to comment begins with the words "*Om ity etad akṣaram*" etc., and that it consists of a quartet of *prakaraṇas*. Since it is the Māṇḍūkya which begins with the words "*Om ity etad akṣaram*" etc., Subbiah concluded quite sensibly — given his premisses — that the *bhāṣya-kāra* believed that the author of the prose *mantras* of the

Māṇḍūkya was identical with the author of the *kārikās* of all four *prakaraṇas*, i.e. that Gauḍapāda wrote what we now know as the Māṇḍūkyopaniṣad.

This engaging line of reasoning loses much of its force, however, once it is realized that the *bhāṣya-kāra* tells us explicitly that he is commenting on a quartet of *prakaraṇas* (*prakaraṇa-catuṣṭaya*) and not on a four-chaptered work. Furthermore, Subbiah's line of argument was undermined in 1933 by Y. Subrahmanya Sarma, who pointed out that Sureśvara, Śaṃkara's immediate disciple, cites Māṇḍ. 6 in his Vārttika on Śaṃkara's Bṛhad-āraṇyakopaniṣad-bhāṣya, and describes it there as a saying from the *śruti* (*śruti-vacas*).[7] Subbiah's argument was intended to show that Śaṃkara himself did not regard the Māṇḍūkya as *śruti*, but Sarma's observation proved that there must be something wrong with Subbiah's reasoning, since we know that Sureśvara, Śaṃkara's immediate disciple, did regard the Māṇḍūkya as *śruti*.

Nārāyaṇāśramin (fl. 1595), a follower of the Śaṃkara school who lived in the late medieval period, also seems to have been aware of the difficulties involved in assuming that the Āgama-śāstra was a unitary work. In his 1933 paper, Venkatasubbiah cited a commentary on the Āgama-śāstra by Nārāyaṇāśramin, who began his commentary with the following words:

> The words *Om ity etad akṣaram idaṃ sarvam*...mark the beginning of the Māṇḍūkyopaniṣad which consists of four sections (*khaṇḍa*). Reading it in sections, the teacher Gauḍapāda, through the favor of Nārāyaṇa, explained it by means of verses which are in four series and are introduced by the words *atraite ślokā bhavanti*. Thus, since the first section consisting of the *śruti* and its explanation consists mostly of the *śruti*, the practice grew up among Veda-knowers of calling it an "Upaniṣad." Similarly in the case of the latter three *prakaraṇas* too that treat of the same matters. This collection of four *prakaraṇas* is an epitome of the essence of the Vedānta-śāstra. And therefore there is no need to state separately the *saṃbandha*, *abhidheya* and *prayojana*.[8]

Here Nārāyaṇāśramin is obviously trying to explain several things which must have puzzled him. First, he is trying to explain why Śaṃkara, the *bhāṣya-kāra*, says in the opening words of his commentary that the *whole* treatise on which he is going to comment is a *prakaraṇa-catuṣṭaya* which begins with the words *Om ity etad* etc. As we have seen, this is a problem, because the statement seems to imply that the *kārikās* and the Māṇḍūkya are on the same level and that both are by a human author, whereas the Māṇḍūkya is traditionally regarded as *śruti*. Furthermore, Nārāyaṇāśramin wants to explain why the verses, which part of the tradition regards as being by Gauḍapāda, are regarded by others as being an Upaniṣad (i.e. *śruti*). He also wants to explain why some people within his tradition want to regard the *kārikās* of all *four prakaraṇas* as an Upaniṣad.

Nārāyaṇāśramin's attempt to deal with these problems is unconvincing. First of all, he attempts to avoid the conclusion that Śaṃkara did not regard the Māṇḍūkya as *śruti* by interpreting the term *prakaraṇa-catuṣṭaya* to mean — at least in part — that the Māṇḍūkyopaniṣad itself had four sections (*māṇḍūkyopaniṣac catuḥ-khaṇḍā)*. However, it is surely incorrect to interpret the opening words of the *bhāṣya-kāra* to mean that the *Māṇḍūkya* has four sections. In the first place, the *bhāṣya-kāra* clearly uses the term "*prakaraṇa-catuṣṭaya*" to refer to *everything* on which he is going to comment. Secondly, it is untrue that the Māṇḍūkyopaniṣad consists of four sections. What Nārāyaṇāśramin undoubtedly had in mind here is the fact that the Āgama-prakaraṇa comments on the Māṇḍūkya in four different sets of verses. But this does not mean that the Māṇḍūkya consists of four different parts.[9]

I believe that the Āgama-śāstra was put together as a unitary work, not by Śaṃkara, but by someone who postdated Śaṃkara. It is this hypothesis which best explains all the foregoing, divergent traditions about this text.

For one thing, the fact that the *bhāṣya-kāra* states that the Āgama-śāstra (which he never names) is a composite work is a very strong reason for thinking that Śaṃkara was not the *bhāṣya-kāra*. As I have previously noted, the other commentaries which are attributed to Śaṃkara are commentaries on the *prasthāna-traya* (i.e. the Upaniṣads, the Brahma-sūtra and the Bhagavad-gītā). There is no other example in the corpus of works attributed to Ādi Śaṃkara of a *bhāṣya* on a Vedānta-śāstra, and certainly no other commentary in which Śaṃkara has *constructed* a text by taking four different treatises and stringing them together.

Secondly, it is this hypothesis which best explains the fact that some of the other schools in India never accepted all four *prakaraṇas* as a single work. Puruṣottama, one of the leading figures of the Śuddhādvaita or Vallabhācārya school of the Vedānta, did regard all four *prakaraṇas* as comprising a single work, but the Madhva school (Dvaitins) and the Rāmānuja school (Viśiṣṭādvaitins) did not. Madhva and Kūranārāyaṇa (a follower of the Viśiṣṭādvaita), for example, wrote commentaries on the Māṇḍūkya and the twenty-nine commentarial verses of the Āgama-prakaraṇa, but never even referred to the last three *prakaraṇas* of the Āgama-śāstra. *Could* they have done so if there had ever been a strong tradition to the effect that all four *prakaraṇas* were a single work by a single author? Would someone write a commentary on one chapter of a four-chaptered work, and not even bother to mention that it was only *part* of the whole work?

Actually, the situation is even stranger than this, for, as the passage from Nārāyaṇāśramin shows, there was disagreement in later centuries *within* the Śaṃkara school about the status of the various parts of the "Āgama-śāstra." Yet, according to the prevailing view, the Āgama-śāstra and the Āgama-śāstra-vivaraṇa are texts that belonged specifically to the Śaṃkara school. It is hard to believe that the Śaṃkara school itself could have been guilty of elevating the Āgama-prakaraṇa to the status of *śruti* if there had been a tradition about Śaṃkara's authorship of the ĀŚV and about Gauḍapāda's authorship of the "Āgama-śāstra" which dated from Śaṃkara's day. And it is equally unlikely on this hypothesis that other schools would have been able to ignore the last three *prakaraṇas* (which contain doctrines which are unacceptable to them) and elevate the first *prakaraṇa* to the status of *śruti*. All these facts, it seems to me, are much harder to explain if we suppose that it was Ādi Śaṃkara (and not a later and less famous writer) who constructed the *prakaraṇa-catuṣṭaya* and wrote the Āgama-śāstra-vivaraṇa.

X

In the previous chapter, I have argued that the *bhāṣya-kāra* who wrote the Āgama-śāstra-vivaraṇa (ĀŚV) created the work known as the "Āgama-śāstra" out of four separate works for his own expository purposes. This, I have suggested, provides grounds for thinking that the ĀŚV was not written by Ādi Śaṃkara. In this chapter I discuss a number of other reasons for thinking that Ādi Śaṃkara was not the author of the ĀŚV.

1. There are two benedictory stanzas at the beginning of the *bhāṣya*, and three at the end. It is unusual for very old treatises — which this one would be if it were by Śaṃkara — to have such benedictory stanzas. It is true that this is not a decisive consideration, since at least two other works which are ascribed to Śaṃkara — the Bhagavad-gītā-bhāṣya and the Upadeśa-sāhasrī —also have such stanzas. Nevertheless, such a practice was not common in the very early period of Indian history.

Furthermore, there are too many feet in one of the lines of the second introductory verse. Śaṃkara-bhagavat-pāda has demonstrated elsewhere that he was a very competent versifier. Hence, it has been argued, it is unlikely that the benedictory verses are by him.

2. In the introduction to the ĀŚV, the *bhāṣya-kāra* says that the first *prakaraṇa* of the collection of four treatises (i.e. the Āgama-prakaraṇa) is an investigation (*nirṇaya*) into the meaning of the sacred syllable *Aum.* He then asks: How can the investigation of the meaning of the *praṇava* be a means to the attainment of the true nature of the Self (*ātma-tattva*)? He answers his own question as follows:

> The *Oṃkāra* is the substratum of the imagination of the *prāṇas* etc., which pertain to the domain of words (*vāk-prapañca*). The *praṇava* is the very essence of the Self (*ātma-svarūpa*), for it is the name or designation for the Self. All things — like the imaginations by the Self of the *prāṇas* etc. — are signified by sounds which are modifications of the *Oṃkāra*, and as such they cannot exist apart from their names.

The *bhāṣya-kāra* then cites Chānd. 6.1.4 (*vācā "rambhaṇaṃ vikāro nāmadheyam*). Then, after citing Māṇḍ. 1, he continues:

> All things exist because they are signified as the denotation of words since they are not different from their names. And since names are not different from the *Oṃkāra*, the *Oṃkāra* alone is said to be the primary means to the *para-brahman*, both as the name and the thing that is named.

As P. P. Subrahmanya Sastri pointed out in his Foreword to the 1937 edition of Maṇḍanamiśra's Brahma-siddhi, this is very similar to, if not identical with, the *sphoṭa-vāda* or *śabda-brahma-vāda* (word-mysticism) of writers like Bhartṛhari (530-630) and Maṇḍanamiśra.[1] Yet Śaṃkara in his Brahma-sūtra-bhāṣya condemns the *sphoṭa-vāda* in unmistakable terms.[2] Since we can be certain that the Brahma-sūtra-bhāṣya is by Śaṃkara (almost by definition), this is a reason for rejecting the ĀŚV as a work of Śaṃkara's.

In general, the Āgama-śāstra-vivaraṇa is a work which does not measure up to the high standards established by Śaṃkara in his definitive works, like the Brahma-sūtra-bhāṣya and the Bṛhadāraṇyakopaniṣad-bhāṣya. This point has been conceded even by many scholars who regard the ĀŚV as an authentic work of Śaṃkara's, and these scholars have therefore hypothesized that the ĀŚV must be an early and immature work of the master. I cannot present all of the reasons for thinking that the ĀŚV is an inferior work of Śaṃkara's (or, as others believe, that it is not a work of his at all), but I will present a couple of examples. The example in section 3 is taken from the ĀŚV's commentary on ĀP 6-9; the one in section 4 is taken from its commentary on ADP 25.

3. *Kārikās* 6-9 of the ALP, as we have seen in chapter 1, provide a commentary on Mand. 6 (*eṣa sarveśvara...*). As I argued in chapter 1, these verses do not support the Māyāvāda. The author of the ĀŚV, who wants to show that the *kārikās* do teach the Māyāvāda, has some problems with ĀP 6, in particular. At one point in the commentary he says:

> Origination of all the things that really exist, i.e., of all the entities which are the differentiated forms of waking, dreaming and sleeping, is of the nature of illusory names and forms made of ignorance. Thus it is said later (ADP 3.28cd): "The son of a barren woman is born neither in reality nor in illusion." For if the birth

> of things were from a non-entity, there would be the absurd result that there would be no way of knowing *brahman*, which is known from experience (*vyavahārya*). For it is seen that the rope is real, from which the snake etc. arise as from a seed (*bīja*) which is made of ignorance. For no one perceives a rope-snake or a mirage which does not have a substratum (*āspada*). Just as the pre-existent snake when it arises in the rope has the nature of a rope and does not exist as a snake, so it is with regard to the origination of all beings: their reality consists of their pre-existence as the seed of *prāṇa* only.[3]

Here the view that the effect is real and pre-exists in the cause (*satkārya-vāda*) is combined — in a very confusing way — with the very different view that the effect is an unreal appearance of the underlying cause (*vivarta-vāda*). Could the Śaṃkara who wrote the Brahma-sūtra-bhāṣya and the Bṛhad-āraṇyakopaniṣad-bhāṣya have been capable of such a muddle?

4. The *bhāṣya-kāra* in his commentary on ADP 25 cites Īśāvāsyopaniṣad (ĪU) 12, and gives it an interpretation which cannot be correct. Furthermore, the interpretation cannot be reconciled with the interpretation given in the *bhāṣya* on the Īśāvāsyopaniṣad which has been ascribed to Śaṃkara.

ADP 25 says "By the denial of birth, becoming is denied" (*sambhūter apavādāc ca saṃbhavaḥ pratiṣidhyate*). This is probably a citation of ĪU 12, which says:

> Into blind darkness enter those who worship the unmanifested (*asaṃbhūti*)
>
> And those who worship the manifested (*saṃbhūti*) enter, as it were, into even greater darkness.
>
> *andhaṃ tamaḥ praviśanti ye 'saṃbhūtim upāsate*
> *tato bhūya iva te tamo ya u saṃbhūtyāṃ ratāḥ*[4]

The *bhāṣya-kāra* cites only the first half of this verse(12ab), which he gives as follows: *andhaṃ tamaḥ praviśanti ye saṃbhūtim upāsate*. It is clear from the commentary that follows that he interprets this to mean: "Those who worship the *manifested* (*saṃbhūti*) enter blind darkness." But this interpretation of the passage is untenable. For it is Īśāvāsyopaniṣad 12*cd* which says: "They enter into greater darkness who worship the *manifested*" (*tato bhūya iva te tamo ya u saṃbhūtyāṃ ratāḥ*). Īśā 12ab means: "Those who worship the *un*manifested (*asaṃbhūti*) enter into blinding darkness." (This interpretation is confirmed by ĪU 9, 11 and 14 as well.) If the *bhāṣya-kāra* had wanted to take the *kārikā* on which he was commenting to refer to ĪU 12, he should have cited ĪU 12cd rather than 12ab. It is unlikely that Ādi Śaṃkara would have been misread a *śruti* text in this way.

5. Two of the main theses of the last three *prakaraṇas* of the ĀŚ are (1) that there is no real distinction to be drawn between sleeping and waking, and (2) that everything is nothing but the activity or vibration (*spandana*) of the mind (*vijñāna*, *citta*). Both of these propositions were held by the Vijñānavāda school of Buddhists. The ĀŚV, which comments on these *prakaraṇas*, fully endorses these views.

Since these views (as we shall now see) are criticized by Śaṃkara in his Bṛhad-āraṇyakopaniṣad-bhāṣya (BUB) and Brahma-sūtra-bhāṣya (BSB), it is unlikely that he wrote the ĀŚV, and also unlikely that he had a *parama-guru* (Gauḍapāda) who wrote the last three *prakaraṇas* of the Āgama-śāstra. Since the point is an important one, I shall discuss the texts in considerable detail. We will begin with the Bṛhad-āraṇyakopaniṣad-bhāṣya (BUB).

5a. Śaṃkara begins the Bṛhad-āraṇyakopaniṣad-bhāṣya with the statement that the subject matter of all the Upaniṣads is the true nature of the Self. Śaṃkara says that the Self is not an object of perception (*pratyakṣa-viṣaya*), and that this is why the Buddhists and the materialists (Lokāyatas), in spite of the fact that they also say "I am," deny the existence of the Self.

Somewhat later, in his commentary on BU 2.3.6, Śaṃkara says that the self which the *vaināśikas* (i.e. the Buddhists) say is unreal is not the Self (*ātman*) at all. What the Buddhists deny, Śaṃkara says, is only the subtle body (*kāraṇātma liṅga rūpa*). He says of this body that it is made of impressions (*vāsanā-maya*), and that it is produced by the union of the *vijñānamaya* (i.e. that which is made of consciousness), on the one hand, and the impressions of gross and subtle things, on the other. This "self," he says, is like an illusion, magical appearance or mirage (*māyā-indrajāla-mṛgatṛṣṇika*), and it is entirely based on illusion (*sarva-vyāmoha-āspada*). The

Vijñānavādin nihilists, he says, are deluded in thinking that the true Self (*ātman*) is this and nothing more.

These two passages set the stage for the extended critique of the Buddhist system — and especially of the Vijñānavāda — in BUB 4.3.7.

Bṛhad-āraṇyakopaniṣad 4.3.7 describes the Self (*ātman*) as the "person (*puruṣa*) who consists of mind (*vijñānamaya*), who is the light within the sense-organs." One of Śaṃkara's main concerns in his commentary on this passage is to show that the true Self is *not* this *vijñānamaya ātman*. Śaṃkara regards the *vijñānamaya ātman* as unreal: it is only what Buddhists and others erroneously take to be the Self. Hence he argues in his commentary on BU 4.3.7 that "*vijñānamaya*" does not mean "consisting of *vijñāna*" or "made of *vijñāna*." What it means instead is that the Self is *identified* with the intellect (*vijñāna*) through a failure to distinguish the Self from the mind or intellect, which is only its limiting adjunct (*upādhi*). Śaṃkara uses this rather unnatural interpretation of "*vijñānamaya*" to interpret the second part of BU 4.3.7 also, which speaks of the dreaming state. According to Śaṃkara's interpretation, the Self cannot be said to dream: it is the intellect (*vijñāna*) which dreams. The Self appears to dream (*iva*), but that is only because it is similar in some respects to the intellect, and because the essential difference between the Self and the *vijñāna* is not perceived due to ignorance.

At this point, the *pūrvapakṣin* (i.e. the Buddhist idealist) objects that there is no such thing as the "light of the Self" (i.e. the *ātman* of the Vedānta) which is different from the mind. The *pūrvapakṣin* objects that perception and inference (the two means of knowledge recognized by the Buddhists) reveal only the *vijñāna,* and never anything like the Vedic *ātman*. Furthermore, the Vijñānavādin says, there are no external objects, because what we call an external object is just consciousness which takes a particular form and appears as an external object.The Vijñānavādin argues: if a thing *x* is never perceived apart from a thing *y*, then we infer that *x* is identical with *y*. Since we never see dream objects apart from the dream consciousness, we say that the objects are mind only (*vijñāna-mātra*). Furthermore, the postulation of a Self apart from the intellect (*vijñāna*) involves an infinite regress. Therefore the assertion that there is something apart from *vijñāna* (i.e. the *ātman*) which in turn reveals the *vijñāna*, is untenable.

It is necessary to place this objection in the wider context of Buddhist philosophy as a whole. According to the Buddhists, what we call "mind," "intellect," or "consciousness" (*manas*, *citta*, *vijñāna*) is only a stream of percepts (*vijñapti*). Like the Scottish philosopher David Hume, the Buddhists did not distinguish between impressions, on the one hand, and our consciousness of impressions, on the other.[5] For Śaṃkara, however, this distinction is crucial. On Śaṃkara's view, it makes no more sense to say that a mental impression could be conscious of itself (*svayaṃ-prakāśa*) than it would to say that a rock was self-conscious. For Śaṃkara, a percept or impression (*vijñapti*) is a thing, and it is only due to the proximity and likeness of these impressions to pure consciousness (i.e. the *ātman*) that people suffer from the illusion that they *are* their minds and nothing more. This view is implicit in the opening pages of the BUB (see above), but it becomes explicit when Śaṃkara attacks the Buddhist Vijñānavādins in BUB 4.3.7 on the nature of consciousness and the question of the unreality of the external world.

First of all, Śaṃkara denies that the postulation of a Self which reveals the *vijñāna* (or percepts) involves an infinite regress (*anavasthā*). There is no absolute rule, he says, that if something is revealed by something else there must be a third thing involved. This is admitted by the Vijñānavādin himself, because the Vijñānavādin maintains that the *vijñāna* is itself self-conscious (*svayaṃ-prakāśa*). But for Śaṃkara, as we have seen, the Buddhist view is untenable, because he holds that a percept (which must itself be an object of perception) cannot be *svayaṃ-prakāśa*. According to Śaṃkara, something can be self-conscious if and only if it cannot be the object of *any* perception. In short, according to Śaṃkara, consciousness (*caitanya*) which is inherently self-revealing, is not a property of the *vijñāna*: it is a property of the Upaniṣadic *ātman*.

In response to the claim that a thing like a lamp can be self-revealing, Śaṃkara says:

> The lamp is not a good illustration to show that *vijñāna* is self-revealing (*ātma-grāhya-grāhakatva*). *Vijñāna* is revealed by consciousness (*caitanya*) just as much as an external, inert object

> **is...The other entity which illumines the *vijñāna* is the light of the Self (*ātma jyoti*) which is different from the *vijñāna*.**

According to Śaṃkara, the Buddhist idealists are themselves suffering from the fundamental illusion of superimposing the attributes of the object onto the Self, which is only a pure subject.[6] On Śaṃkara's view, what the Vijñānavādins call consciousness or mind (*vijñāna*) is as external to the *ātman* as rocks and trees and other external objects are to the *vijñāna*.

For Śaṃkara, the whole phenomenal world is an illusory superimposition (*adhyāsa*) on the pure *ātman*. This sounds similar to the Vijñānavāda doctrine, but according to Śaṃkara, it is different for two reasons.

First of all, the Buddhist system, according to Śaṃkara, is nihilistic (*vaināśika*). The whole world and its attendant suffering (*saṃsāra*) is reduced by the Vijñānavādins to a stream of mental impressions. Since this stream of impressions itself involves suffering, the only way to escape suffering is to extinguish the mind (*vijñāna*). But, according to Śaṃkara, since the Buddhists do not believe in the *ātman* which transcends the mind and its suffering, the extinction of the mind means one's annihilation. Śaṃkara finds this view unacceptable. The Buddhist view that the extinction (*nirvāṇa*) of the *vijñāna* is the highest goal of life is untenable, he says, because in that case there is no one to receive the benefit.

Secondly, according to Śaṃkara, the Vijñānavāda position is soteriologically inadequate because it cannot really release us from the bondage to the world and its suffering. The reason, according to Śaṃkara, is that the Vijñānavādin is in no position to say that the world is unreal, since he does not believe in any principle that is permanent and which can be the substratum of the appearances. The only evidence that the Vijñānavādin accepts is what he can see or infer from the sense data (*vijñapti*), and Śaṃkara argues that there is no basis in the sense data themselves for saying that the world is unreal. In short, Śaṃkara argues, we cannot reach the realization of the unreality of the world on the basis of our words and ideas, for these tell us that the world is *real*, not that it is unreal. This is the experience of the idealist philosopher as much as the man in the street, though the Buddhist idealist philosophers do not say so. Reliance on the doctrine of *vijñapti-mātratā*, therefore, lands us either in nihilism or in eternal bondage.

5b. Similar criticisms of the Buddhist idealists are found in Śaṃkara's commentary (BSB) on Brahma-sūtra (BS) 2.2.28-31.

Adhyāya 2, Pāda 2 of the Brahma-sūtras is devoted to a refutation of non-Vedāntist philosophical doctrines. *Sūtras* 18-32 are directed against the Buddhist schools. *Sūtras* 18-27 are directed primarily against the realist Buddhist school (i.e. the Sarvāstivādins), *sūtras* 28-31 are directed against the idealist school (Vijñānavāda), and *sūtra* 32 is a condemnation of the Sugata and his doctrines in general.[7]

Brahma-sūtra 2.2.28 says that external objects cannot be non-existent because they are perceived,[8] and BS 2.2.29 says that the perception of external objects in the waking state are not like dreams because the two are different in nature.[9] By this the *sūtra-kāra* undoubtedly meant that the world is real and not an illusion; it is, instead, a real creation of *brahman*.[10] In his commentary on these two *sūtras*, Śaṃkara makes no attempt to show that the *sūtras* are consistent with his own interpretation of the Vedānta,[11] but he does use them as the occasion for making some very strong criticisms of the Buddhist idealist.

As in the Bṛhad-āraṇyakopaniṣad-bhāṣya, Śaṃkara's criticism of the Vijñānavāda rests on the distinction he draws between the Self (*ātman*) — which Śaṃkara describes as a pure witness (*sākṣin*) — and what the Buddhists call *vijñāna*, which is simply a stream of cognitions, ideas, or impressions (*vijñapti*). According to Śaṃkara, the *vijñāna* is itself a part of the illusory world-appearance, and he contends that it is contradictory to argue from *within* the world appearance that the world appearance is unreal.

The Vijñānavādin says that nothing exists but our cognitions (*vijñapti-mātratā*), and that any inferences which presuppose something outside this stream of cognitions is illegitimate. The Vijñānavādin concludes from this that there is no difference between sleeping and waking and that there are no external objects which are perceived in the waking state. According to Śaṃkara, however, this is incorrect, for according to him our cognitions themselves tell us that there is such a distinction and that the world is real. In short, according to Śaṃkara, the Buddhist cannot rely upon the doctrine that the world is nothing but mind to show that the world is unreal. He himself rejects the view that the world is nothing but mind, but not on the grounds that the world is real. According to Śaṃkara, the world is an *illusory superimposition on the Self*. According to Śaṃkara, this view is different from the *vijñapti-mātratā* of the idealist Buddhists because the Self is a pure witness (*sākṣin*) and not a cognition or a series of cognitions (*vijñāna*).

After setting out the position of the *pūrvapakṣin* in BSB 2.2.28, Śaṃkara says: "It is not possible to maintain that external objects do not exist, for the simple reason that they are actually perceived." The philosopher who attempts to deny this is contradicting his own experience. We would not accept a person's statement that he was not eating if we saw him eating, and similarly we should not credit the idealist philosopher's assertion that he is not seeing anything when his sense organs (*indriyas*) are plainly in contact with external objects.

The Vijñānavādin might reply that he is only asserting that what he sees is not different from cognition itself, rather than the view that nothing is seen at all. Śaṃkara replies that this would make no sense, because it is through perception and perception only that the distinction between perception and an object is made. No one ever says that a pillar or a wall is nothing but a perception (*upalabdhim-eva*), and the idealist Buddhist does not say it either.That is why even the Vijñānavādin says: "that which is an interior form *appears as if* it were something external."[12]

Here is the sum and substance of Śaṃkara's attack against the Vijñānavādin. The Vijñānavādin says that there is nothing but perceptions, and that we must not make inferences which presuppose anything apart from them. But this view is self-defeating, Śaṃkara says, for the cognitions themselves project outward and point to something outside themselves, as the Vijñānavādin himself admits. Hence the cognitions (*vijñāna*) themselves contradict the doctrine of the Vijñānavādin!

In his Ālambana-parīkṣā, the Buddhist idealist Dignāga argued that external objects are not possible. One of his arguments was that such objects are aggregates (*saṃghātas*), and that aggregates cannot be real because they must either be identical with, or different from, their constituent atoms (*paramāṇus*). According to Dignāga, both possibilities are impossible; hence, he concludes, objects are only appearances, and have no existence apart from their cognitions. Śaṃkara has to deal with this argument, for the Vijñānavādin might argue that one cannot argue from the fact that cognitions *appear* to refer to something external that there really are external objects, on the grounds that there is the foregoing argument to show that such objects could not *possibly* exist.

Śaṃkara contends that the Vijñānavādin cannot evade the difficulty in this way. If there is a conflict between perception (*pratyakṣa*) and reasoning, there must be something wrong with the reasoning. The possibility (*saṃbhava*) or impossibility of something is to be based on the antecedent operation of a valid means of knowledge (*pramāṇa*). The Buddhist accepts perception (*pratyakṣa*) as a valid means of knowledge. Hence he cannot argue that the validity or non-validity of perception depends upon the possibility or impossibility of the *objects* of perception. Whatever is actually grasped through perception and the other valid means of knowledge is possible, and that which is never grasped by anyone through any *pramāṇa* is not possible. The Vijñānavādin, therefore, has things the wrong way around.

There is another reason why the contention that there is no difference between a cognition and its object is untenable. According to Śaṃkara, the cognition per se is the common factor in all cognitions, and that is the pure Self (*ātman*) or knowledge itself (*jñāna*). In the case of a cognition of a pot (*ghaṭa-jñāna*) and the cognition of a piece of cloth (*paṭa-jñāna*), the differences are in the pot and the piece of cloth, and not in the cognitions as such. Similarly, in the case of a white bull and a black bull, the difference is only in the whiteness and blackness, and not in "bullness" (*gotva*) itself. Śaṃkara concludes from this that things are different from their perceptions (*tasmād-artha-jñānayor-bhedaḥ).* According to Śaṃkara, the common factor in all cognitions is the Self (*sākṣin*). This principle was not recognized even by the Buddhist Vijñānavādins, for they held that there was nothing but a stream of individual cognitions or impressions, all of which are different from each other.

Śaṃkara concludes his commentary on BS 2.2.28 by arguing (as he does in the BUB) that the cognitions (*vijñāna*) of the Buddhists cannot be self-illuminating (*svayaṃ-prakāśa*). Cognitions themselves cannot be self-luminous like a lamp, Śaṃkara says, because an action cannot act on itself, just as fire cannot burn itself. The obvious fact that external objects are known by cognitions (*vijñāna*) which are different from those objects is widely recognized in the world, and by denying it the Buddhist idealist is just trying to make a big exhibition of his learning (*aho pāṇḍityaṃ mahadarśitam*).

The Vijñānavādin contends that cognitions themselves can be self-luminous, and that to suppose otherwise would lead to an infinite regress (*anavasthā*). But, Śaṃkara says, both these contentions are untenable. First of all, there is no basis for asserting that there is an infinite regress, because cognitions (*vijñāna*) are perceived by the Self (*sākṣin*). This *sākṣin* is its own proof (*svayaṃsiddha*), and it is different in nature from the cognitions; hence there is no infinite regress.

On the other hand, the Buddhist's contention that the cognitions apprehend themselves in untenable. Their contention that the property of being conscious (*anubhava-rūpatva*) belongs essentially to the cognitions must be rejected, for the Buddhists also say that cognitions are originated, are destroyed, and are multiple (*anekatva*), and entities of this nature cannot be self-luminous according to Śaṃkara. Śaṃkara concludes that cognitions, like a lamp, are apprehended by something different from them (i.e. by the witnessing Self).

Then Śaṃkara begins his commentary on BS 2.2.29 by saying: "We must reject the view of those who say that there are no external objects, and that perceptions of pillars etc. in the waking state, like the experiences of dreams, have no external objects corresponding to them, on the grounds that there is no difference between them as experiences."

Śaṃkara claims that the sleeping state and the waking state are different in nature (*vaidharmya*). For one thing, our experiences in the dreaming state are contradicted (*bādhyate*) by the experience of the waking state: when we awaken, we realize that the things we saw in dreams are false, like a magical illusion. However, the things we perceive in the waking state are never contradicted in any state. Secondly, dreams are simply memories (*smṛti*), while what is seen in the waking state is a genuine perception (*upalabdhi*). Consequently, Śaṃkara says, people who actually experience the difference between these two states cannot say: "Perceptions in the waking state are false, *because they are perceived*, just like the perceptions in dreams (*mithyā jāgaritopalabdhir-upalabdhitvāt-svapnopalabdhi-vad iti*).

Those who cannot, on the basis of their own immediate experience, establish the proposition that waking experiences are without external support (*nirālaṃbanatā*) wish to do so on the grounds that waking experiences are similar (*sādharmya*) to dreams. But that which cannot be the self nature of a thing cannot be its nature merely because it is similar to some other thing. Fire, which is experienced to be hot, will not become cold just because it is similar to water. And the difference in nature between dreams and waking experiences, Śaṃkara says, has already been established.

* * *

There are some similarities between Śaṃkara's views in the BUB and the BSB and those of the idealist Buddhists. Both Śaṃkara and the Vijñānavādins, for example, maintain that the world is, in the final analysis, unreal (*mithyā*). However, it would be wrong to infer from this fact that there are no substantive differences between Śaṃkara's views and those of the Vijñānavādins.

For one thing, the nature of reality is fundamentally different in the two systems. In the Vijñānavāda, reality consists of a series of momentary impressions or self-luminous cognitions, and there is nothing outside of them. On Śaṃkara's view, even these cognitions (*vijñāna*, *prajñapti*) are unreal superimpositions (*adhyāsa*) on the underlying reality of the nondual, all-pervading and absolute Self. Hence, according to Śaṃkara, his system is not nihilistic (even though he maintains that the world is unreal), for in his system of thought the absolute reality remains as the substratum when the world-illusion is sublated. According to the Vijñānavādins, however, there is no perceiving Self (*sākṣin*) apart from the stream of cognitions. Hence, according to Śaṃkara, when this stream of cognitions is extinguished (*nirvāṇe*), the result is annihilation, pure and simple.

For our present purposes, however, the most important point to note about these two authentic works of Śaṃkara is that they reject the following two assertions made by the Vijñānavādins: (1) that the world is the creation of the activity of the mind (*vijñāna*, *citta*) and (2) that there is no distinction whatever to be drawn between waking and dreaming experiences. The conclusion which needs to be drawn from these two facts, it seems to me, is that it is unlikely (1) that all of the verses in the last three *prakaraṇas* of the Āgama-śāstra were written by the *parama-guru* of Ādi Śaṃkara, and (2) that it is unlikely that Ādi Śaṃkara was the author of the Āgama-śāstra-vivaraṇa. For the two assertions above are fundamental to these *prakaraṇas*, and were also fully accepted by the author of the ĀŚV.

Some scholars have suggested that the authenticity of the ĀŚV can be reconciled with these apparent divergences. Paul Hacker, for example, has suggested that the ĀŚV belongs to an early (and radical) period of Śaṃkara's activities, and that some of these radical views were later modified or dropped in the later works.[13] Similarly, Mayeda has suggested that the differences between Śaṃkara's Brahma-sūtra-bhāṣya and the ĀŚV are due to the differences between the two texts on which they comment.[14] Thus, Mayeda has suggested that in the Brahma-sūtra-bhāṣya Śaṃkara used his knowledge of Buddhism to attack Buddhist doctrines since the Brahma-sūtra itself attacks them. In the Gauḍapādīya-bhāṣya, however, his purpose is to make Buddhist doctrines Advaita doctrines. Hence the differences between the two works.

I doubt, however, that these views can escape the objections to the traditions of the Śaṃkara school which I have made in earlier chapters. Unless we suppose that Śaṃkara at some time of his life was either a Buddhist or was sympathetic to Buddhism — and there is virtually no reason apart from the Āgama-śāstra and the traditions surrounding it to think that he was — it is imcomprehensible why he should have written the Āgama-śāstra-vivaraṇa at all. Why *would* he have wanted to make "Buddhist doctrines Advaita doctrines?" If anything, he would have wanted to distance his own views from those of the Buddhists as much as possible. As I have previously argued, his motivation would be more understandable if his *parama-guru had* been a Buddhist or had held that the Buddha was a Vedāntist or quasi-Vedāntist. But it is intrinsically improbable that Śaṃkara had such a *parama-guru*.

Furthermore, some of the doctrinal differences between the ĀŚV and other authentic works of Śaṃkara are so great that the foregoing hypotheses would force us to suppose that Śaṃkara underwent a really radical change of views between the writing of the ĀŚV and his other (presumably later) works, and not that he merely modified some of them slightly, perhaps by way of accommodating himself to the texts on which he was commenting. For the suggestion that there was a gradual and natural evolution of views — rather than a radical break with previously held views — becomes less tenable when clear and substantive contradictions can be found between the texts. I have already discussed some of these. But there is one more that is so striking and interesting that we should look at it in more detail.

In the commentary on Vaitathya-prakaraṇa (VP) 4, the *bhāṣyakāra* presents an argument (*anumāna*) against the reality of our waking experiences. It is presented in the form and style of the Indian school of logicians (*nyāya*). The argument goes as follows:

(1) The proposition to be established (*pratijñā*) is the unreality of the objects which are perceived in the waking state (*jāgrad-dṛśyānāṃ bhāvānāṃ vaitathyam iti*).

(2) The reason or ground (*hetu*) is that they are perceived (*dṛśyatvāt*).

(3) The illustration (*dṛṣṭānta*) is that they are like the things which are seen in dream.

(4) Just as in sleep where the objects which are perceived are unreal, so also are the objects which are seen in the waking state. The attribute of being seen is not different in the two cases. This is the relation (*upanaya*) between the reason (*hetu*) and the illustration (*dṛṣṭānta*).

(5) Therefore in the waking state also things are unreal. This is the reiteration of the proposition or the conclusion (*nigamana*).[15]

Then the ĀŚV concludes (among other things): "What is common (to both the things seen in the waking state and the things seen in dreams) is that they are both seen and both non-existent (*dṛśyatvam-asatyatvaṃ cāviśiṣṭam-ubhayatra*)."

Two things should be noted about this argument: (a) it is a transparently fraudulent argument, and (b) it is unlikely that Ādi Śaṃkara could have authored it.

(a) Even if we reject the sense data doctrine (according to which things seen in dream have a mental reality) it certainly does not follow that the things that are seen in dream are non-existent *because* they are seen, which is the reason (*hetu*) of the argument. Furthermore, if the above argument were valid, then any two things which shared any property P would share all of their properties.

A closer examination of this argument reveals that it actually consists of two different arguments. The first of these arguments is valid, but it is also unsound, for one of the premisses is false (or at least doubtful):

All things which are perceived are unreal.
All things seen in the waking state are perceived.
Therefore, all things seen in the waking state are unreal.

The first premise of this argument, which is at least questionable, appears to be the conclusion, in turn, of the following invalid argument:

All dreams are perceived.
All dreams are unreal.
Therefore, all things which are seen are unreal.

(b) It is also implausible that Śaṃkara ever advanced this argument, for it is explicitly repudiated, as we have seen, by Śaṃkara in BSB 2.2.29. The argument in the ĀŚV purports to show that the objects which we seem to perceive in the waking state are unreal *because* (like the things seen in dream) they are perceived. Brahma-sūtra 2.2.29, however, contends that the things we see in the waking state are *real* because they are perceived,[16] and Śaṃkara agrees. Furthermore, he points out that the doctrine that things seen in the waking state are *unreal* because they are seen is a Mahāyānist doctrine, not a Vedāntic one.[17]

In the Brahma-sūtra-bhāṣya, Śaṃkara points out that the argument relies on the *similarity* between the waking state and the dreaming state, and that a reason of this kind does not support the conclusion. Thus, Śaṃkara says, the *pūrvapakṣin* contends that waking experiences are unreal because (1) they are *seen* (like those of dreams) and (2) because dreams are unreal. But, as Śaṃkara points out, one cannot argue that something has a property just because it is similar in some respect to some other thing that has that property. In other words, Śaṃkara in the BSB repudiates not only the conclusion (*nigamana*) of the argument that is presented by the unknown author of the Āgama-śāstra-vivaraṇa: he also repudiates the reasoning that is given in that argument. It would be hard to find a sharper disagreement between two works than this.

XI

We have been led by the evidence to abandon many of the traditions of the Śaṃkara school regarding the Āgama-śāstra and the Āgama-śāstra-vivaraṇa. Clearly, the waters here are so treacherous that none of these traditions should be taken for granted. In this chapter, therefore, I will try to determined what we can say with reasonable certainty about Gauḍapāda if we rely solely on the oldest and most reliable texts.

There are four very old works of the Advaita Vedānta school which are of interest to us, because they either (1) mention the "Gauḍas," "the teacher of the Gauḍas" (*gauḍācārya*) etc., or (2) cite *kārikās* which can be found in the Āgama-śāstra. These four works are: the Brahma-sūtra-bhāṣya (BSB) of Śaṃkara, the Brahma-siddhi of Maṇḍanamiśra, and the Naiṣkarmya-siddhi (NKS) and Bṛhad-vārttika (BV) of Sureśvara. If there is anything to the claim that Gauḍapāda was the *parama-guru* of Ādi Śaṃkara, or that he wrote the Āgama-śāstra, or that he was the first Māyāvādin etc., we might expect to find evidence for it in these early texts. In this chapter we will examine these four texts; in the next two chapters we will attempt to draw the appropriate conclusions from our investigation.

I shall first list the *kārikās* that are cited by these authors, giving also the places in their works where the verses are cited. If a *kārikā* has been asterisked, it means that the verse was not only cited, but also attributed to Gauḍapāda.

ĀP 3a-c — *Viśva*, indeed is the always the enjoyer of the gross, *taijasa* is the enjoyer of the refined; *prājña*, likewise, is the enjoyer of bliss.

Sureśvara cites this verse in BV 1.4.744, p. 582, where he says that it is a teaching of the Vedāntic tradition (*āgama-śāsana*):

viśvo hi sthūlabhuṅ-nityaṃ taijasaḥ praviviktabhuk
ānandabhuk-tathā prājña iti cā''gama-śāsanam.

ĀP 11* — The two — *viśva* and *taijasa* — are considered to be bound by cause and effect. *Prājña*, on the other hand, is bound by cause alone. These two do not exist in *turya*.

This verse is cited in three places. Maṇḍanamiśra cites it in the Brahma-siddhi,[1] and Sureśvara cites it in NKS 4.41 and in BV 1.4.712.[2]

Maṇḍanamiśra simply introduces the verse with the words "Thus it is said" (*tad-uktam*), and in the Bṛhad-vārttika the verse is included as part of the text, without being cited or attributed to anyone. In the Naiṣkarmya-siddhi, however, Sureśvara connects the verse with Gauḍapāda, for he says: "This is declared by the 'Gauḍas' and the 'Drāviḍas' whom we revere" (*evaṃ gauḍair drāviḍair naḥ pūjyair ayam arthaḥ prabhāṣitaḥ*).

ĀP 14 Waking and dreaming are joined with dream and sleep; *prājña*, likewise, is bound with sleep but not with dream. Those with firm conviction see neither sleep nor even dream in *turya*.

Sureśvara cites this verse in BV 1.4.615, p. 556 where he says: "This is a well-established teaching of the Vedānta" (*vedāntoktau viniścitaḥ*):

svapna-nidrā-yutāv-ādyau prājñas-tv-asvapna-nidrayā
ity-ādi-sthāna-bhedo'pi vedāntoktau viniścitaḥ.

In his Ṭīkā on the Bṛhad-vārttika, Ānandagiri apparently cites this verse of the Āgama-prakaraṇa as *śruti*.

ĀP 15* Dream is for one comprehending otherwise (i.e. falsely); sleep is for one who does not know reality (*tattva*). When these two errors are destroyed, one attains *turīya*.

This verse is quoted (along with ĀP 11 and a verse which is found in the Upadeśa-sāhasrī) in Naiṣkarmya-siddhi 4.42, where it is ascribed to the *gauḍa* teacher or teachers whom Sureśvara reveres.

Although ĀP 11 is the only *kārikā* found in the Āgama-śāstra which Maṇḍanamiśra actually cites, the discussion in the

Brahma-siddhi before and after his citation of ĀP 11 recalls ĀP 15 as well. Thus, in his commentary on ĀP 11, Maṇḍanamiśra recognizes two different kinds of nescience (*avidyā*), i.e., non-apprehension (*agrahaṇa*) and misapprehension (*anyathā-grahaṇa*). He also calls wrong apprehension "*vikṣepa*," and associates it with the states of waking and dreaming, whereas sleep, he says, is characterized by "merging" (*laya-lakṣaṇa*). The similarity between these views and ĀP 15 is quite striking. It is not certain that Maṇḍanamiśra had ĀP 15 in mind when he wrote this passage of the Brahma-siddhi, but it is a definite possibility.

ĀP 16 When the individual (*jīva*) who is asleep owing to the beginningless *māyā* awakens, he awakens to the birthless, sleepless, dreamless nonduality.

Śaṃkara quotes this verse in BSB 2.1.9, where he says that it is a saying by the teacher (or teachers) who know the tradition of the meaning of the Vedānta (*atroktaṃ vedāntārtha-saṃpradāya-vidbhir-ācāryaiḥ*).

VP 17* As a rope not definitely ascertained in the dark is imagined to be things like a snake, a line of water, etc., so also is the Self imagined.

Sureśvara cites the first three words of this verse in BV 1.4.389, p. 510:

The fearlessly declared maxim (*nyāya*) 'As a rope is not definitely ascertained etc.,' has been set forth clearly in the sayings of Gauḍapāda (*gauḍapādīyaṃ vacas*)

aniścitā yathā rajjur-iti nyāyopabṛṃhitam
sphuṭārthaṃ gauḍapādīyaṃ vaco 'rthe 'traiva gīyate.

VP 38* Having seen the reality (*tattva*) within as well as the reality without, becoming one with the reality, delighting in it, one should not deviate from reality.

In BV 4.4.886, p. 1866, Sureśvara refers to the verses of Gauḍapāda and to the doctrines which have been clearly taught by those who themselves know the correct tradition of the Vedānta:

ślokāṃś-ca gauḍapādāder-yathoktārthasya sākṣiṇaḥ
adhīyate 'tra yatnena saṃpradāyavidaḥ svayam.

Then in the next verse (BV 4.4.887) he cites VP 38 verbatim.

ADP 15* The creation (*sṛṣṭi*) which has been expounded by the examples of clay, gold, metal, sparks of fire etc. is only a means of introducing the real subject. There is no difference whatsoever.

This verse is cited by both Śaṃkara and Sureśvara. Śaṃkara cites it in BSB 1.4.14, where he says: "This is what is said by those who know the tradition of the Vedānta" (*tathā-ca saṃpradāyavido vadanti*). In BV 2.1.386, p. 951 Sureśvara says:

This is the teaching of those who know the true meaning of the Vedas. This matter has been taught by the *gauḍa* teacher (or *gauḍa* teachers) just as it is by us.

niḥśeṣa-veda-siddhānta-vidvadbhir-api bhāṣitam
gauḍācāryair-idaṃ vastu yathā 'smabhiḥ prapañcitam.

Then he cites (BV 2.1.387) ADP 15 verbatim.

ADP 46 When the mind does not go under, and when again it is not distracted, then that, motionless and without appearances, becomes *brahman*.

Sureśvara cites this verse in BV 4.4.888, after citing VP 38 in BV 4.4.887 (see above). Both these verses follow BV 4.4.886, which refers to the verses of Gauḍapāda and to the doctrines which have been clearly taught by those who themselves know the correct tradition of the Vedānta.

Verses which can now be found in the Āgama-śāstra are cited by these three authors twelve times. Śaṃkara cites two verses, Maṇḍanamiśra cites one, and Sureśvara cites nine. The following verses are cited once: ĀP 3, 14, 15 and 16; VP 17 and 38; and ADP 46. ADP 15 is cited twice, and ĀP 11 is cited three times.

ĀP 3, 14 and 16 are mentioned without attribution. However, ĀP 11, ĀP 15, VP 17, VP 38, ADP 15, and ADP 46 are associated specifically with Gauḍapāda, either directly or indirectly. When part of a *kārikā* is cited in the same verse where Gauḍapāda's name is mentioned, we can be certain of the attribution; but even in the other cases, where a *kārikā* of the Āgama-śāstra is found before or after a verse which mentions the name "Gauḍapāda," we must also attribute the verse to Gauḍapāda.

Śaṃkara and Maṇḍanamiśra cite some verses, but do not mention Gauḍapāda in connection with them. So far as the oldest and most reliable texts are concerned, the association of Gauḍapāda with *any* of the verses now found in the Āgama-śāstra rests on the two works of Sureśvara: the Naiṣkarmya-siddhi and the Bṛhad-vārttika.

Note also that all the verses cited by these authors which can be found in the Āgama-prakaraṇa are in ĀP 11-16, except for ĀP 3. In other words, nearly all of the *kārikās* in the Āgama-prakaraṇa which are cited in the oldest sources are from the ĀP's commentary on Māṇḍ. 7.[3] Furthermore, none of these writers cite ĀP 17 and 18, which are the most problematic of the verses of the Āgama-prakaraṇa. These are, as I have argued in chapter 1, the only *kārikās* of the ĀP which contain unequivocally Māyāvādin (even Śūnyavādin) teachings, so it is particularly interesting that these writers (who all held Māyāvādin views) do not cite them.

The following questions need to be asked about the above verses and their citations by these Advaitins:

(a) Do the verses that are cited necessarily support the doctrine of *māyā* and the TI interpretation of the Māṇḍūkya?

(b) Do the foregoing authors always interpret the cited verses in a Māyāvādin way themselves?

(c) Finally, is there anything in these passages which permits us to infer that Gauḍapāda wrote all the verses of the Āgama-śāstra or that he was the *parama-guru* of Ādi Śaṃkara?

(a) Two of the *kārikās* fail to throw any light on the first point at all. ĀP 3 simply speaks of the three-fold enjoyment, and VP 38 simply says that one should not deviate from the reality after having seen it and should become one with it. These verses do not even raise the question of whether they should be interpreted in a Māyāvādin way or not.

ĀP 11 says that *viśva* and *taijasa* are bound by cause and effect, that *prājña* is bound by cause alone, and that these two (*dvau tau*) do not exist in *turya*. This *kārikā* is a little obscure. On one possible reading, the *kārikā* assserts that causation is unreal, on the grounds that neither cause nor effect exists in *turya*, which is the absolute reality. However, the words "these two" (*dvau tau*) may also refer, not to cause and effect as such, but to the bondage (*baddha*) of cause and the bondage of effect. Thus, the verse may simply mean that the states of waking (*viśva*) and dreaming (*taijasa*) are bound by cause and effect; that deep sleep (*prājña*) is bound by cause alone (because all effects are latent in this state); and that *turya* is beyond the bondage of both cause and effect, because it is the ultimate cause itself (*kāraṇa-svarūpa*).

Either reading of the verse seems to me to be possible. However, the latter reading is the more natural one if the verse is interpreted in context, i.e. in connection with ĀP 10 and ĀP 12 (verses which are not cited by either Śaṃkara, Sureśvara or Maṇḍanamiśra). Since the early writers we are considering here never mention the Āgama-śāstra, and in fact never cite anything but isolated sayings (*vacas*), this consideration is not decisive. Nevertheless, it is worth noting that ĀP 10 says:

> The ordainer (*īśāna*) of the cessation of suffering, the Lord (*prabhu*), immutable, without a second (*advaita*), the god of all beings (*sarvabhāvānāṃ deva*): *turya* (the fourth) is held to be all-pervading (*vibhu*).

Similarly, ĀP 12 says that *turya* is all-seeing (*sarva-dṛś*), a term that is plainly connected with Māṇḍ. 6, which refers to *īśvara*. ĀP 10 and 12, in other words, are compatible with the interpretation of ĀP 11 I have suggested, while the strict Māyāvādin interpretation is not.

ĀP 14 says that there is neither sleep nor dream in *turya*. This is true even on the IC interpretation. In the classical Upaniṣads (which adhere to this interpretation) sleeping and dreaming are described as two of the embodied states of the Self, and both are said to be different from the fourth state, i.e., the disembodied state which is attained only by the individual who has freed himself from all desires.

ĀP 15 is also equally compatible with the TI and IC interpretations of the four states of the Self, since it merely says that both dream (which involves false perception) and sleep (which involves ignorance of the reality) are absent in *turya*.

ĀP 16 asserts that when the individual who is asleep owing to the beginningless illusion (*māyā*) awakens, he awakens to the birthless, sleepless, dreamless nonduality. Note that this verse refers to the *individual* who awakens from the illusion of difference and of individuality. It does not say that the world itself is unreal, but only that duality is an illusion. This is compatible, of course, with the view that the world is unreal, but it is also compatible with the view that the world is real but also nondual.

VP 17 is similar to ĀP 16. It asserts that the Self is imagined (*vikalpita*) to be the non-Self, just as a rope in the dark is imagined through ignorance to be a snake. This, too, is compatible with the non-Māyāvādin explanation that it is merely the *individual's* ignorance which imposes duality or differences on the world, which is only the nondual *brahman*.

ADP 15 says that the analogies of clay, gold, sparks of fire etc. by which the *śruti* explains the nature of creation (*sṛṣṭi*) is merely a means of introducing that subject, and that there is in fact no difference (*bheda*) whatever. This verse does not preclude a Māyāvādin explanation, but I do not think that it requires one either. The verse can perfectly well be interpreted to mean that all such analogies are ultimately inadequate to explain the relationship between *brahman* and the world. In the case of the sparks analogy, the sparks fly off and become spatially separated from the fire, and for this reason the teaching in question does not provide a perfect analogy for the relation between *brahman* and the world, for there can be no separation — spatial or otherwise — between the world and *brahman*. The analogies of pots made out of clay, or jewels made out of gold, are also inadequate. For one thing, mud and gold, and the artifacts made out of them, are inert, whereas *brahman* is pure consciousness (*cit*). Secondly, such analogies refer to articles that, according to our everyday, practical experience (*vyavahāra*) are separate, distinct entities, whereas from the highest point of view they are just *brahman*. As the verse says, from the point of view of *brahman*, there really are no differences.

ADP 46 says that when the mind is neither merged nor distracted, and is motionless and without appearances (*anābhāsa*), it becomes *brahman*. This is somewhat reminiscent of BU 4.4.6, which says that the man without desires goes to *brahman* because he is *brahman*. In the Bṛhad-āraṇyakopaniṣad, the state of merging (laya), or sleep, is only a prelude to the postmortem state, which (in the case of the man without desires) involves merging into *brahman* and *īśvara*, which are regarded as identical.[4] Similarly, ADP 46 says that *turya* is beyond even the state of merging (*laya*) or sleep, and that it is without appearances (*anābhāsa*) because the subject-object distinction has been transcended. This verse is compatible with both the TI and IC interpretations of the doctrine of the four states of the Self.

(b) I have been arguing that the verses of Gauḍapāda which are cited by these early Advaitins can be given non-Māyāvādin interpretations. Interestingly, this is confirmed even by Śaṃkara himself, for (as we shall see below) when he cites ADP 15 he gives it such an interpretation. It is also instructive to consider his remarks in connection with ĀP 16. Although he gives ĀP 16 a clearly Māyāvādin interpretation, the context of his citation shows that a non-Māyāvādin interpretation is the preferable one.

1. Śaṃkara's citation of ADP 15 occurs in Brahma-sūtra-bhāṣya 1.4.14. BS 1.4.14 says that *brahman* is the cause of space and all the rest of the world (*kāraṇatvena cākāśādiṣu yathā-vyapadiṣṭokteḥ*). Śaṃkara attempts to defend this *sūtra* against the objection that the *śruti* gives conflicting accounts about the order of creation. Since the order of creation varies from passage to passage in Tait. 2.1, Chānd. 6.2.3, Pra. 6.4, Ait. 4.1.2, Chānd. 3.19.1, Chānd. 6.2.1, BU 1.4.7 etc., the *pūrvapakṣin* (who in this instance is a Sāṃkhyavādin, according to Śaṃkara) argues that the *śruti* cannot be regarded as authoritative on the matter of the creation of the world, and that one therefore has no choice but to rely on the *smṛtis* and reasoning (*nyāya*). These two authorities, the *pūrvapakṣin* says, tell us that the cause of the world is the subtle matter (*pradhāna*) of the Sāṃkhya system.

In his reply to this objection, Śaṃkara says that, while there may be apparent discrepancies in the *śruti* concerning the order of the things which are created by *brahman* (e.g. the *ākāśa* etc.), there is no conflict about the essential thing, i.e. the creator (*sraṣṭi*). All the passages from the *śruti* hold that the world has such a creator, and they tell us that that creator is *brahman*. Śaṃkara takes the phrase "*yathā-vyapadiṣṭokteḥ*" of the *sūtra* to mean that *brahman* is consistently described in the *śruti* as omniscient, the lord of all, the one self of all, and the one without a second (*sarvajñaḥ sarveśvaraḥ sarvātmaiko 'dvitīyaḥ*). He also cites Tait. 2.6, which says that this *brahman* thought "May I be many and may I procreate myself."

According to Śaṃkara, this means that there is no difference between the modifications which are created and their creator (*sṛjyamānānāṃ vikārāṇāṃ sraṣṭur-abhedam*). There is therefore no discrepancy in the Vedānta because all the texts are in agreement about the cause itself (*kāraṇa-svarūpa*). On the other hand, he says, there are discrepancies about the things which arise as effects (*kārya-viṣaya*). But this is no real fault, according to Śaṃkara, because the aim of the *śruti* is to tell us about *brahman*, and not to describe the world process or to give the details of *how* the world is created. The illustrations given in the Vedānta of things made out of clay, gold etc. (as in Chānd. 6.1.4-6) are merely intended to tell us that the created world (*sṛṣṭy-ādi-prapañca*) is not different, as an effect, from its cause (*kāryasya kāraṇenābheda*). Then Śaṃkara says: "This is what is said by those who know the tradition of the Vedānta (*tathā-ca saṃpradāyavido vadanti*), and then he cites ADP 15.

Note that Śaṃkara does not cite this verse in order to show that creation is unreal, or to show that there is no creation (*sṛṣṭi*). On the contrary, the whole commentary on BS 1.4.14 is intended to defend the view that *brahman* is the sole cause of the world.

As I argued earlier, ADP 15 cannot be used to show that Gauḍapāda was a Māyāvādin. What is perhaps even more surprising is that Śaṃkara's citation of ADP 15 in BSB1.4.14 cannot even be used to show that *Śaṃkara* thought that he was.

2. The second citation by Śaṃkara of a *kārikā* occurs in BSB 2.1.9.

BS 2.1.9 is a reply to an objection, which, according to Śaṃkara, is raised by a follower of the Sāṃkhya system. Like the Vedāntin, the Sāṃkhyavādin maintains that there is no real difference between the cause and the effect, either before or after the emergence of the effect.[5] The *pūrvapakṣin* argues that this renders the doctrine of *brahman's* causality untenable, for *brahman*, according to the Vedānta, is pure intelligence, nondual, free from the opposites of pleasure and pain etc. Furthermore, the Upaniṣads, *smṛtis*, *purāṇas* etc. hold that the world is periodically dissolved (*pralaya*) in its source or cause. If the effect were identical with the cause, then when this *pralaya* occurs, *brahman* would be tainted with the properties that belong to the phenomenal world. But this conclusion the Vedāntin will not and cannot accept. Hence *brahman* cannot be the cause of the world.

The *sūtra-kāra* responds to this objection in 2.1.9 by saying: "It is not so, because there are examples for it" (*na tu dṛṣṭānta-bhāvāt*). Śaṃkara takes this to mean that the *pūrvapakṣin's* objections have no force because there are examples which show that when an effect merges into its cause it does not contaminate the cause with its own qualities. For example, things like pots which are made of clay, and which as modifications exist in the state of being separate (*vikārā vibhāgāvasthā*), do not impart their own properties to the clay when they are resorbed into the clay. In fact, Śaṃkara says, the objection makes no sense because, if the special qualities of the effect continued to exist and affect the cause, no dissolution or absorption would occur at all. Furthermore, while the cause is the self of the effect (*kāryasya kāraṇātmatva*), the converse is not true. Hence the question of the cause being tainted by its effects does not arise.

Śaṃkara also attempts to answer the *pūrvapakṣin's* objection by arguing that the qualities (*dharmas*) of the effect are merely the illusory superimpositions on the cause by ignorance (*avidyādhyāropitatva*). Here too, he says, there are examples. Just as a magician is never affected by his own magical illusion (*māyā*), so the supreme Self (*paramātman*) is never affected by the illusory *saṃsāra*, since it (like the magician's illusions) are not real. Just as a person who dreams is not affected (*saṃspṛśyate*) by the illusory dream visions because these do not persist in the states of waking and deep sleep, so also the one, single witness (*sākṣy-eka*) of the three states of waking, dreaming and sleeping is not affected by them. For this appearance of the *paramātman* as the Self of the three states is a mere illusion (*māyā-mātra*), like the proverbial snake in respect to the rope. Then Śaṃkara says that in this connection there is a saying by the teacher (or teachers) who know the Vedānta (*atroktaṃ vedāntārtha-saṃpradāyavidbhir ācāryaiḥ*), and he cites the following verse:

> When the individual who is asleep owing to the beginningless *māyā* awakens, he awakens to the birthless, sleepless, dreamless nonduality.

This verse is identical with the sixteenth *kārikā* of the Āgama-prakaraṇa.

It is clear from the context in which he cites this verse that Śaṃkara interpreted ĀP 16 to mean that the world is entirely unreal and that it vanishes when the truth of its unreality is recognized. However, all the verse says is that the deluded person who awakens realizes the "sleepless, dreamless nonduality." This does not necessarily mean that the world *as such* disappears. A more natural and much less problematic way of reading the *kārikā* is to say that when the true nature of things is realized, the world — which is a manifestation of *brahman* — is realized to be nondual and non-different from *brahman*. In other words, when a person attains Self-realization, it is not the world as such but his misapprehension and misperception of the nature of the world that is sublated.

Śaṃkara cites this *kārikā* to support his contention that *brahman* can remain "untainted" by the phenomenal world-appearance both before and after it is dissolved in the universal *pralaya*. It is not at all clear, however, that the verse supports this contention, for there is a difference between a magician and his illusion, on the one hand, and a dreamer and his dreams on the other. The magician, as Śaṃkara properly says, is not in the least affected by his legerdemain: he knows (or hopes) that his audience will be deceived by his actions, but he does not see what they see. The illustration of the dreamer and his dreams is different. The dreamer is affected by his dreams, even though the dream-objects have no existence outside the dreamer's mind.

In short, Śaṃkara cites the verse to show that the dreamer is unaffected by his dreams because they are unreal, whereas the more natural way of interpreting it is to say that a dreamer is affected by his dream-creations even though they have no existence apart from him. Dreams are not just pictures which get painted on the screen of the mind when we are asleep: they are things with which we are involved and which we actually experience in some paradoxical fashion.[6]

(c) The third question which needs to be asked about the verses cited in the oldest sources and their references to Gauḍapāda is whether or not we can infer from them that Gauḍapāda was the author of all the verses of the Āgama-śāstra or whether he was the *parama-guru* of Ādi Śaṃkara. These identifications, it turns out, have to rest on two works of Sureśvara — the Naiṣkarmya-siddhi (NKS) and the Bṛhad-vārttika (BV) — for it is only in these two works that any link is made between verses now found in the Āgama-śāstra and the name Gauḍapāda.

(1) As I have already mentioned, NKS 4.41 cites ĀP 11, NKS 4.42 cites ĀP 15, and NKS 4.43 cites a verse which is identical with verse 17.26 of the Upadeśa-sāhasrī which is attributed to Ādi Śaṃkara:

(41) These two — *viśva* and *taijasa* — are considered to be bound by cause and effect. *Prājña*, on the other hand, is bound by cause alone. These two do not exist in *turya*.

(42) Dream is for one comprehending erroneously; sleep is for one who does not know reality. When these two errors are destroyed, one attains the fourth state (*turīya*).

(43) The darkness or ignorance which is called deep sleep is the cause (lit. "seed") of the waking and dreaming states. When it is burnt by the fire of Self-knowledge (*ātma-bodha*) it is like a seed which is burnt and hence non-existent.[7]

Then Sureśvara says: "This is declared by the 'Gauḍas' and the 'Drāviḍas' whom we revere" (*evaṃ gauḍair-drāviḍair-naḥ pūjyair-ayam-arthaḥ prabhāṣitaḥ*).

Max Walleser argued in 1910 that in this passage Śaṃkara does not mention two different individuals, but rather two different schools of the Vedānta: one belonging to the Gauḍas (a part of Bengal) and one belonging to the Drāviḍa country in the south, and that there is therefore no reason to assume that there ever was an individual by the name of "Gauḍapāda."[8]

This suggestion appears to be untenable. The use of plurals in names and descriptions as an honorific was customary in classical Sanskrit writings. Furthermore, we have the testimony of BV 1.4.389, which shows Sureśvara citing a verse from the sayings of Gauḍapāda (*gauḍapādīyaṃ vacas*), and this expression probably means that Sureśvara thought he was citing a saying of an individual teacher named "Gauḍapāda." Finally, it is reasonably certain on the basis of NKS 4.41-44 alone that Sureśvara thought that Gauḍapāda was an individual teacher. For NKS 4.43 cites a verse which can be found in the Upadeśa-sāhasrī of Śaṃkara, who (according to tradition) was from the Drāviḍa country in the south. Hence, Sureśvara probably means that the teachings presented were taught by his own *guru* Śaṃkara, who was from the Drāviḍa country, as well as by the one from the Gauḍas, both of whom Sureśvara reveres.

Although Walleser's suggestion must be rejected, it is significant, I think, that Sureśvara does not say that this "Gauḍa" was the grand-teacher of his own *guru*, Śaṃkara. What he says is that he reveres *both* teachers. This is compatible with the traditional account, according to which Gauḍapāda was the *parama-guru* of Ādi Śaṃkara; however, the verse does not entail this interpretation. Another possible interpretation is that Sureśvara reveres the one from the Gauḍas *as well as* his own *guru*, Śaṃkara. On the basis of some other passages from the BV (to which we now turn), I think that this is what it does mean.

(2) BV 2.1.386 (p. 951) says:

> This is the teaching of those who know the true meaning of the Vedas. This matter has been taught by the *gauḍa* teacher (or *gauḍa* teachers), just as it is by us.

This, I think, would be a rather odd way of referring to the *parama-guru* of one's own *guru*. Here Sureśvara does not regard the identity of doctrine as something that can be taken for granted, but rather as a matter of significance. This reading of the verse is reinforced by the verse which we will consider next (BV 4.4.886), which also suggests that Sureśvara was not in a lineage (*saṃpradāya*) which connected him directly with Gauḍapāda.

(3) BV 4.4.886 (p. 1866) refers to the verses of "Gauḍapāda and others" (*gauḍapādādi*) who, he says, teach the same doctrine as he does, and it refers to those who themselves know the correct tradition of the Vedānta. It is significant that Sureśvara refers to "Gauḍapāda *and others*" who teach the same doctrine as he does and who know the *saṃpradāya*. This, too, would be a rather odd way of referring to the *parama-guru* of one's own *guru*. Here Gauḍapāda is described merely as one of a number of teachers who belong to the true lineage of the Vedānta. It is the same general *saṃpradāya*, Sureśvara says, as the one to which he belongs. However, there is nothing in the passage to suggest that Sureśvara (and therefore Śaṃkara) was *directly* connected with him. In fact, the wording of BV 4.4.886 and BV 2.1.386 provides some evidence against this supposition.[9]

XII

The last chapter discussed the oldest available sources which mention Gauḍapāda and/or cite verses which are found in the work called "Āgama-śāstra" which is attributed to him. In this chapter, we turn to evidence of a different kind which has been adduced to show that Gauḍapāda was the *parama-guru* of Ādi Śaṃkara. In this chapter I shall discuss in turn (1) the two benedictory verses at the conclusion of the ĀŚV, (2) the traditional *guru-paramparā* verses of the Śaṃkara school which state that Gauḍapāda was the *parama-guru* of Ādi Śaṃkara, (3) Upadeśa-sāhasrī 2.18.2, and (4) Chāndogyopaniṣad-bhāṣya 8.12.1.

(1) Some scholars, like A. Venkatasubbiah and T. M. P. Mahadevan, have argued that the benedictory verses at the end of the ĀŚV itself show that Gauḍapāda was the *parama-guru* of Śaṃkara, but this seems to me unlikely.[1]

The first of these verses praises the unborn (*aja*) and nondual (*eka*) *brahman*, which appears as many to the deluded because of its divine power (*aiśvarya-yoga*). Then the second verse says:

> I bow down to the feet of that (*amuṃ*) *parama-guru* who is the adorable of the adorable, who, seeing all beings sinking in the terrible ocean filled with the crocodiles of unceasing birth, and who, out of compassion for them, extracted this from the ocean of the Vedas, which is hard even for the gods to obtain, by churning it with the churning-rod of his illumined reason.

The third verse says:

> I bow down to those holy feet that dispel the fear of births and deaths and which make all those who take shelter in them attain the scriptures (*śruti*), peace and right conduct; who destroyed the enveloping darkness of my mind through his illumined reason; and who destroyed *my* appearance and disappearance in the terrible, frightening ocean (of *saṃsāra*).

According to scholars like Venkatasubbiah and Mahadevan, the term "*parama-guru*" in the second verse refers to Gauḍapāda, i.e., Śaṃkara's *parama-guru* in the sense of "teacher of his teacher." This follows the traditional interpretation of these closing verses, according to which (1) the verses were written by Ādi Śaṃkara, (2) the term "*parama-guru*" in the second verse denotes Gauḍapāda, and (3) the teacher who is praised in the third verse is Govinda, the immediate teacher of Śaṃkara.

However, this is not the only possible interpretation of these verses. Note that the second verse does not *say* that this teacher was directly related to the author of the verse through a lineage. The verse refers to *that parama-guru* who is adorable etc. This wording does not exclude the interpretation that the teacher in question was the author's grand-teacher, but it certainly does not entail it.

Another interpretation is that the verse is dedicated to the supreme (*parama*) *guru* Nārāyaṇa, an incarnation or human form of Viṣṇu. There is support for this interpretation in the *bhāṣya-kāra's* own commentary on ALP 1, where he takes the phrase "best of bipeds" (*dvipadāṃ varam*) to mean "*puruṣottama*," i.e. Nārāyaṇa. Alternatively, the verse could praise Śukadeva, an even earlier *guru* in the *saṃpradāya* than Gauḍapāda. There is also some support for this interpretation in the fact that Upaniṣadbrahmayogin, a late member of the Śaṃkara school, takes the term "*dvipadāṃ varam*" of ALP 1 to refer to Śukadeva, an *avatāra* of Nārāyaṇa.

The third verse is the only one of the three in which the author refers to himself. This verse pays obeisance to the feet which saved *him* from the cycle of births and deaths. If, as I believe, the *bhāṣya-kāra* was a later writer of the Śaṃkara school, this verse would simply refer to the *bhāṣya-kāra's* teacher — whoever he was. The verse certainly does not mention Govinda, just as the preceding verse does not mention Gauḍapāda.[2]

According to this interpretation, the first verse refers to *brahman*, the second refers to the *ṛṣi* and *avatāra* Nārāyaṇa, and the third refers to the *bhāṣya-kāra's* own *guru* (whoever he was); accordingly, none of the three verses praises Gauḍapāda. It might be objected that this is a serious weakness of the interpretation, because there is a tradition going back at least to the time of Sureśvara that Gauḍapāda was the author of at least some of the *kārikās*, and because there was (at least in later times) a tradition that Gauḍapāda was inspired by Nārāyaṇa to explain the Māṇḍūkya with his four-chaptered set of verses. Hence, one would not expect the *bhāṣya-kāra* to omit praising Gauḍapāda in a verse.

We should note, however, that the *bhāṣya-kāra* never mentions the name "Gauḍapāda," either in the text itself or in the verses which tradition ascribes to him. No doubt he was aware of the fact that tradition ascribed at least some of the verses to Gauḍapāda, but he never tells us that *all* of the verses were by a single author. All he tells us is that he has put together a *prakaraṇa-catuṣṭaya*, and this certainly allows for the possibility that the *prakaraṇas* were by different authors, who may have included sayings (*vacas*) by Gauḍapāda as well as others. Hence it is quite possible that the *bhāṣya-kāra* does not praise any particular *guru* in the lineage in either the first or second verses, but simply praises *brahman* in the first verse and Nārāyaṇa (or Śukadeva) in the second verse as the ultimate authorities for *all* of the teachers who adhere to the true teachings of the Vedānta.

(2) Once again, then, we find that there is no evidence that Gauḍapāda was the *parama-guru* of Ādi Śaṃkara apart from the *traditions* of the Śaṃkara school. If we could convince ourselves that these traditions were credible, we might hesitate to deny that there was a direct, lineal relationship between these two early Advaitins. However, even a cursory inspection of the traditions of the Śaṃkara school on this matter shows that they are not evidential. I will cite briefly two examples.

T. M. P. Mahadevan cites a verse which gives the following list of the earliest teachers of the Śaṃkara school: Nārāyaṇa, the lotus-born Brahmā, Vasiṣṭha, Śakti, his son Parāśara, Vyāsa, Śuka, the great Gauḍapāda, Govinda-yogīndra, his disciple Śaṃkarācārya, and then Śaṃkara's four pupils Padmapāda, Hastāmalaka, Troṭaka and the Vārttika-kāra (i.e. Sureśvara).[3] The Śaṃkara-dig-vijaya of Vidyāraṇya (fl. 1350 C.E.), which gives the Śaṃkara school's traditional account of the life and activities of Ādi Śaṃkara, gives a slightly more truncated list: Vyāsa, Śuka, Gauḍapāda, Govinda-bhagavat-pāda, and Śaṃkara. Each is said to have been the immediate teacher of his successor.

There is nothing in either of these lists to inspire confidence in them. In Mahadevan's list, the first two figures are deities, and the next five are mythical or quasi-mythical figures. The first figure in this list who may have been an historical figure at all is Gauḍapāda. The lists are also of very doubtful credibility even for the Gauḍapāda and post-Gauḍapāda (i.e. historical) period. According to the Dig-vijaya for example, Govinda-bhagavatpāda is identical with Patañjali, the author of the Mahābhāṣya. This assertion cannot be credited, however, since Śaṃkara probably lived around the first half of the 8th century, whereas Patañjali is now placed much earlier than that, about 150 B.C.E. (Cardona (1976: 266)).[4]

(3) The Upadeśa-sāhasrī is a work that is usually ascribed to Ādi Śaṃkara, and parts of it, at least, are almost certainly authentic. US 2.18.2 praises a great mendicant (*yatīndra*) who is said to be of great intellect, who protected the true import of the Vedas against its enemies. US 2.18.2d says: "*namo yatīndraya guror-garīyase*," and many scholars have interpreted this to mean: "I bow down to that great ascetic (*yatīndra*) who is the teacher of my teacher (*guror-garīyase*)," and have taken this to mean Gauḍapāda, the teacher of Govinda, Śaṃkara's own *guru*.[5]

Since "*garīyas*" in Sanskrit is the comparative of "*guru*," one of the meanings of which is "teacher," this meaning cannot be ruled out. On the other hand, it is not the only possible meaning, nor, I think, the most natural one. "*Guru*" (as an adjective) also means "heavy," "important," "great," "venerable," "highly prized." "*Guror-garīyas*," therefore, can simply mean "extremely great teacher," "he who is greater than a (mere) *guru*," "he who is dearer than a *guru*," or simply "highly venerable *guru*."[6]

It seems to me, therefore, that the interpretation "*guru* of my *guru*" is unwarranted. On purely linguistic grounds this reading cannot be excluded, but it would be a much less common usage of the phrase "*guror-garīyase*" than the latter ones. Furthermore, since there is nothing in this part of the US that indicates that the author was specifically talking about Gauḍapāda, the most natural thing to suppose is that he was talking about Govinda, for it is customary in texts to praise one's *own guru*. In the absence of any specific reason for referring to Gauḍapāda rather than Govinda, the assumption that the author was referring to the *guru* of his *guru* would appear to be somewhat invidious, for there is no other verse in the text that refers to the *immediate guru* of the author. For these reasons, it seems to me that "*guror-garīyase*" in US 2.18.2 should not be interpreted to mean "the *guru* of my *guru*."

(4) S. L. Pandey (1974: 30-31) has adduced 8.12.1 of the Chāndogyopaniṣad-bhāṣya that is ascribed to Ādi Śaṃkara as evidence that Gauḍapāda was the *parama-guru* of Ādi Śaṃkara. Pandey translates the concluding passage of CUB 8.12.1 as follows:

> The reality of self which can be known only from such past masters of the philosophy of the Vedānta as have given up all desires for external things, have sought shelter into [sic] the identity of Ātman and have adopted the highest stage of a mendicant's life, as has been described by the most revered follower of the school of Prajāpati in the four *prakaraṇas*. He alone is teaching it these days and nobody else is doing so.[7]

He then draws the following conclusion:

> The last citation of Śaṃkara's ... proves that the Four *Prakaraṇas*, viz. the *Āgamaśāstra* which is termed as Four *Prakaraṇas* (by Śaṃkara in the introductory sentence of his commentary theron) were written by one and the same person who alone was teaching the traditional philosophy of Vedānta during the life-time of Śaṃkara.

This purported evidence is perhaps the weakest of all, for Pandey's reading of "*prakaraṇa-catuṣṭayena*" is taken out of context. Not only is his reading of "*prakaraṇa*" as "treatise" arbitrary; it is also more or less *excluded* by the language of the *bhāṣya* itself.

Chānd. 8.11-12, as I pointed out in chapter 4, form the conclusion of an extended passage of the Chāndogya which begins with Chānd. 8.7. In this section of the Upaniṣad, Prajāpati instructs Indra about the Self which is "free from evil, ageless and deathless." Four instructions are given by Prajāpati to Indra in succession: (1) the Self is the body, (2) the Self is the one who dreams, (3) the Self is the one who sleeps and (4) the Self is the one who is bodiless (*aśarīra*) and who is released at death. The first three teachings are said to be false teachings, and are used to test Indra. According to the Upaniṣad, the fourth teaching, that the Self is bodiless, is the correct teaching.

The *bhāṣya* (though not the Upaniṣad) uses the term "*prakaraṇa*" to refer to these four different sections, instructions or teachings.[8] It also uses this term interchangeably with the terms "*prakāra*" and "*paryāya*," which mean "method," "manner," "way of proceeding," or a figure of speech which is circumlocutory or periphrastic. This terminology of the *bhāṣya* is justified by the fact that Prajāpati's teaching is indirect, involving three false teachings at the beginning, the first of which (i.e. that the Self is the same as the body) is introduced by asking Indra to look at himself in a mirror or pan of water. Thus, in its commentary on 8.7.1 (p. 472 of the *ASS* edition) the CUB says that Prajāpati took up the following *prakāra* to explain the Self that obtains all the worlds and all desires; in its commentary on 8.11.3 (p. 490) Prajāpati refers to the three synonyms (*paryāya*) which he has previously used (i.e. Self as body, Self as dreamer and Self as sleeper) to explain the Self; in its commentary on 8.12.1 (p. 495) it refers to the three previous expressions (*paryāya*) that were used and to the fourth *paryāya* which leads the listener from the body to incorporeality; and on p. 498 it refers to the fourth explanation and to all the four explanations (*paryāyāḥ*).

The passage that Pandey cites forms the conclusion of the *bhāṣya's* commentary on Chānd. 8.12.1. The term "*prakaraṇa-catuṣṭaya*" in this passage is clearly taken by Ānandagiri in his Ṭīkā to refer to Prajāpati's four teachings to Indra concerning the nature of the Self, for he says that the three states and the fourth are the object of the four explanations (*sthāna-trayaṃ turīyaṃ cety-etad-viṣayaṃ prakaraṇa-catuṣṭayam*). Accordingly, Ganganatha Jha (1899) translated the passage simply and straightforwardly as follows:

> Therefore the Supreme Reality of the unity of the Self can be rightly comprehended only by those Paramahaṃsa-Renunciates who have renounced all desire for the external world, who have nothing else to fall back upon, who have accepted the highest state of life, who are engaged only with the conception of the Vedānta, — the highly revered ones, following as they do the doctrine laid down by Prajāpati in the aforesaid sections; and hence today too, it is only such revered ones, and none others, that teach this doctrine.

Pandey's interpretation, on the other hand, seems arbitrary. After all, the *bhāṣya* is commenting on the Upaniṣad, and the Upaniṣad refers to Prajāpati, not Gauḍapāda. Since Pandey's interpretation of the passage apparently fails to apply to the *bhāṣya's* commentary on Chānd. 8.7- 8.12 as a whole, it would appear to be an untenable one.

Unless we want to exert ourselves by grasping at straws, it seems that we must simply abandon the attempt to validate the tradition that Gauḍapāda was the *parama-guru* of Ādi Śaṃkara. Since we cannot take it for granted that Gauḍapāda was the grand-teacher of Śaṃkara, we cannot take it for granted that he taught the same doctrines as Śaṃkara, either. What can we say about his doctrines on the basis of the four early texts which were examined in the previous chapter?

One thing that we can say about Gauḍapāda with some certainty is that he was especially interested in the doctrine of the four states (*pādas*, *avasthās*) of the Self. At any rate this is a natural thing to conclude on the assumption that the citations of his *kārikās* by Śaṃkara, Maṇḍanamiśra and Sureśvara can be taken as an indication of his philosophical interests, for on many of the occasions when these writers cite Gauḍapāda or Gauḍapādīya *kārikās*, they cite *kārikās* which mention these states.

Secondly, Gauḍapāda clearly upheld a very strict nondualistic (Advaitin) interpretation of the Upaniṣads. In spite of this, however, it would be incautious to assume that he also taught a strict illusionistic (Māyāvādin) doctrine.

In addressing this question it is important to note which *kārikās* are *not* cited by the earliest Advaitin writers. Significantly, neither Śaṃkara, Sureśvara nor Maṇḍanamiśra cites any *kārikās* from the ALP, which is the most problematic of all of the *prakaraṇas* of the "Āgama-śāstra." Nor do any of these writers cite *kārikās* which clearly uphold the view — which is the special theme of the VP — that there is no real difference between the experiences of the waking state and the dreaming state. Nor do they cite ĀP 17 and 18, which are the most problematic verses of the Āgama-prakaraṇa.

As I argued in the last chapter, the *kārikās* which are cited do not necessarily imply a strict illusionistic doctrine. For example, ADP 15 may simply mean what Śaṃkara takes it to mean in BSB 1.4.14, i.e., that the Upaniṣads uphold the doctrine of the creation of the world from (and out of) *brahman*, but deny that the world is separate from *brahman*. Similarly ĀP 16, as I have previously argued, may simply mean that when the *jīva* awakens from the sleepless, dreamless *māyā*, the misperception that the world is different from *brahman* and that it is a multiplicity vanishes, though the world (as a manifestation of *brahman*) does not itself vanish. Similarly, ĀP

11 may simply mean that *turya* is not *bound* by any cause, and not that there is no causality at all. Similar interpretations, I believe, can be applied to all of the verses that are cited in the oldest texts by Śaṃkara, Sureśvara and Maṇḍanamiśra.

To be sure, the particular *kārikās* cited by Śaṃkara, Maṇḍanamiśra and Sureśvara do not *exclude* a strict Māyāvāda interpretation. However, the main reason for not interpreting them in this way is that other *kārikās* of the Āgama-prakaraṇa, like the ones discussed in chapter 1, preclude the TI or Māyāvāda interpretation. It is true that the oldest texts do not tell us that all of these *kārikās* were written by Gauḍapāda, but if some of them were, then one would have to interpret the *kārikās* that Śaṃkara, Maṇḍanamiśra and Sureśvara do cite in a non-Māyāvādin way also. Furthermore, if we confine ourselves to only the best and oldest sources, there is nothing intrinsically improbable in the suggestion that Gauḍapāda was both a nondualist and a realist, as were the Advaitins of the Śuddhādvaita school and the school of Kāśmīra Śaivism in later periods of Indian history. This assumption, it seems to me, is the only one which is capable of accommodating the kinds of *kārikās* which Śaṃkara, Maṇḍanamiśra and Sureśvara do cite as well as ĀP 6-9, 10, 12, and 26-28.

Since the Māṇḍūkya is specifically concerned with the four states of the Self and Gauḍapāda was especially interested in this doctrine, it would seem fairly natural to conclude that Gauḍapāda wrote the Āgama-prakaraṇa as a single work, and as a commentary on the Māṇḍūkya. However, we are not really entitled to this conclusion. For one thing, the oldest sources — which are the only ones, it seems to me, on which we can rely with any certainty — never mention the Āgama-prakaraṇa, nor do they mention Gauḍapāda as having had any special connection with the Māṇḍūkya. This is a very striking fact, for even in ancient and medieval India works were commonly given titles — and were referred to by their titles — just as they have been in the rest of the world. If Gauḍapāda had been the author of a work like the Āgama-prakaraṇa, it is rather strange that these early writers of the Advaita school do not mention it. This is particularly striking in the case of Sureśvara. He cites the Māṇḍūkya (and even names it), and occasionally mentions "Gauḍapāda," "the teachers of the Gauḍas," etc., but he does not appear to connect Gauḍapāda or the verses of the ĀP specifically with the Māṇḍūkya.[9] Hence one cannot exclude the possibility that Gauḍapāda did not write the Āgama-prakaraṇa as such, or, if he did, that he did not write *all* of it. A later writer might have taken his isolated sayings and constructed a commentary on the Māṇḍūkya out of them, somewhat in the fashion of the author of the ĀŚV, who constructed the "Āgama-śāstra" as a *prakaraṇa-catuṣṭaya* out of four different *texts*.

The hypothesis that there was more than one author of the *kārikās* which we find in the ĀP would provide an explanation for the highly anomalous seventeenth and eighteenth *kārikās* of the Āgama-prakaraṇa. These are, as I pointed out in chapter 1, virtually impossible to explain according to any interpretation. They appear to be straightforward Buddhist Śūnyavāda teachings, yet they appear in what is manifestly a Vedāntic text.

What may have happened is that some *kārikās* from another tradition were introduced into the commentary on the Māṇḍūkya by another writer — perhaps the *bhāṣya-kāra*. When the *bhāṣya-kāra* tells us that he is constructing a *prakaraṇa-catuṣṭaya*, he may mean that he took four different texts *as he found them* and simply strung them together. But what he actually says does not preclude the possibility that he had a hand in constructing the *prakaraṇas* themselves. The hypothesis that he did have a hand in them, furthermore, would explain how Śūnyavāda teachings got into the commentary on the Māṇḍūkya. What may have happened is that the author of the ĀŚV put them there in order to create a more unified work by linking the Māṇḍūkya and the ĀP with the very Buddhist-sounding teachings of the ALP.[10]

Whether it was the *bhāṣya-kāra* or some other writer who interpolated the seventeenth and eighteenth verses into the ĀP, the inclusion appears to have gained wide currency by the 13th century, for the early medieval commentators on the ĀP (e.g. Ānandagiri, Madhva and Kūranārāyaṇa) treated ĀP 17 and 18 as verses of the Āgama-prakaraṇa. It is striking, too, that both Madhva and Kūranārāyaṇa felt that they could write commentaries on the Āgama-prakaraṇa at this date without even mentioning Gauḍapāda, the reputed *parama-guru* of Ādi Śaṃkara.

XIII

The main points of the discussion in the preceding chapters may be summarized as follows:

(1) Māṇḍ. 6 belongs with Māṇḍ. 7 rather than with Māṇḍ. 5 (chapters 1-6 of Part I). Hence, the Māṇḍūkya is not a Māyāvāda text.

(2) The Āgama-prakaraṇa, the oldest commentary on the Māṇḍūkya, supports the IC rather than the TI interpretation of the Māṇḍūkya, except for two highly anomalous verses, ĀP 17 and ĀP 18. These are very Buddhist sounding verses, and in fact on a literal reading belong to the Śūnyavāda (chapter 1).

(3) The Alāta-śānti-prakaraṇa could not have been written by Gauḍapāda, the reputed grand-guru (*parama-guru*) of Ādi Śaṃkara. The interpretation of Buddhism which is found in the ALP was not the one held by Śaṃkarācārya (chapters 7-8).

(4) The traditions of the Saṃkara school are almost certainly unreliable as to the purported relations between Śaṃkarācārya and Gauḍapāda. There is nothing in these traditions, nor anything in the oldest and most authoritative texts which refer to Gauḍapāda or which cite *kārikās* which can be found in the Āgama-śāstra, to make us think that Gauḍapāda wrote the ALP or even all the *kārikās* of the Vaitathya-prakaraṇa and the Advaita-prakaraṇa. The *kārikās* which are cited show that Gauḍapāda was a nondualist, but there is no evidence in them that clearly supports the view that he was a Māyāvādin, or that he was the individual who introduced the TI interpretation of the Māṇḍūkya into the tradition of the Vedānta (chapters 11-12).

(5) Originally, the work we now know as the "Āgama-śāstra" was not a single treatise at all. It was, instead, a quartet of treatises (*prakaraṇa-catuṣṭaya*). Its individual components were strung together by the author of the Āgama-śāstra-vivaraṇa for his own didactic purposes (chapter 9).

(6) There are many compelling reasons for thinking that Ādi Śaṃkara did not write the Āgama-śāstra-vivaraṇa (chapters 8-10).

This virtually wholesale rejection of the traditional account may seem to leave us with a very incoherent picture. However, it seems to me that it is possible to provide an adequate explanation of all of these texts (i.e. the Māṇḍūkya, the four treatises of the "Āgama-śāstra" and the Āgama-śāstra-vivaraṇa). All the difficulties of interpretation disappear as soon as we (1) assign the *prakaraṇa-catuṣṭaya* and its Vivaraṇa to the post-Śaṃkara period, and (2) give up the tradition of the Śaṃkara school which tells us that the author of the ĀŚ was the *parama-guru* of Ādi Śaṃkara.

Let me now outline an alternative scenario which I think provides a far more plausible scenario of events than the traditional account:

(1) We have no reason to doubt that the verses ascribed to Gauḍapāda by Sureśvara are his. The verses of the Āgama-śāstra which are ascribed simply to the "knowers of the traditions" etc. in the early writings are probably also by Gauḍapāda, although this is somewhat inferential. However, I suggest that Gauḍapāda did not write all of the "Āgama-śāstra," and in fact that he may never have written *all* of the Āgama-prakaraṇa. In any case, he was not the author of the Alāta-śānti-prakaraṇa.[1]

(2) The ĀŚV was not written by Ādi Śaṃkara, but by a post-Śaṃkara writer of the Śaṃkara school. We may never know exactly when the ĀŚV was written, but the available evidence allows for a very late date. It is surely significant that the earliest work which mentions the ĀŚV is the commentary (Ṭīkā) on the ĀŚV by Ānandagiri, who flourished around 1300 C.E. This leaves an interval of about six hundred years — between the approximate date of Gauḍapāda and the date of Ānandagiri — in which the ĀŚV could have been written.[2]

(3) As we have seen, the author of the Vivaraṇa was more than a mere *bhāṣya-kāra*: he was also a *prakaraṇa-catuṣṭaya-kāra*, in the sense that he took four independent texts and strung them together to form a collected work on which to write his commentary. The *bhāṣya-kāra's* inclusion of the ALP in this *prakaraṇa-catuṣṭaya* was a particularly bold move on his part. His commentary on the ALP shows that he frequently misunderstood or deliberately distorted the text, but (as I shall argue shortly) his inclusion of this text was an essential part of his plan for providing a Māyāvāda interpretation of the Māṇḍūkya and for differentiating even his own very radical Māyāvādin views from those of the Buddhists.

There are two objections which might be raised against this suggested scenario. First, it might be objected that it, too, fails to provide an adequate explanation for the discrepancy between the ALP and its interpretation by the ĀŚV. Thus, it might be argued, any later writer of the Śaṃkara school would have been able to see that the ALP in general, and parts of the VP and ADP as well, set forth views which are indistinguishable in many respects from those of the Vijñānavāda Buddhists — views which were explicitly and forcefully criticized by Śaṃkara in his definitive and most important works. Consequently, the problem of the discrepancy between the ĀŚV and the last three *prakaraṇas* (especially the ALP) simply reappears in this hypothesis in a new guise. Second, it might be argued that it is more likely that the Alāta-śānti-prakaraṇa is a *pre*-Śaṃkara work, for it has undoubtedly been greatly influenced by Mahāyāna doctrines. A critic might use this fact to argue that a work like the ALP was probably written in the pre-Śaṃkara period (when Buddhism was very strong) rather than in the post-Śaṃkara period (when it seems to have been comparatively weak).

I think that both of these objections can be met. I shall begin with the second objection.

(a) So far as Buddhist influence on the Vedānta is concerned, it must be noted that the evidence from other writers and other works shows clearly that the first response of the Vedic tradition to Buddhism was highly negative and critical — a response which is understandable given that Buddhism as a spiritual and religious force was in many respects quite alien to the Vedic tradition. In this early period, it is the differences between the two systems which are stressed. The earliest extant works from the Vedic tradition which refer to Buddhism in any detail consistently adopt this attitude towards it. Important examples are the Brahma-sūtra, Kumārila Bhaṭṭa's Śloka-vārttika (ca. 660 C.E.), and the definitive and well-authenticated writings of Ādi Śaṃkara. It is probably true that in the earlier period Buddhism was much more powerful than it was in the post-Śaṃkara period, when its power seems to have been in decline; but it is equally important to note that the evidence strongly indicates that in the early period the reaction of the Vedic tradition towards Buddhism was consistently negative.

Śaṃkara, of course, is often regarded as an exception to this general rule. Śaṃkara has always been subject to the charge of being a crypto-Buddhist (*pracanna-bauddha*), mainly because he advocated the doctrine that the world is unreal (*māyāvic*). Since the doctrine that the world is an illusion probably originated within

Buddhism, Śaṃkara, it is thought, may very well have had Buddhist leanings and been influenced by Buddhist doctrines.

It is undoubtedly true that Śaṃkara's treatment of *māyā* as illusion — rather than as a real *śakti* or power of transformation — and his frequent use of Mahāyānist analogies like the rope-snake illusion (*rajju-sarpa*), illusory cities in the sky (*gandharva-nagara*) etc. to explain the nature of the world-appearance, shows Buddhist influence. However, in Śaṃkara's definitive writings these analogies — and the interpretation of *māyā* as illusion — are *adapted* to the Vedānta. In the Brahma-sūtra-bhāṣya and the Bṛhad-āraṇyakopaniṣad-bhāṣya, at least, Śaṃkara is very careful to distinguish his own views from the views of the Buddhists, which he regards as wholly alien to the Vedānta.[3]

It is likely that the ALP represents a later stage than the one represented by Śaṃkara's authoritative writings, for the ALP does more than simply adopt (and adapt) some features of a system which is clearly recognized as different. According to the ALP, there *is* no difference between the two systems. This interpretation of Buddhism could be quite late, for at an early period, when Buddhism was being fought tooth and nail, it is unlikely that any philosophically sophisticated person could have taken the ALP's interpretation of the teachings of the Buddha seriously. It is more likely that this kind of interpretation was put forward at a later period of Indian history, when Buddhist views had been more thoroughly assimilated into the Śaṃkara school of the Vedānta, and when the nature of the doctrinal differences between Buddhism and the Vedānta were less clearly understood.[4]

The ĀŚV is probably a much later work than even the ALP. It is one thing to say that the Buddha was a crypto-Vedāntist (which is the view of the ALP), and quite another to take a text which clearly asserts this, and to interpret it in such a way that the doctrines are attributed to Nārāyaṇa rather than to Gautama Buddha. It seems to me that this could have happened only when Buddhist doctrines had penetrated the Vedānta to an even greater extent, and when the understanding of the crucial doctrinal differences between the two systems had reached a rather abysmal state. It is even possible that this interpretation of the ALP was written after Buddhism had virtually disappeared as an active force from Indian religious and social life. It could have been advanced, for example, after the

Muslims had invaded large parts of India and destroyed many of the Buddhist texts and the centers of Buddhist learning. One cannot dismiss the possibility that the ĀŚV was written at such a late date, for the earliest text (so far as we know) which refers to the ĀŚV is Ānandagiri's Ṭīkā, which was written ca. 1300 C.E. There appears to be nothing in the present state of research which precludes us from supposing that the ĀŚV was written within a couple of hundred years of this date.

Some support for the foregoing scenario may be found by comparing the views of the ĀŚV towards Buddha and Buddhism with the view of the Buddha which may be found in later Vaiṣṇava writings like the Gīta-govinda of Jayadeva. Although there is undoubtedly no direct connection between the ĀŚV and works like the Gīta-govinda, it is of interest for our present purposes to note that the later medieval Vaiṣṇavas regarded the Buddha as an *avatāra* of Viṣṇu. Furthermore, their interpretation of the Buddha and his teachings are about as unconvincing as the ĀŚV's interpretation of the ALP. For example, the later Vaiṣṇavas held that the Buddha *avatāra* was notable for having accomplished two things: (1) he stopped the animal sacrifices of the Vedic *karma-kāṇḍa*, and (2) he succeeded in deceiving people with non-Vedic doctrines. The first accomplishment is regarded by the Vaiṣṇavas with approval, but the second accomplishment is ambiguous at best, for how could Viṣṇu have wanted to deceive anyone?

This is a good example of the bizarre ways in which one tradition can try to accommodate itself to another tradition which is really alien to it: if the motive is strong enough, virtually anything can happen. This example shows, I think, that the hypothesis for the ĀŚV that I am propounding is not intrinsically implausible. There is not such a great distance, after all, between the later Vaiṣṇavas, who maintained that the Buddha was an incarnation of Viṣṇu, and the views of the unknown author of the ĀŚV, who ascribes the teachings of the ALP to Nārāyaṇa.[5]

(b) Let us turn now to the other objection. According to the alternative scenario I have been outlining, the *bhāṣya-kāra* was a later writer of the Śaṃkara school. This later writer linked the four *prakaraṇas* together, and then wrote a commentary (the ĀŚV) on the "Āgama-śāstra." It might be objected that this suggestion is implausible, for the unknown author of the ĀŚV, as a follower of the

Śaṃkara school of the Advaita, would have had strong reasons for not linking the ALP, with its patently Buddhist terminology, with the other *prakaraṇas*.

I think, however, that there were perfectly sensible reasons for the *bhāṣya-kāra's* having done what I suggest he did.

It is likely that some Vedāntic *śāstras* which had promulgated the Māyāvāda had been elevated to the status of *śruti* by the time the ĀŚV was written, so the TI interpretation of the Māṇḍūkya may already have entered (at least implicitly) the tradition of the Vedānta. Furthermore, the Māṇḍūkya itself had undoubtedly grown in importance since the time of Śaṃkara, and there was therefore a strong motive to apply the TI interpretation directly to the Māṇḍūkya itself. However, as I have already argued at some length, the TI interpretation of the Māṇḍūkya is a rather unnatural and implausible reading of the Upaniṣad, and the weight of the Vedāntic tradition was against it. Hence, it is understandable that the *bhāṣya-kāra* would have been tempted to enlist the support of the the strongly Māyāvādin verses in the Vaitathya-prakaraṇa and the Advaita-prakaraṇa, and even some of the strongly Mādhyamika- and Vijñānavādin-sounding views which are found in the Alāta-śānti-prakaraṇa, in carrying out this project. The result was (except for the Āgama-prakaraṇa) not a commentary on the Māṇḍūkya in the strict sense. Nevertheless, the "Āgama-śāstra" that resulted is a text that does move from the classicism of the Māṇḍūkya to very extreme Māyāvādin views in a reasonably convincing fashion.

The hypothesis, then, is that the *bhāṣya-kāra* included the last three *prakaraṇas* of the Āgama-śāstra because these treatises made his case for the TI interpretation of the Māṇḍūkya more convincing. Since the doctrines of the last three *prakaraṇas* obviously owe a great deal to Mahāyānist views, however, the *bhāṣya-kāra* was leaving himself open to the charge of being one of the "*pracanna-bauddhas*" (Buddhists in disguise). This is particularly true, of course, of the last *prakaraṇa*, the ALP. It is unlikely that the *bhāṣya-kāra* was unaware of this fact, so his attitude towards Buddhism is central to ascertaining his motives, both as a *prakaraṇa-catuṣṭaya-kāra* and as a *bhāṣya-kāra*.

I suggest that one of the *bhāṣya-kāra's* ulterior motives in using the last three *prakaraṇas* (and especially the ALP) was to meet *head on* the persistent charge that Śaṃkara (to whose school he undoubtedly belonged) was a crypto-Buddhist.

The issue of "crypto-Buddhism" is raised even more sharply by the last three *prakaraṇas* and in the *bhāṣya-kāra's* own version of the Vedānta than it is in Śaṃkara's writings, of course, for the *bhāṣya-kāra* accepts a very extreme formulation of the Māyāvāda, including views that Śaṃkara criticized at length in his Brahmasūtra-bhāṣya and the Bṛhad-āraṇyakopaniṣad-bhāṣya. In spite of this I think it is possible to discern a motive for what the *bhāṣya-kāra* did. What the *bhāṣya-kāra* may have wanted to show was that even *his* views were different from the Mahāyāna. If he could show this, then a fortiori he would have clearly absolved the whole Śaṃkara school of the charge of crypto-Buddhism.

Although the *bhāṣya-kāra* is guilty of frequently misinterpreting the ALP, it has to be said in his favor that he is in one important respect a far more reliable guide to Buddhist doctrines than the text on which he is commenting. As I argued in chapter 7, the Buddhist terminology of the Alāta-śānti-prakaraṇa must not be taken at face value. While the language of the *prakaraṇa* is consistently Buddhist, the underlying intent is to show that the Buddha taught an eternalist doctrine. According to the ALP, when the mind ceases to "vibrate" and becomes pure, it becomes one with an all-pervading, non-*dharmic*, changeless reality which is, in effect, identical with *brahman* (though in the ALP it is never called *brahman*). This eternalist and substantialist interpretation of the Buddha *dharma* must be rejected, and the *bhāṣya-kāra* sees that it must be rejected. Even though he accepts the view that the world is the imaginary creation of the moving mind and that there is no substantive difference between waking and dreaming, he notes in his commentary to ALP 99 that the doctrine of the ALP is not really a Buddhist doctrine. There he says:

> For the *śruti* says: 'The knowledge of the seer is never lost.' This supreme, nondual reality (*paramārtha-tattvam-advayam*), devoid of the distinction between knowledge, knower and what is known, was not taught by the Buddha. The view (of the Buddhists) that there are no external objects (*bāhyārtha*) and that everything is mind only (*jñānamātra-kalpanā*) is similar to the nondual reality (*advaya-vastu*). However, this nondual supreme reality

(*paramārtha-tattvam-advaitam*) is learned from the Vedānta alone.

The *bhāṣya-kāra* was perceptive enough to see that the ALP does not really teach a Buddhist doctrine, even though it purports to do so. His fateful mistake, however, was to make this perfectly valid point by writing a commentary on a text which does not exactly *say* what he wants it to say. Indeed, the text on which he comments actually implies that the Buddha held the views of the Māyāvāda Vedānta and that the Buddha believed in the eternal and unchanging reality of an all-pervading consciousness etc. Thus, although the *bhāṣya-kāra* wanted to defend even his version of the Vedānta against the charge of crypto-Buddhism, his mistaken reading of the ALP has led — through a series of events which he could not possibly have foreseen — to the opposite result. I suggest that what happened was the following.

First of all, legends started forming in the Śaṃkara school about the Gauḍapāda that Sureśvara mentions occasionally in his Naiṣkarmya-siddhi and Bṛhad-vārttika, some of whose *kārikās* are included in the Āgama-śāstra. Eventually, the fact that the *bhāṣya-kāra* was a *prakaraṇa-catuṣṭaya-kāra* was overlooked, and the so-called "Āgama-śāstra" came to be viewed as a single work by a single author, Gauḍapāda. Furthermore, a tradition about the early teachers of the school was formed, according to which Śaṃkara was the direct student of Govinda, who was the direct student of Gauḍapāda, who was the direct student of the mythical and quasi-divine Śukadeva etc. The *bhāṣya-kāra* himself came to be identified with Śaṃkara, and his reference in the second of the closing verses of the Vivaraṇa to "that *great* teacher" etc. was interpreted as a reference to Śaṃkara's *grand* teacher, Gauḍapāda.[6]

The problems which were inherent in these developments all along went undetected, apparently, until 1910, when the Buddhist scholar de La Vallée Poussin read the Alāta-śānti-prakaraṇa and noted that the *maṅgalācaraṇa* was undoubtedly to Gautama Buddha rather than to Nārāyaṇa, and that the phrase "*naitad buddhena bhāṣitam*" certainly does *not* mean: "This is different from what was taught by the Buddha." At this point, things began to unravel in a really sinister way. Vidusekhara Bhattacharya followed up on Poussin's insight in a number of works, in which he was able to draw freely from Buddhist works which had been preserved in the Tibetan Bstang-'gyur. In these publications Bhattacharya scandalized the orthodox by arguing that the ALP was written in praise of the Buddha and that Gauḍapāda was himself a Buddhist or — at the very least — that he must have identified the Buddha's doctrines with his own. This was just the modern incarnation of the old charge against Śaṃkara that he was a crypto-Buddhist. Now, however, the charge had to be taken very seriously, for now it was solidly based on scholarly research on the Buddhist texts, many of which had been unavailable in India for centuries.

The *bhāṣya-kāra*, who no doubt meant well, could not have foreseen any of these developments. However, I believe that it is this later and presently unknown writer of the Śaṃkara school who is ultimately responsible for the present state of affairs. Now, as a result of his efforts, modern scholars can seriously discuss the question whether the *guru* of Śaṃkara's *guru* was a Buddhist.

PART III

XIV

We may now return to the consideration of the Māṇḍūkya. In this chapter I begin with a review of the doctrine of the four states of the Self. I first compare the TI and IC interpretations of this doctrine. I then contrast the doctrine of *māyā* which belongs to the IC interpretation (according to which *māyā* is a unique power of self-transformation on the part of *brahman*) with the doctrine of *māyā* according to the TI interpretation (according to which *māyā* is simply illusion). I also discuss at this point two different analyses of causation, since the two interpretations of *māyā* are closely connected with differing views about causality. I conclude the section with some philosophical objections to the Māyāvāda.

The Doctrine of the Four States of the Self

Although the Māṇḍūkya is based on earlier Upaniṣadic teachings, the underlying teachings are not immediately apparent because they have been compressed tremendously into the compass of twelve short *mantras*. Interpreting the Māṇḍūkya is largely a matter of "unpacking" or "reconstructing" the full scope of the underlying teachings from these twelve sentences. That this is not an entirely straightforward matter is shown by the fact that there have been two very different interpretations of the Māṇḍūkya in the history of the Vedānta — what I have called the TI and the IC interpretations.

According to the TI interpretation, Māṇḍ. 6, which speaks of the lord of all (*sarveśvara* etc.), is connected with Māṇḍ. 5, which speaks of the state of deep sleep. According to this interpretation, there is in the Māṇḍūkya a steady progression from the outwardly oriented waking state of consciousness to a state of complete isolation from the phenomenal world (*kaivalya*). Thus, the mind is more introverted in the dreaming state than it is in the waking state; more introverted yet in the sleeping state; and totally withdrawn or isolated in the fourth state (*caturtha*, *turīya*). According to the Āgamaśāstra-vivaraṇa, which adheres to this interpretation, all of our waking and dreaming experiences are unreal. The ultimate cause (literally, "seed" or *bīja*) of these experiences is the sleeping state. In the state of subjectivity which we call deep sleep, this seed lies latent, but even this "seed" is destroyed in the *samādhi* state (*turīya*).

According to the IC interpretation, however, the underlying structure of the Māṇḍūkya is considerably more complicated. According to this interpretation, Māṇḍ. 6 and Māṇḍ. 7 are both connected with the supreme state, and both *mantras* are, therefore, connected with Māṇḍ. 1 and 2. There is no steady progression from extroversion to introversion; in fact, on this reading, Māṇḍ. 3-5 are essentially an interruption of the main line of the teaching of the Upaniṣad, as they are essentially concerned with the *embodied* states of the Self. Māṇḍ. 6 and 7, on the other hand, are principally concerned with the absolute and disembodied state of the Self.

The essential features of the IC interpretation can be set forth in the following way. First, highlight the fact that Māṇḍ. 3-5 describe the three different states of the *embodied* self by indenting them from the rest of the text; and second, treat Māṇḍ. 6 and 7 as a single *mantra*. What we get for the first seven *mantras* of the Māṇḍūkya is the following:

***

Aum: this syllable is all this. A clear exposition of it is: what was, what is and what will be: all this is only *Aum*. And whatever else is beyond the three times: that also is only *Aum*.

All this, indeed is *brahman*. This Self is *brahman*. This Self itself has four quarters:

> (1) The waking state, outwardly cognitive, having seven limbs, having nineteen mouths, enjoying the gross, the universal: this is the first quarter.
>
> (2) The dreaming state, inwardly cognitive, having seven limbs, having nineteen mouths, enjoying the refined, the brilliant: this is the second quarter.
>
> (3) Where one, asleep, does not desire any desire whatever, sees no dream whatever, that is deep sleep. The sleeping state, which has become one, just a cognition mass, made of bliss,

verily an enjoyer of bliss, whose face is thought: *prājña* is the third quarter.

(4) This is the lord of all, this is the knower of all, this is the inner controller, this is the source of all, indeed the origin and the end of all beings: not inwardly cognitive, not outwardly cognitive, not cognitive both ways, not a cognition mass, not cognitive, not non-cognitive, unseen, beyond speech, ungraspable, without any distinctive marks, unthinkable, undesignatable, the essence of the knowledge of the one Self, the cessation of the phenomenal world, quiescent, auspicious, nondual: such they think is the fourth. He is the Self. He is to be known.

***

Combining Māṇḍ. 6 and 7 in this way is, in fact, the most natural way of reading the Māṇḍūkya simply as a syntactical or textual matter, since there is a clear pattern in the text of naming a state as the first, second, third or fourth state *after* the state itself has been described. Furthermore, as I noted in chapter 2, there is textual support for this straightforward way of reading the Māṇḍūkya in the Nṛsiṃha-pūrva-tāpanīya and Rāmottara-tāpanīya Upaniṣads. The texts of these Upaniṣads, which cite the Māṇḍūkya, consistently run Māṇḍ. 6 and 7 together (i.e. without a major break, or with no break at all), whereas they insert breaks where the terms "this is the first state" (*prathama pāda*), "this is the second state" (*dvitīya pāda*), "this is the third state" (*tṛtīya pāda*) and "this is the fourth state" (*caturtha pāda*) occur.

Since Māṇḍ. 6 and 7 both describe the same state of the Self (i.e. the fourth), there is no reason why the "positive" attributes of Māṇḍ. 6 should be mentioned separately from the "negative" attributes of Māṇḍ. 7. This, I think, is a purely inessential feature of the text. According to the IC interpretation, the meaning of the text would remain unchanged (and in some respects would even be clearer) if we mixed the terms together indiscriminately, as follows:

> *This is the lord of all*, not inwardly cognitive, not outwardly cognitive, not a cognition mass, not cognitive, not non-cognitive; *this is the knower of all*, unseen, beyond speech; *this is the inner control-*

> *ler*, ungraspable, without any distinctive marks; *this is the source of all*, unthinkable, undesignatable; *this is the origin and the end of all beings*, the essence of the conviction of the one Self, the cessation of the phenomenal world, quiescent, auspicious, nondual: this they think, is the fourth. He is the Self. He is to be known.

As I noted in chapter 6, this is exactly how the "negative" attributes of the absolute *ātman* and the "positive" attributes of *īśvara* are treated in the Maitrī Upaniṣad.

If we look at the Māṇḍūkya in this way, it is clear that there is no reason to suppose that the sleeping state is any closer to the highest state of the Self (*turīya*) than the waking state is. According to the classical Upaniṣads, the sleeping state may be said to be closer to the *turīya* in one sense, because when the individual is in this state he is more detached from the body than he is in the normal, waking state of consciousness. However, in another sense the individual in the sleeping state is even *further* removed from the *turīya* than he is in the waking state, because the sleeping state (unlike the waking state) is a state of ignorance.[1,2]

The Doctrine of *Māyā* and the Analysis of Causality

According to the Upaniṣads, the world is the self-transformation (*ātmakṛteḥ pariṇāma*) of the supreme Self, or God (*paramātman*); and since *paramātman* is essentially pure consciousness and intelligence, it is not entirely illegitimate to say that on this view the world is a dream or self-transformation of the Absolute. However, putting the matter this way certainly does not mean that the world is somehow unreal, for while it might make sense to say that something that has no existence outside *my* mind is purely illusory, it would make no sense to say that something that had no existence outside of *God's* mind was purely illusory. If we are to use the analogy of dreaming, it is essential to distinguish between ordinary dreaming and *paramātman's* "dreaming." According to the Upaniṣads, the self in the dreaming state is *in* the body, whereas the fourth state of the Self (the *paramātman*) is not in the body at all.

These two different interpretations of *māyā* (i.e. *māyā* as illusion and *māyā* as self-transformation) are intimately connected with two different theories of causation in Indian philosophy. According to the Māyāvādins of the Śaṃkara school, causality is a purely phenomenal notion that will not bear examination. On this point they were wholly indebted to the Mahāyāna Buddhists like Nāgārjuna. The best example of this, in fact, is the Alāta-śānti-prakaraṇa, which uses the dialectical arguments of Nāgārjuna in order to establish the doctrine of *ajāti*, according to which nothing arises and nothing perishes.

It is surprising, however, to find such arguments in a Vedāntic work. It is true that the Upaniṣads occasionally refer to a principle of *māyā*, but in the Upaniṣads "*māyā*" means a unique power (*śakti*) by which *brahman* transforms itself into the apparent multiplicity of the world, rather than a principle of ignorance or illusion. A good example of a passage which illustrates what I mean is BU 2.5.19, which quotes Ṛgveda 6.47.18:

> He became corresponding in form to every form.
> This is to be looked upon as a form of him.
> Indra by his magic powers (*māyā*) goes about in many forms.
> Yoked are his hundred and ten steeds.

Then the Bṛhad-āraṇyaka says:

> He (the *ātman*) is verily the steeds. He, verily, is tens and thousands, many and endless. This *brahman* is without an earlier and without a later, without an inside and without an outside. This self is *brahman* (*ayam ātmā brahma*), the all-perceiving.[3]

Here "*māyā*" does not mean "illusion": it is instead a power (*śakti*) of transformation.

In the Vedic Saṃhitās and Brāhmaṇas, Indra and the other gods are said to transform themselves into various forms in order to go about incognito. Thus in Ṛgveda 8.2.40 and Śatapatha Brāhmaṇa 3.3.4.18, Indra is said to have appeared before Medhātithi in the form of a ram, and in Ṣaḍviṃśa Brāhmaṇa 1.1 Indra is said to have abducted Medhātithi in the form of a ram. There is an exact correspondence between such myths and the myths of Greek mythology, where, for example, Zeus is said to have transformed himself into a bull in order to abduct Europa. There is no more reason in the case of the Vedic myth to suppose that Medhātithi's abduction is a mere appearance than there is to suppose that in the Greek myth it only *seems* to Europa that she is carried across the Mediterranean from Phoenicia to Crete on the back of a white bull. Even a common magician or hypnotist can create false appearances, but — unlike *brahman* or the Vedic deities — a common magician does not have a genuine power of self-transformation. The concept of "self-transformation" is genuinely Vedic, whereas the acausality of the Māyāvāda must be traced back to the no-self (*anātman*) doctrine of early Buddhism.

We ordinarily think, on the basis of our everyday, immediate experience, that there is an "I" or self which underlies all our experiences and which remains unchanged through time. This the Buddhists denied. Furthermore, according to the Mahāyāna there are no substances. What other philosophies have regarded as substances are regarded by the Buddhists as collections (*skandhas*) of *dharmas*.[4] The Hīnayānists accepted the reality of these *dharmas*, but in the Mahāyāna even this concept of a *dharma* was rejected, and everything was held to be void (*sarva-dharma-śūnyatā*).

This Mahāyānist doctrine was probably an inevitable development within Buddhism, for if the Buddhist arguments against the notion of an enduring self are valid, then they should be valid against any substance or postulated entity whatsoever. In any case, the Mahāyāna is as alien to the world of thought of the Upaniṣads as the *dharma*-theory of the Hīnayāna. In Buddhism the intention was to use the concept of *dharmas* to replace the notion of underlying substances and entities. The Vedānta, on the other hand, is entirely based on the notions of Self (*ātman*) and substance (*dravya*). The Vedānta clearly appeals to the notion of substance in its theory of causality, called the *satkārya-vada*, which holds that the effect is simply the transformation or manifestation of the underlying substance (i.e. the cause), and has no existence apart from it.

The Buddhist paradigm for causation, on the other hand, is that of one thing "originating from" or "giving birth to" another thing.[5] The *satkārya-vāda* of the Vedānta is quite different. In fact, the Buddhist point of view cannot even be *stated* within the terms of the *satkārya-vāda*. For example, when milk is transformed into curds, we do not say that the milk has "given birth" to the curds, and when water turns into ice when the temperature falls below freezing, we do not say that the water (or the fall in temperature) has "given birth" to ice. In the water/ice case, for example, it is just that the mass of H_2O molecules that in one physical state had the properties of "water" has the properties of "ice" in another physical state.[6]

Although the Vedānta uses such examples to illustrate the doctrine that the world is nothing but *brahman*, it is important to note that such analogies are imperfect ones in two respects. First of all, in the ordinary examples of water/ice, milk/curds etc., the cause is itself an effect of a previous cause. But this cannot be the case with *brahman*, for *brahman*, according to the Upaniṣads, is the absolute, first, unmoved cause of all things: its transformations, as the Brahma-sūtra succinctly says, are self-caused (*ātmakṛteḥ pariṇāma*). Secondly, the analogies are imperfect because *brahman*, unlike milk, seeds, fire, mud etc., is essentially a conscious and intelligent entity. Indeed, it is described in the Upaniṣads as *absolute* consciousness and intelligence.

The Upaniṣadic doctrine, in short, is an idealist doctrine, according to which the world is mere thought, consciousness or intelligence (*cetā-mātra*). Maitrī 6.17 captures the essence of this doctrine well:

> Verily, in the beginning this world was *brahman*, the limitless one: limitless to the east, limitless to the south, limitless to the west, limitless to the north, and above and below, limitless in every direction. Truly, for him east and the other directions exist not, nor across, nor below, nor above.
>
> Incomprehensible is that supreme self (*paramātman*), unlimited, unborn (*aja*), not to be reasoned about, unthinkable (*acintya*) — he whose self is space (*ākāśātman*). In the dissolution of the world he alone remains awake. From that space he, assuredly, awakens the world (*bodhayati*), which is a mass of thought (*cetā-mātra*). It is thought by him (*dhyāyate*), and in him it disappears.[7]

The Maitrī, like the Vedāntic passages which compare *brahman's* creation of the world to milk and curds, fire and sparks, mud and pots etc., is committed to the *satkārya-vada*, according to which the world is nothing but a transformation or modification (*vikāra*, *pariṇāma*) of *brahman*. However, the Maitrī specifies that the world is a modification of God's *mind* or *consciousness*. It is also implied that the modifications are self-caused (*ātmakṛteḥ pariṇāma*), for the Maitrī says that the world is thought by *brahman*, and that the world has no existence outside his mind. Finally, the important point is made that *brahman* also transcends the world, for the passage says that when the world is dissolved (*kṛtsna-kṣaye*), the supreme Self continues to exist and remain awake.

Maitrī 6.17 might, on a superficial reading, look similar to the Buddhist idealist and Śūnyavāda doctrines, but in fact the doctrine it teaches is incompatible with them. For one thing, the Buddhists did not accept the Vedāntic doctrine of *brahman* or *īśvara*, so it could not be said that on their view the world is in *God's* mind. Furthermore, the metaphysics of Maitrī 6.17 is an absolutist and realist idealism. This doctrine is based on the *satkārya-vāda*, according to which the effect is simply a modification or special state of an underlying cause. The Buddhists, however, rejected the *satkārya-vāda*. Consequently, when the Buddhist idealists said that the world was nothing but mind, they did *not* mean that it was nothing but a modification (*vikāra*) of an underlying and unchanging mental or spiritual substance.

The same differences which I described earlier between the *satkārya-vāda* and the *dharma* theory of the Buddhists apply when it is mind or conscious that is in question, rather than physical things like milk and curds, water and ice, mud and pots etc. On the Buddhist view, it is incorrect to say that curds are nothing but milk or that pots are nothing but mud. Similarly, the Vedāntic doctrine that the world is nothing but *brahman* (*sarvaṃ khalvidaṃ brahma*), and that the world is a manifestation of God's mind, cannot even be *stated* within the parameters of Buddhist philosophy.

The *dharma* theory of the Buddhists leads to one of two possibilities. Either things do arise and perish (there being no unchanging substances underlying them) or things do not arise and perish at all. The former view was held by the Hīnayāna Abhidharma and the latter view was held by the Mahāyānists. Neither position is compatible with the Vedānta, which holds that the world is the modification or manifestation of *brahman*. Even the Mahāyāna view is incompatible with this doctrine, for according to the Mahāyāna, the world is not the manifestation of an Absolute at all: it is simply *unreal*.

One can see very clearly from the Alāta-śānti-prakaraṇa how the Mahāyānist analysis of causation leads to the doctrine that the world is unreal, rather than to the Vedāntic doctrine that the world is a manifestation or modification of a supreme consciousness (*paramātman*, *brahman*). In interpreting what the ALP says about mind, the nature of the world and causality, it is essential to keep in mind that it adopts the *dharma* theory of the Buddhists, except that (unlike the Buddhists) it does not treat mind or consciousness itself as a *dharma* or as a collection of *dharmas*. According to the ALP, the world is entirely illusory and non-existent. The mind, on the other hand, is real but it is not a thing (*dharma*), and it is eternal and unchanging. The consequences of this doctrine emerge clearly in ALP 45-61, which I summarize as follows:

***

45. What we call *things* are — like the things we regard as purely mental creations — simply the appearances (*ābhāsa*) of the mind (*vijñāna*), which is in essence unborn and unmoving.

46. Therefore all *dharmas* are unborn (*ajāta*), i.e. unreal.

47. It is only when consciousness is in motion that it has the appearance of being the perceiver and the perceived, just as it is only when a burning stick (*alāta*) is in motion that it creates the illusion of a straight or crooked line of fire in the sky etc.

49. The appearances do not arise from the moving fire-brand nor is it the case that, being different from the fire-brand, they enter it when it is not moving.

51. Similarly, when the mind vibrates the appearances do not in reality arise from it or enter into it.

50,52. The appearances which seem to arise from the fire-brand and the mind when they are in motion have no substance (*dravya*). There is in fact no relationship of cause and effect in either case; hence appearances are unthinkable.

53. Something can be the cause of another thing only when it is a substance (*dravya*) and different from the effect; and it is impossible to say that there is a cause-effect relationship between *dharmas* according to either criterion.

54. The mind (*citta*) is not born from the *dharmas*, and the *dharmas* are not born from the mind.[8]

55, 56. Cause and effect (*hetu-phala*) and the whole world of suffering (*saṃsāra*) only arise as long as the mind is preoccupied with them; when this preoccupation comes to an end, both are no longer possible.

58. Those which are said to be born are in reality not born. Their birth is like an illusion, and even that illusion does not exist (*sā ca māyā na vidyate*).

61. Dreams and waking experiences are both unreal, and the appearance of duality (*dvayābhāsa*) in both states is due simply to the illusory activity of the mind.

***

The argument that there is no difference between dreaming and waking then continues from ALP 61 through ALP 71.

It is argued in the foregoing verses that all perceptions in the waking and dreaming states are unreal because (it is said) no cause-effect relation can be established between mind and the *dharmas* (which are only the appearances of the mind). This argument is based on an analysis of causality which cannot even be coherently stated within the parameters of the Upaniṣadic doctrines, which adhere to the *satkārya-vada*. On the Vedāntic view, causality is not a relation between *dharmas* in the first place. It is a transformation (*pariṇāma*, *vikāra*) of the underlying cause.

The ALP contends that no cause-effect relation can be established between the *dharmas*, or between mind and the *dharmas*, and it concludes from this that all *dharmas* are unreal. This is not what a Vedāntist would be likely to conclude from this argument. A Vedāntist who adhered strictly to the Upaniṣads would treat the conclusion that the world is unreal as absurd, and conclude that the argument shows that the no-substance (*adravya*, *niḥsvabhāva*) view of the Buddhists is untenable.

On the Upaniṣadic view, the question of the unreality of the world cannot arise. According to the Upaniṣadic way of looking at things, the world might be said to be real precisely *because* it is a manifestation or modification of the one, eternal being — which is called *sat*, *brahman*, *paramātman*, etc.

Philosophical Objections to the Māyāvāda

There are some fundamental (and rather obvious) philosophical objections to the *māyā* doctrine. The difficulties emerge as soon as we ask: Whose mind is the illusory world supposed to be in? Here there are two possible answers, and both of them raise problems for the Māyāvāda.

On the one hand, there are obvious objections to saying that the world is in *my* mind or *your* mind (i.e. in the individual's mind). If I go to sleep, my consciousness of the world may vanish, but surely the world itself does not vanish.[9] On the other hand, the Māyāvādin cannot say that the world is in *God's* mind, for if it were in God's mind, it could not be said that the world is unreal, for there is nothing outside of *īśvara* by which he could be deluded. It is a logical point that *parameśvara* could not be subject to perceptual illusions like the rope-snake (*rajju-sarpa*). An individual could find out that he was mistaken in thinking that there was a snake lying in the path ahead of him by investigating the matter further and finding that the object was in fact a rope. But in the case of *parameśvara*, this possibility does not arise, for the rope and everything else does not have any existence apart from God's mind. Hence, while it might be said that *parameśvara* imagines snakes, ropes etc., he could not really be *mistaken* about them.

Other problems arise for the Māyāvāda because it holds that *brahman* (which, it is said, is the only thing that exists) is essentially inactive. This makes it impossible to explain the fact, which we certainly know from our own experience, that *something* is going on in the world.

According to the Māyāvāda, the *īśvara* that is regarded by other schools of the Vedānta as the creator (*kartṛ*, *kāraṇa*) of the world is as illusory as the world-appearance itself. However, we cannot have an Absolute *without īśvara*, for *īśvara* is essentially the active power (*śakti*) which connects the Absolute with the phenomenal world which we experience through our physical senses — and the reality of this phenomenal world cannot sensibly be denied.

This is the *philosophical* reason why Māṇḍ. 6 cannot be detached from Māṇḍ. 7. It is not, as Belvalkar and Ranade would have it, that "God is sundered from the Absolute as with a hatchet." Instead, *brahman* and *īśvara* are regarded in the Māṇḍūkya as complementary descriptions of the same thing: *brahman* is *īśvara*, and the creator is itself the Absolute. Māṇḍ. 6 speaks of the lord of all, the source of all, the beginning and end of all creatures etc., and Māṇḍ. 7 simply completes this description by describing this *sarveśvara* as unseen, ungraspable, without any distinctive marks, unthinkable, undesignatable etc. Here Māṇḍ. 7 is simply stating what is logically implied by the concept which is presented in Māṇḍ. 6. For how *could* the Lord of all etc. be seen or grasped? To say that God could be seen would be self-contradictory. Such an assertion would imply that there was something which was not God (e.g. you or me) by which he could be seen. But in that case God would not be Absolute, not omnipresent, not nondual etc., which would contradict the conception of God which is implicit in the Upaniṣadic world-view.

But doesn't the doctrine that the world is nothing but *brahman* entail that *brahman* becomes tainted by involvement in the world's sufferings? This is one of Śaṃkara's main concerns, and it is one of the main reasons why he resorts to the doctrine of *māyā* or illusion. According to the strict Māyāvādin, *brahman* cannot be implicated in any way with the phenomenal world; hence, Śaṃkara argues, the phenomenal world must be unreal.

It seems to me that this insistence on the absolute purity of *brahman* has resulted in a doctrine that subtly but pervasively distorts the world of thought of the classical Upaniṣads. According to the Māyāvādin, *brahman* cannot be said to have any *saṃsāric* experiences whatever. According to the Upaniṣads, however, *brahman* really has these experiences, although it also transcends them. There are, after all, many Upaniṣadic passages which assert that *brahman* is involved in the experiences that it creates for itself. Maitrī 7.11.8, for example, says explicitly that the great Self (*mahātman*) has a "dual nature (*dvaitībhava*) for the sake of experiencing the true and the false."[10]

It is true that Māṇḍ. 7 describes a transcendent state of the Self, but the assertion that the *ātman* of the fourth state is transcendent does not mean that the Self does not have any experiences. A useful analogy here is that of dreaming. Dreams are very real subjective experiences, but the dreamer also transcends them, for the dream objects are in *his* own mind, so that the dreamer himself is — paradoxically — the cause of his own fright and the other experiences which he has in the dreaming state. That is why on awaking we say things like: "So that was only a dream," "I was only dreaming that I was being chased by a tiger," etc. There is no question here of denying the reality of dreams *as experiences*. Similarly, there is no question, on the Upaniṣadic view, of denying the reality of worldly experience.

The Māṇḍūkya asserts that the essential nature of the Self (*ekātma-pratyaya-sāra*) transcends the embodied states of waking, dreaming and sleeping, and that these latter states (in all bodies and for all beings) are simply the manifestation of this nondual and absolute reality. On this view, the experiences of all beings in all bodies are *brahman's* experiences, but they do not exhaust its nature. In fact, they comprise only a small part of it.[11]

Whether the Upaniṣadic view is true (or even philosophically tenable) I do not know, but in any case I am convinced that it is a different view — and philosophically a more defensible view — than the one which has been traditionally ascribed to the Māṇḍūkya, both by the Śaṃkara school and by modern scholarship. According to the prevailing interpretation, Māṇḍ. 6 (which describes the Lord of all) belongs with Māṇḍ. 5 (which describes the state of deep sleep) rather than with Māṇḍ. 7 (which describes the nondual, formless and ungraspable nature of the supreme Self). I am convinced that this interpretation of the Māṇḍūkya is mistaken. If I am right about this, it means that the Māyāvāda cannot be supported textually by citing a single classical Upaniṣad — including the Māṇḍūkya.

APPENDIXES

MĀṆḌŪKYOPANIṢAD

Om-ity-etad-akṣaram-idaṃ sarvaṃ tasyopavyākhyānaṃ bhūtaṃ bhavad-bhaviṣyad-iti sarvam-oṃkāra eva / yac-cānyat-trikālātītaṃ tad-apy-oṃkāra eva // 1 // sarvaṃ hy-etad-brahmāyam-ātmā brahma so 'yam-ātmā catuṣpāt // 2 // jāgarita-sthāno bahiṣ-prajñaḥ saptāṅga ekonaviṃśati-mukhaḥ sthūla-bhug-vaiśvānaraḥ prathamaḥ pādaḥ // 3 // svapna-sthāno 'ntaḥ-prajñaḥ saptāṅga ekonaviṃśati-mukhaḥ pravivikta-bhuk-taijaso dvitīyaḥ pādaḥ // 4 // yatra supto na kaṃcana kāmaṃ kāmayate na kaṃcana svapnaṃ paśyati tat-suṣuptam / suṣupta-sthāna ekī-bhūtaḥ prajñāna-ghana evā ''nandamayo hy-ānanda-bhuk-cetomukhaḥ prājñas-tṛtīyaḥ pādaḥ // 5 // eṣa sarveśvara eṣa sarvajña eṣo 'ntaryāmy-eṣa yoniḥ sarvasya prabhavāpyayau hi bhūtānām // 6 // nāntaḥ-prajñaṃ na bahiṣ-prajñaṃ nobhayataḥ-prajñaṃ na prajñāna-ghanaṃ na prajñaṃ nāprajñam / adṛṣṭam-avyavahāryam-agrāhyam-alakṣaṇam-acintyam-avyapadeśyam-ekātma-pratyaya-sāraṃ prapañcopaśamaṃ śāntaṃ śivam-advaitaṃ caturthaṃ manyante sa ātmā sa vijñeyaḥ // 7 // so 'yam-ātmā 'dhyakṣaram-oṃkāro 'dhimātraṃ pādā mātrā mātrāś-ca pādā akāra ukāro makāra iti // 8 // jāgarita-sthāno vaiśvānaro 'kāraḥ prathamā mātrā ''pter-ādimattvād-vā ''pnoti ha vai sarvān-kāmān-ādiś-ca bhavati ya evaṃ veda // 9 // svapna-sthānas-taijasa ukāro dvitīyā mātrotkarṣād-ubhayatvād-votkarṣati ha vai jñāna-saṃtatiṃ samānaś-ca bhavati nāsyābrahmavit-kule bhavati ya evaṃ veda // 10 // suṣupta-sthānaḥ prājño makāras-tṛtīyā mātrā miter-apīter-vā minoti ha vā idaṃ sarvam-apītiś-ca bhavati ya evaṃ veda // 11 // amātraś-caturtho 'vyavahāryaḥ prapañcopaśamaḥ śivo 'dvaita evam-oṃkāra ātmaiva saṃviśaty-ātmanā ''tmānaṃ ya evaṃ veda // 12 //

ĀGAMA-PRAKARAṆA

1. *bahiṣprajño vibhur-viśvo hy-antaḥprajñas-tu taijasaḥ /*
ghanaprajñas-tathā prājña eka eva tridhā smṛtaḥ //

2. *dakṣiṇākṣi-mukhe viśvo manasy-antas-tu taijasaḥ /*
ākāśe ca hṛdi prājñas-tridhā dehe vyavasthitaḥ //

3. *viśvo hi sthūlabhuṅ-nityaṃ taijasaḥ praviviktabhuk /*
ānandabhuk-tathā prājñas-tridhā bhogaṃ nibodhata //

4. *sthūlaṃ tarpayate viśvaṃ praviviktaṃ tu taijasam /*
ānandaś-ca tathā prājñaṃ tridhā tṛptiṃ nibodhata //

5. *triṣu dhāmasu yad-bhojyaṃ bhoktā yaś-ca prakīrtitaḥ /*
vedaitad-ubhayaṃ yas-tu sa bhuñjāno na lipyate //

6. *prabhavaḥ sarvabhāvānāṃ satām-iti viniścayaḥ /*
sarvaṃ janayati prāṇaś-cetoṃśūn-puruṣaḥ pṛthak //

7. *vibhūtiṃ prasavaṃ tv-anye manyante sṛṣṭi-cintakāḥ /*
svapna-māyā-sarūpeti sṛṣṭir-anyair-vikalpitā //

8. *icchā-mātraṃ prabhoḥ sṛṣṭir-iti sṛṣṭau viniścitāḥ /*
kālāt-prasūtiṃ bhūtānāṃ manyante kāla-cintakāḥ //

9. *bhogārthaṃ sṛṣṭir-ity-anye krīḍārtham-iti cāpare /*
devasyaiṣa svabhāvo 'yam-āpta-kāmasya kā spṛhā //

10. *nivṛtteḥ sarva-duḥkhānām-īśānaḥ prabhur-avyayaḥ /*
advaitaḥ sarva-bhāvānāṃ devas-turyo vibhuḥ smṛtaḥ //

11. *kārya-kāraṇa-baddhau tāv-iṣyete viśva-taijasau /*
prājñaḥ kāraṇa-baddhas-tu dvau tau turye na sidhyataḥ //

12. *nā "tmānaṃ na parāṃś-caiva na satyaṃ nāpi cānṛtam /*
prājñaḥ kiṃcana saṃvetti turyaṃ tat-sarvadṛk-sadā //

13. *dvaitasyāgrahaṇaṃ tulyam-ubhayoḥ prājña-turyayoḥ /*
bīja-nidrā-yutaḥ prājñaḥ sā ca turye na vidyate //

14. *svapna-nidrā-yutāv-ādyau prājñas-tv-asvapna-nidrayā /*
na nidrāṃ naiva ca svapnaṃ turye paśyanti niścitāḥ //

15. *anyathā gṛhṇataḥ svapno nidrā tattvam-ajānataḥ /*
viparyāse tayoḥ kṣīṇe turīyaṃ padam-aśnute //

16. *anādi-māyayā supto yadā jīvaḥ prabudhyate /*
ajam-anidram-asvapnam-advaitaṃ budhyate tadā //

17. *prapañco yadi vidyeta nivarteta na saṃśayaḥ /*
māyā-mātram-idaṃ dvaitam-advaitaṃ paramārthataḥ //

18. *vikalpo vinivarteta kalpito yadi kenacit /*
upadeśād-ayaṃ vādo jñāte dvaitaṃ na vidyate //

19. *viśvasyātva-vivakṣāyām-ādi-sāmānyam-utkaṭam /*
mātrā-saṃpratipattau syād-āpti-sāmānyam-eva ca //

20. *taijasasyotva-vijñāna utkarṣo dṛśyate sphuṭam /*
mātrā-saṃpratipattau syād-ubhayatvaṃ tathā-vidham //

21. *makāra-bhāve prājñasya māna-sāmānyam-utkaṭam /*
mātrā-saṃpratipattau tu laya-sāmānyam-eva ca //

22. *triṣu dhāmasu yat-tulyaṃ sāmānyaṃ vetti niścitaḥ /*
sa pūjyaḥ sarva-bhūtānāṃ vandyaś-caiva mahāmuniḥ //

23. *akāro nayate viśvam-ukāraś-cāpi taijasam /*
makāraś-ca punaḥ prājñaṃ nāmātre vidyate gatiḥ //

24. *oṃkāraṃ pādaśo vidyāt-pādā mātrā na saṃśayaḥ /*
oṃkāraṃ pādaśo jñātvā na kiṃcid-api cintayet //

25. *yuñjīta praṇave cetaḥ praṇavo brahma nirbhayam /*
praṇave nitya-yuktasya na bhayaṃ vidyate kvacit //

26. *praṇavo hy-aparaṃ brahma praṇavaś-ca paraḥ smṛtaḥ /*
apūrvo 'nantaro 'bāhyo 'naparaḥ praṇavo 'vyayaḥ //

27. *sarvasya praṇavo hy-ādir-madhyam-antas-tathaiva ca /*
evaṃ hi praṇavaṃ jñātvā vyaśnute tad-anantaram //

28. *praṇavaṃ hīśvaraṃ vidyāt-sarvasya hṛdi saṃsthitam /*
sarva-vyāpinam-oṃkāraṃ matvā dhīro na śocati //

29. *amātro 'nanta-mātraś-ca dvaitasyopaśamaḥ śivaḥ /*
oṃkāro vidito yena sa munir-netaro janaḥ //

VAITATHYA-PRAKARAṆA

1. *vaitathyaṃ sarva-bhāvānāṃ svapna āhur-manīṣiṇaḥ /*
antaḥsthānāt-tu bhāvānāṃ saṃvṛtatvena hetunā //

2. *adīrghatvāc-ca kālasya gatvā deśān-na paśyati /*
pratibuddhaś-ca vai sarvas-tasmin-deśe na vidyate //

3. *abhāvaś-ca rathādīnāṃ śrūyate nyāya-pūrvakam /*
vaitathyaṃ tena vai prāptaṃ svapna āhuḥ prakāśitam //

4. *antaḥsthānāt-tu bhedānāṃ tasmāj-jāgarite smṛtam /*
yathā tatra tathā svapne saṃvṛtatvena bhidyate //

5. *svapna-jāgarita-sthāne hy-ekam-āhur-manīṣiṇaḥ /*
bhedānāṃ hi samatvena prasiddhenaiva hetunā //

6. *ādāv-ante ca yan-nāsti vartamāne 'pi tat-tathā /*
vitathaiḥ sadṛśāḥ santo 'vitathā iva lakṣitāḥ //

7. *saprayojanatā teṣāṃ svapne vipratipadyate /*
tasmād-ādy-antavattvena mithyaiva khalu te smṛtāḥ //

8. *apūrvaṃ sthāni-dharmo hi yathā svarga-nivāsinām /*
tān-ayaṃ prekṣate gatvā yathaiveha suśikṣitaḥ //

9. *svapna-vṛttāv-api tv-antaś-cetasā kalpitaṃ tv-asat /*
bahiś-cetogṛhītaṃ sad-dṛṣṭaṃ vaitathyam-etayoḥ //

10. *jāgrad-vṛttāv-api tv-antaś-cetasā kalpitaṃ tv-asat /*
bahiś-cetogṛhītaṃ sad-yuktaṃ vaitathyam-etayoḥ //

11. *ubhayor-api vaitathyaṃ bhedānāṃ sthānayor-yadi /*
ka etān-budhyate bhedān-ko vai teṣāṃ vikalpakaḥ //

12. *kalpayaty-ātmanā "ātmānam-ātmā devaḥ svamāyayā /*
sa eva budhyate bhedān-iti vedānta-niścayaḥ //

13. *vikaroty-aparān-bhāvān-antaś-citte vyavasthitān /*
niyatāṃś-ca bahiś-citta evaṃ kalpayate prabhuḥ //

14. *citta-kālā hi ye 'ntas-tu dvaya-kālāś-ca ye bahiḥ /*
kalpitā eva te sarve viśeṣo nānya-hetukaḥ //

15. *avyaktā eva ye 'ntas-tu sphuṭā eva ca ye bahiḥ /*
kalpitā eva te sarve viśeṣas-tv-indriyāntare //

16. *jīvaṃ kalpayate pūrvaṃ tato bhāvān-pṛthag-vidhān /*
bāhyān-ādhyātmikāṃś-caiva yathā-vidyas tathā-smṛtiḥ //

17. *aniścitā yathā rajjur-andhakāre vikalpitā /*
sarpa-dhārādibhir-bhāvais-tadvad-ātmā vikalpitaḥ //

18. *niścitāyāṃ yathā rajjvāṃ vikalpo vinivartate /*
rajjur-eveti cādvaitaṃ tadvad-ātma-viniścayaḥ //

19. *prāṇādibhir-anantaiś-ca bhāvair-etair-vikalpitaḥ /*
māyaiṣā tasya devasya yayā saṃmohitaḥ svayam //

20. *prāṇā iti prāṇa-vido bhūtānīti ca tad-vidaḥ /*
guṇā iti guṇa-vidas-tattvānīti ca tad-vidaḥ //

21. *pādā iti pāda-vido viṣayā iti tad-vidaḥ /*
lokā iti loka-vido devā iti ca tad-vidaḥ //

22. *vedā iti veda-vido yajñā iti ca tad-vidaḥ /*
bhokteti ca bhoktṛ-vido bhojyam-iti ca tad-vidaḥ //

23. *sūkṣma iti sūkṣma-vidaḥ sthūla iti ca tad-vidaḥ /*
mūrta iti mūrta-vido 'mūrta iti ca tad-vidaḥ //

24. *kāla iti kāla-vido diśa iti ca tad-vidaḥ /*
vādā iti vāda-vido bhuvanānīti tad-vidaḥ //

25. *mana iti mano-vido buddhir-iti ca tad-vidaḥ /*
cittam-iti citta-vido dharmādharmau ca tad-vidaḥ //

26. *pañca-viṃśaka ity-eke ṣaḍ-viṃśa iti cāpare /*
eka-triṃśaka ity-āhur-ananta iti cāpare //

27. *lokāṃl-loka-vidaḥ prāhur-āśramā iti tad-vidaḥ /*
strī-puṃna-puṃsakaṃ laiṅgāḥ parāparam-athāpare //

28. *sṛṣṭir-iti sṛṣṭi-vido laya iti ca tad-vidaḥ /*
sthitir-iti sthiti-vidaḥ sarvaṃ ceha tu sarvadā //

29. *yaṃ bhāvaṃ darśayed-yasya taṃ bhāvaṃ sa tu paśyati /*
taṃ cāvati sa bhūtvā 'sau tad-grahaḥ samupaiti tam //

30. *etair-eṣo 'pṛthag-bhāvaiḥ pṛthag-eveti lakṣitaḥ /*
evaṃ yo veda tattvena kalpayet-so 'viśaṅkitaḥ //

31. *svapna-māye yathā dṛṣṭe gandharva-nagaraṃ yathā /*
tathā viśvam-idaṃ dṛṣṭaṃ vedānteṣu vicakṣaṇaiḥ //

32. *na nirodho na cotpattir-na baddho na ca sādhakaḥ /*
na mumukṣur-na vai mukta ity-eṣā paramārthatā //

33. *bhāvair-asadbhir-evāyam-advayena ca kalpitaḥ /*
bhāvā apy-advayenaiva tasmād-advayatā śivā //

34. *nā ''tma-bhāvena nānedaṃ na svenāpi kathaṃcana /*
na pṛthaṅ-nāpṛthak-kiṃcid-iti tattva-vido viduḥ //

35. *vītarāga-bhaya-krodhair-munibhir-veda-pāragaiḥ /*
nirvikalpo hy-ayaṃ dṛṣṭaḥ prapañcopaśamo 'dvayaḥ //

36. *tasmād-evaṃ viditvainam-advaite yojayet-smṛtim /*
advaitaṃ samanuprāpya jaḍaval-lokam-ācaret //

37. *nistutir-nirnamaskāro niḥsvadhākāra eva ca /*
calācala-niketaś-ca yatir-yādṛcchiko bhavet //

38. *tattvam-ādhyātmikaṃ dṛṣṭvā tattvaṃ dṛṣṭvā tu bāhyataḥ /*
tattvībhūtas-tad-ārāmas-tattvād-apracyuto bhavet //

ADVAITA-PRAKARAṆA

1. *upāsanāśrito dharmo jāte brahmaṇi vartate /*
prāg-utpatter-ajaṃ sarvaṃ tenāsau kṛpaṇaḥ smṛtaḥ //

2. *ato vakṣyāmy-akārpaṇyam-ajāti samatāṃ gatam /*
yathā na jāyate kiṃcij-jāyamānaṃ samantataḥ //

3. *ātmā hy-ākāśavaj-jīvair-ghaṭākāśair-ivoditaḥ /*
ghaṭādivac-ca saṃghātair-jātāv-etan-nidarśanam //

4. *ghaṭādiṣu pralīneṣu ghaṭākāśādayo yathā /*
ākāśe sampralīyante tadvaj-jīvā ihā"tmani //

5. *yathaikasmin-ghaṭākāśe rajodhūmādibhir-yute /*
na sarve saṃprayujyante tadvaj-jīvāḥ sukhādibhiḥ //

6. *rūpa-kārya-samākhyāś-ca bhidyante tatra tatra vai /*
ākāśasya na bhedo 'sti tadvaj-jīveṣu nirṇayaḥ //

7. *nā "kāśasya ghaṭākāśo vikārāvayavau yathā /*
naivā "tmanaḥ sadā jīvo vikārāvayavau tathā //

8. *yathā bhavati bālānaṃ gaganaṃ malinaṃ malaiḥ /*
tathā bhavaty-abuddhānām-ātmā 'pi malino malaiḥ //

9. *maraṇe saṃbhave caiva gaty-āgamanayor-api /*
sthithau sarva-śarīreṣu ākāśenāvilakṣaṇaḥ //

10. *saṃghātāḥ svapnavat-sarve ātma-māyā-visarjitāḥ /*
ādhikye sarva-sāmye vā nopapattir-hi vidyate //

11. *rasādayo hi ye kośā vyākhyātās-taittirīyake /*
teṣām-ātmā paro jīvaḥ khaṃ yathā saṃprakāśitaḥ //

12. *dvayor-dvayor-madhu-jñāne paraṃ brahma prakāśitam /*
pṛthivyām-udare caiva yathā "kāśaḥ prakāśitaḥ //

13. *jīvātmanor-ananyatvam-abhedena praśasyate /*
nānātvaṃ nindyate yac-ca tad-evaṃ hi samañjasam //

14. *jīvātmanoḥ pṛthaktvaṃ yat-prāg utpatteḥ prakīrtitam /*
bhaviṣyad-vṛttyā gauṇaṃ tan-mukhyatvaṃ na hi yujyate //

15. *mṛl-loha-visphuliṅgādyaiḥ sṛṣṭir-yā coditā 'nyathā /*
upāyaḥ so 'vatārāya nāsti bhedaḥ kathaṃcana //

16. *āśramās-trividhā hīna-madhyamotkṛṣṭa-dṛṣṭayaḥ /*
upāsanopadiṣṭeyaṃ tad-artham-anukampayā //

17. *svasiddhānta-vyavasthāsu dvaitino niścitā dṛḍham /*
parasparaṃ virudhyante tair-ayaṃ na virudhyate //

18. *advaitaṃ paramārtho hi dvaitaṃ tad-bheda ucyate /*
teṣām-ubhayathā dvaitaṃ tenāyaṃ na virudhyate //

19. *māyayā bhidyate hy-etan-nānyathā 'jaṃ kathaṃcana /*
tattvato bhidyamāne hi martyatām-amṛtaṃ vrajet //

20. *ajātasyaiva bhāvasya jātim-icchanti vādinaḥ /*
ajāto hy-amṛto bhāvo martyatāṃ katham-eṣyati //

21. *na bhavaty-amṛtaṃ martyaṃ na martyam-amṛtaṃ tathā /*
prakṛter-anyathābhāvo na kathaṃcid-bhaviṣyati //

22. *svabhāvenāmṛto yasya bhāvo gacchati martyatām /*
kṛta-kenāmṛtas-tasya kathaṃ sthāsyati niścalaḥ //

23. *bhūtato 'bhūtato vā 'pi sṛjyamāne samā śrutiḥ /*
niścitaṃ yukti-yuktaṃ ca yat-tad-bhavati netarat //

24. *neha nāneti cā "mnāyād-indro māyābhir-ity-api /*
ajāyamāno bahudhā māyayā jāyate tu saḥ //

25. *saṃbhūter-apavādāc-ca saṃbhavaḥ pratiṣidhyate /*
ko nv-enaṃ janayed-iti kāraṇaṃ pratiṣidhyate //

26. *sa eṣa neti netīti vyākhyātaṃ nihnute yataḥ /*
sarvam-agrāhya-bhāvena hetunā 'jaṃ prakāśate //

27. *sato hi māyayā janma yujyate na tu tattvataḥ /*
tattvato jāyate yasya jātaṃ tasya hi jāyate //

28. *asato māyayā janma tattvato naiva yujyate /*
vandhyā-putro na tattvena māyayā vā 'pi jāyate //

29. *yathā svapne dvayābhāsaṃ spandate māyayā manaḥ /*
tathā jāgrad-dvayābhāsaṃ spandate māyayā manaḥ //

30. *advayaṃ ca dvayābhāsaṃ manaḥ svapne na saṃśayaḥ /*
advayaṃ ca dvayābhāsaṃ tathā jāgran-na saṃśayaḥ //

31. *manodṛśyam-idaṃ dvaitaṃ yat-kiṃcit-sacarācaram /*
manaso hy-amanībhāve dvaitaṃ naivopalabhyate //

32. *ātma-satyānubodhena na saṃkalpayate yadā /*
amanastāṃ tadā yāti grāhyābhāve tad-agrahāt //

33. *akalpakam-ajaṃ jñānaṃ jñeyābhinnaṃ pracakṣate /*
brahma-jñeyam-ajaṃ nityam-ajenājaṃ vibudhyate //

34. *nigṛhītasya manaso nirvikalpasya dhīmataḥ /*
pracāraḥ sa tu vijñeyaḥ suṣupte 'nyo na tat-samaḥ //

35. *līyate hi suṣupte tan-nigṛhītaṃ na līyate /*
tad-eva nirbhayaṃ brahma jñānālokaṃ samantataḥ //

36. *ajam-anidram-asvapnam-anāmakam-arūpakam /*
sakṛd-vibhātaṃ sarvajñaṃ nopacāraḥ kathaṃcana //

37. *sarvābhilāpa-vigataḥ sarva-cintā-samutthitaḥ /*
supraśāntaḥ sakṛj-jyotiḥ samādhir-acalo 'bhayaḥ //

38. *graho na tatra notsargaś-cintā yatra na vidyate /*
ātma-saṃsthaṃ tadā jñānam-ajāti samatāṃ gatam //

39. *asparśa-yogo vai nāma durdarśaḥ sarva-yogibhiḥ /*
yogino bibhyati hy-asmād-abhaye bhaya-darśinaḥ //

40. *manaso nigrahāyattam-abhayaṃ sarvayogiṇām /*
duḥkha-kṣayaḥ prabodhaś-cāpy-akṣayā śāntir-eva ca //

41. *utseka udadher-yadvat-kuśāgreṇaika-bindunā /*
manaso nigrahas-tadvad-bhaved-aparikhedataḥ //

42. *upāyena nigṛhṇīyād-vikṣiptaṃ kāma-bhogayoḥ /*
suprasannaṃ laye caiva yathā kāmo layas-tathā //

43. *duḥkhaṃ sarvam-anusmṛtya kāma-bhogān-nivartayet /*
ajaṃ sarvam-anusmṛtya jātaṃ naiva tu paśyati //

44. *laye saṃbodhayec-cittaṃ vikṣiptaṃ śamayet-punaḥ /*
sakaṣāyaṃ vijānīyāt-samaprāptaṃ na cālayet //

45. *nā ''svādayet-sukhaṃ tatra niḥsaṅgaḥ prajñayā bhavet /*
niścalaṃ niścarac-cittam-ekī kuryāt-prayatnataḥ //

46. *yadā na līyate cittaṃ na ca vikṣipyate punaḥ /*
aniṅganam-anābhāsaṃ niṣpannaṃ brahma tat-tadā //

47. *svasthaṃ śāntaṃ sanirvāṇam-akathyaṃ sukham-uttamam /*
ajam-ajena jñeyena sarvajñaṃ paricakṣate //

48. *na kaścij-jāyate jīvaḥ sambhavo 'sya na vidyate /*
etat-tad-uttamaṃ satyaṃ yatra kiṃcin-na jāyate //

ALĀTA-ŚĀNTI-PRAKARAṆA

1. *jñānenā "kāśakalpena dharmān-yo gaganopamān /*
jñeyābhinnena saṃbuddhas-taṃ vande dvipadāṃ varam //

2. *asparśa-yogo vai nāma sarva-sattva-sukho hitaḥ /*
avivādo 'viruddhaś-ca deśitas-taṃ namāmy-aham //

3. *bhūtasya jātim-icchanti vādinaḥ kecid-eva hi /*
abhūtasyāpare dhīrā vivadantaḥ paras-param //

4. *bhūtaṃ na jāyate kiṃcid-abhūtaṃ naiva jāyate /*
vivadanto dvayā hy-evam-ajātiṃ khyāpayanti te //

5. *khyāpyamānām-ajātiṃ tair-anumodāmahe vayam /*
vivadāmo na taiḥ sārdham-avivādaṃ nibodhata //

6. *ajātasyaiva dharmasya jātim-icchanti vādinaḥ /*
ajāto hy-amṛto dharmo martyatāṃ katham-eṣyati //

7. *na bhavaty-amṛtaṃ martyaṃ na martyam-amṛtam tathā /*
prakṛter-anyathābhāvo na kathaṃcid-bhaviṣyati //

8. *svabhāvenāmṛto yasya dharmo gacchati martyatām /*
kṛta-kenāmṛtas-tasya kathaṃ sthāsyati niścalaḥ //

9. *sāṃsiddhikī svābhāvikī sahajāpy akṛtā ca yā /*
prakṛtiḥ seti vijñeyā svabhāvaṃ na jahāti yā //

10. *jarā-maraṇa-nirmuktāḥ sarve dharmāḥ svabhāvataḥ /*
jarā-maraṇam-icchantaś-cyavante tan-manīṣayā //

11. *kāranaṃ yasya vai kāryaṃ kāraṇaṃ tasya jāyate /*
jāyamānaṃ katham-ajaṃ bhinnaṃ nityaṃ kathaṃ ca tat //

12. *kāraṇād-yady-ananyatvam-ataḥ kāryam-ajaṃ yadi /*
jāyamānād-dhi vai kāryāt-kāraṇaṃ te kathaṃ dhruvam //

13. *ajād-vai jāyate yasya dṛṣṭāntas-tasya nāsti vai /*
jātāc-ca jāyamānasya na vyavasthā prasajyate //

14. *hetor-ādiḥ phalaṃ yeṣām-ādir-hetuḥ phalasya ca /*
hetoḥ phalasya cānādiḥ kathaṃ tair-upavarṇyate //

15. *hetor-ādiḥ phalaṃ yeṣām-ādir-hetuḥ phalasya ca /*
tathā janma bhavet-teṣām putrāj-janma pitur-yathā //

16. *saṃbhave hetu-phalayor-eṣitavyaḥ kramas-tvayā /*
yugapat-saṃbhave yasmād-asaṃbandho viṣāṇavat //

17. *phalād-utpadyamānaḥ san-na te hetuḥ prasidhyati /*
aprasiddhaḥ kathaṃ hetuḥ phalam-utpādayiṣyati //

18. *yadi hetoḥ phalāt-siddhiḥ phala-siddhiś-ca hetutaḥ /*
katarat-pūrva-niṣpannaṃ yasya siddhir-apekṣayā //

19. *aśaktir-aparijñānaṃ krama-kopo 'tha vā punaḥ /*
evaṃ hi sarvathā buddhair-ajātiḥ paridīpitā //

20. *bījāṅkurākhyo dṛṣṭāntaḥ sadā sādhyasamo hi saḥ /*
na hi sādhyasamo hetuḥ siddhau sādhyasya yujyate //

21. *pūrvāparāparijñānam-ajāteḥ paridīpakam /*
jāyamānād-dhi vai dharmāt-kathaṃ pūrvaṃ na gṛhyate //

22. *svato vā parato vā 'pi na kiṃcid-vastu jāyate /*
sad-asat-sadasad-vā 'pi na kiṃcid-vastu jāyate //

23. *hetur-na jāyate 'nādeḥ phalaṃ cāpi svabhāvataḥ /*
ādir-na vidyate yasya tasya hy-ādir-na vidyate //

24. *prajñapteḥ sanimittatvam-anyathā dvaya-nāśataḥ /*
saṃkleśasyopalabdheś-ca paratantrāstitā matā //

25. *prajñapteḥ sanimittatvam-iṣyate yukti-darśanāt /*
nimittasyānimittatvam-iṣyate bhūta-darśanāt //

26. *cittaṃ na saṃspṛśaty-arthaṃ nārthābhāsaṃ tathaiva ca /*
abhūto hi yataś-cārtho nārthābhāsas-tataḥ pṛthak //

27. *nimittaṃ na sadā cittaṃ saṃspṛśaty-adhvasu triṣu /*
animitto viparyāsaḥ kathaṃ tasya bhaviṣyati //

28. *tasmān-na jāyate cittaṃ citta-dṛśyaṃ na jāyate /*
tasya paśyanti ye jātiṃ khe vai paśyanti te padam //

29. *ajātaṃ jāyate yasmād-ajātiḥ prakṛtis-tataḥ /*
prakṛter-anyathābhāvo na kathaṃcid-bhaviṣyati //

30. *anāder-antavattvaṃ ca saṃsārasya na setsyati /*
anantatā cā "dimato mokṣasya na bhaviṣyati //

31. *ādāv-ante ca yan-nāsti vartamāne 'pi tat-tathā /*
vitathaiḥ sadṛśāḥ santo 'vitathā iva lakṣitāḥ //

32. *saprayojanatā teṣāṃ svapne vipratipadyate /*
tasmād-ādy-antavattvena mithyaiva khalu te smṛtāḥ //

33. *sarve dharmā mṛṣā svapne kāyasyāntar nidarśanāt /*
saṃvṛte 'smin pradeśe vai bhūtānāṃ darśanaṃ kutaḥ//

34. *na yuktaṃ darśanaṃ gatvā kālasyāniyamād-gatau /*
pratibuddhaś-ca vai sarvas-tasmin-deśe na vidyate //

35. *mitrādyaiḥ saha saṃmantrya saṃbuddho na prapadyate /*
gṛhītaṃ cāpi yat-kiṃcit-pratibuddho na paśyati //

36. *svapne cāvastukaḥ kāyaḥ pṛthag-anyasya darśanāt /*
yathā kāyas-tathā sarvaṃ citta-dṛśyam-avastukam //

37. *grahaṇāj-jāgaritavat-tad-dhetuḥ svapna iṣyate /*
tad-dhetutvāt-tu tasyaiva saj-jāgaritam-iṣyate //

38. *utpādasyāprasiddhatvād-ajaṃ sarvam-udāhṛtam /*
na ca bhūtād-abhūtasya saṃbhavo 'sti kathaṃcana //

39. *asaj-jāgarite dṛṣṭvā svapne paśyati tan-mayaḥ /*
asat-svapne 'pi dṛṣṭvā ca pratibuddho na paśyati //

40. *nāsty-asad-dhetukam-asat-sad-asad-dhetukaṃ tathā /*
sac-ca sad-dhetukaṃ nāsti sad-dhetukam-asat-kutaḥ //

41. *viparyāsād-yathā jāgrad-acintyān-bhūtavat-spṛśet /*
tathā svapne viparyāsād-dharmāṃs-tatraiva paśyati //

42. *upalambhāt-samācārād-asti-vastutva-vādinām /*
jātis-tu deśitā buddhair-ajātes-trasatāṃ sadā //

43. *ajātes-trasatāṃ teṣāṃ-upalambhād-viyanti ye /*
jāti-doṣā na setsyanti doṣo 'py-alpo bhaviṣyati //

44. *upalambhāt-samācārān-māyā-hastī yathocyate /*
upalambhāt-samācārād-asti vastu tathocyate //

45. *jāty-ābhāsaṃ calābhāsaṃ vastv-ābhāsaṃ tathaiva ca /*
ajācalam-avastutvaṃ vijñānaṃ śāntam-advayam //

46. *evaṃ na jāyate cittam-evaṃ dharmā ajāḥ smṛtāḥ /*
evam-eva vijānanto na patanti viparyaye //

47. *ṛju-vakrādikābhāsam-alāta-spanditaṃ yathā /*
grahaṇa-grāhakābhāsaṃ vijñāna-spanditaṃ tathā //

48. *aspandamānam-alātam-anābhāsam-ajaṃ yathā /*
aspandamānaṃ vijñānam-anābhāsam-ajaṃ tathā //

49. *alāte spandamāne vai nā ''bhāsā anyatobhuvaḥ /*
na tato 'nyatra nispandān-nālātaṃ praviśanti te //

50. *na nirgatā alātāt-te dravyatvābhāva-yogataḥ /*
vijñāne 'pi tathaiva syur-ābhāsasyāviśeṣataḥ //

51. *vijñāne spandamāne vai nā ''bhāsā anyatobhuvaḥ /*
na tato 'nyatra nispandān-na vijñānaṃ visanti te //

52. *na nirgatās-te vijñānād-dravyatvābhāva-yogataḥ /*
kārya-kāraṇatābhāvād-yato 'cintyāḥ sadaiva te //

53. *dravyaṃ dravyasya hetuḥ syād-anyad-anyasya caiva hi /*
dravyatvam-anyabhāvo vā dharmāṇām nopapadyate //

54. *evaṃ na citta-jā dharmāś-cittaṃ vā 'pi na dharma-jam /*
evaṃ hetu-phalājātiṃ praviśanti manīṣiṇaḥ //

55. *yāvad-dhetu-phalāveśas-tāvad-dhetu-phalodbhavaḥ /*
kṣīne hetu-phalāveśe nāsti hetu-phalodbhavaḥ //

56. *yāvad-dhetu-phalāveśaḥ saṃsāras-tāvad-āyataḥ /*
kśīṇe hetu-phalāveśe saṃsāraṃ na prapadyate //

57. *saṃvṛtyā jāyate sarvaṃ śāśvataṃ nāsti tena vai /*
sad-bhāvena hy-ajaṃ sarvam-ucchedas-tena nāsti vai //

58. *dharmā ya iti jāyante jāyante te na tattvataḥ /*
janma māyopamaṃ teṣāṃ sā ca māyā na vidyate //

59. *yathā māyāmayād-bījāj-jāyate tan-mayo 'ṅkuraḥ /*
nāsau nityo na cocchedī tadvad-dharmeṣu yojanā //

60. *nājeṣu sarva-dharmeṣu śāśvatāśāśvatābhidhā /*
yatra varṇā na vartante vivekas-tatra nocyate //

61. *yathā svapne dvayābhāsaṃ cittaṃ calati māyayā /*
tathā jāgrad-dvayābhāsaṃ cittaṃ calati māyayā //

62. *advayaṃ ca dvayābhāsaṃ cittaṃ svapne na saṃśayaḥ /*
advayaṃ ca dvayābhāsaṃ tathā jāgran-na saṃśayaḥ //

63. *svapna-dṛk-pracaran-svapne dikṣu vai daśasu sthitān /*
aṇḍajān-svedajān-vā 'pi jīvān-paśyati yān-sadā //

64. *svapna-dṛk-citta-dṛśyās-te na vidyante tataḥ pṛthak /*
tathā tad-dṛśyam-evedaṃ svapna-dṛk-cittam-iṣyate //

65. *carañ-jāgarite jāgrad-dikṣu vai daśasu sthitān /*
aṇḍajān-svedajān-vā 'pi jīvān-paśyati yān-sadā //

66. *jāgrac-cittekṣaṇīyās-te na vidyante tataḥ pṛthak /*
tathā tad-dṛśyam-evedaṃ jāgrataś-cittam-iṣyate //

67. *ubhe hy-anyonya-dṛśye te kiṃ tad-astīti nocyate /*
lakṣaṇāśūnyam-ubhayaṃ tan-matenaiva gṛhyate //

68. *yathā svapnamayo jīvo jāyate mriyate 'pi ca /*
tathā jīvā amī sarve bhavanti na bhavanti ca //

69. *yathā māyāmayo jīvo jāyate mriyate 'pi ca /*
tathā jīvā amī sarve bhavanti na bhavanti ca //

70. *yathā nirmitako jīvo jāyate mriyate 'pi ca /*
tathā jīvā amī sarve bhavanti na bhavanti ca //

71. *na kaścij-jāyate jīvaḥ saṃbhavo 'sya na vidyate /*
etat-tad-uttamaṃ satyaṃ yatra kiṃcin-na jāyate //

72. *citta-spanditam-evedaṃ grāhya-grāhakavad-dvayam /*
cittaṃ nirviṣayaṃ nityam-asaṅgaṃ tena kīrtitam //

73. *yo 'sti kalpita-saṃvṛtyā paramārthena nāsty-asau /*
paratantrābhisaṃvṛtyā syān-nāsti paramārthataḥ //

74. *ajaḥ kalpita-saṃvṛtyā paramārthena nāpy-ajaḥ /*
paratantrābhiniṣpattyā saṃvṛtyā jāyate tu saḥ //

75. *abhūtābhiniveśo 'sti dvayaṃ tatra na vidyate /*
dvayābhāvaṃ sa buddhvaiva nirnimitto na jāyate //

76. *yadā na labhate hetūn-uttamādhama-madhyamān /*
tadā na jāyate cittaṃ hetv-abhāve phalaṃ kutaḥ //

77. *animittasya cittasya yā 'nutpattiḥ samā 'dvayā /*
ajātasyaiva sarvasya citta-dṛśyaṃ hi tad-yataḥ //

78. *buddhvā 'nimittatāṃ satyāṃ hetuṃ pṛthag-anāpnuvan /*
vītaśokaṃ tathā 'kāmam-abhayaṃ padam-aśnute //

79. *abhūtābhiniveśād-dhi sadṛśe tat-pravartate /*
vastv-abhāvaṃ sa buddhvaiva niḥsaṅgaṃ vinivartate //

80. *nivṛttasyāpravṛttasya niścalā hi tadā sthitiḥ /*
viṣayaḥ sa hi buddhānāṃ tat-sāmyam-ajam-advayam //

81. *ajam-anidram-asvapnaṃ prabhātaṃ bhavati svayam /*
sakṛd-vibhāto hy-evaiṣa dharmo dhātu-svabhāvataḥ //

82. *sukham-āvriyate nityaṃ duḥkhaṃ vivriyate sadā /*
yasya kasya ca dharmasya graheṇa bhagavān-asau //

83. *asti nāsty-asti nāstīti nāsti nāstīti vā punaḥ /*
cala-sthirobhayābhāvair-āvṛṇoty-eva bāliśaḥ //

84. *koṭyaś-catasra etās-tu grahair-yāsāṃ sadā ''vṛtaḥ /*
bhagavān-ābhir-aspṛṣṭo yena dṛṣṭaḥ sa sarva-dṛk //

85. *prāpya sarvajñatāṃ kṛtsnāṃ brāhmaṇyaṃ padam-advayam /*
anāpannādi-madhyāntaṃ kim-ataḥ param-īhate //

86. *viprāṇāṃ vinayo hy-eṣa śamaḥ prākṛta ucyate /*
damaḥ prakṛti-dāntatvād-evaṃ vidvāñ-śamaṃ vrajet //

87. *savastu sopalambhaṃ ca dvayaṃ laukikam-iṣyate /*
avastu sopalambhaṃ ca śuddhaṃ laukikam-iṣyate //

88. *avastv-anupalambhaṃ ca lokottaram-iti smṛtam /*
jñānaṃ jñeyaṃ ca vijñeyaṃ sadā buddhaiḥ prakīrtitam //

89. *jñāne ca trividhe jñeye krameṇa vidite svayaṃ /*
sarvajñatā hi sarvatra bhavatīha mahādhiyaḥ //

90. *heya-jñeyāpya-pākyāni vijñeyāny-agrayāṇataḥ /*
teṣām-anyatra vijñeyād-upalambhas-triṣu smṛtaḥ //

91. *prakṛtyā ''kāśavaj-jñeyāḥ sarve dharmā anādayaḥ /*
vidyate na hi nānātvaṃ teṣāṃ kvacana kiṃcana //

92. *ādibuddhāḥ prakṛtyaiva sarve dharmāḥ suniścitāḥ /*
yasyaivaṃ bhavati kṣāntiḥ so 'mṛtatvāya kalpate //

93. *ādiśāntā hy-anutpannāḥ prakṛtyaiva sunirvṛtāḥ /*
sarve dharmāḥ samābhinnā ajaṃ sāmyaṃ viśāradam //

94. *vaiśāradyaṃ tu vai nāsti bhede vicaratāṃ sadā /*
bheda-nimnāḥ pṛthag-vādās-tasmāt-te kṛpaṇāḥ smṛtāḥ //

95. *aje sāmye tu ye kecid-bhaviṣyanti suniścitāḥ /*
te hi loke mahājñānās-tac-ca loko na gāhate //

96. *ajeṣv-ajam-asaṃkrāntaṃ dharmeṣu jñānam-iṣyate /*
yato na kramate jñānam-asaṅgaṃ tena kīrtitam //

97. *aṇumātre 'pi vaidharmye jāyamāne 'vipaścitaḥ /*
asaṅgatā sadā nāsti kim-utā ''varaṇa-cyutiḥ //

98. *alabdhāvaraṇāḥ sarve dharmāḥ prakṛti-nirmalāḥ /*
ādau buddhās-tathā muktā budhyanta iti nāyakāḥ //

99. *kramate na hi buddhasya jñānaṃ dharmeṣu tāyinaḥ /*
sarve dharmās-tathā jñānaṃ naitad-buddhena bhāṣitam //

100. *durdarśam-atigambhīram-ajaṃ sāmyaṃ viśāradam /*
buddhvā padam-anānātvaṃ namas-kurmo yathābalam //

NOTES

NOTES

CHAPTER I

1. Belvalkar, S. K. and R. D. Ranade, *History of Indian Philosophy* (1974: 325).

2. Among these are: P. Deussen (1906: 296-312); R. D. Ranade (1926: 139-141, 335-336); V. Bhattacharya (1943); T. M. P. Mahadevan (1975: 100); S. Radhakrishnan (1974: 697); C. Conio (1971: 36-45); P. Hacker (1972: 119).

3. If the use of the term "*vikalpita*" *is* intended to be ironic, the irony is very deft, for in that case the verse would mean that those who hold that the world is a dream and an illusion are themselves imagining things.

4. The implied argument of ĀP 17 seems to be: (1) If the world existed, it could be said to disappear when its true nature is discovered; but (2) it does not exist; (3) therefore it cannot be said to ever disappear. When the argument is made explicit, it can be seen that ĀP 17ab commits the logical fallacy of negating the antecedent of a counterfactual. The valid argument (*modus tollendo tollens*) would negate the disappearance of the world, from which the nonexistence of the world would be inferred.

5. This interpretation is found in R. D. Karmakar (1953: 61); and T. M. P. Mahadevan (1975: 45).

6. This theme is pursued further in chapter 13.

7. Chapter 11 contains a discussion of ĀP 3, 11, 14, 15 and 16. There I reach the conclusion that an analysis of these verses supports the same conclusion.

8. Even here, however, a distinction of some sort is usually drawn between the prose *mantras* of the Māṇḍūkya and the twenty-nine verses. According to Madhva (ca. 1199-1278 C.E.), for example, the Māṇḍūkyopaniṣad itself, strictly speaking, consisted at first of the twelve prose *mantras* alone. These were seen by Varuṇa in the shape of a frog (*maṇḍūka* means "frog"), while the twenty-nine verses were seen by a seer. Since the verses explained the prose *mantras*, according to Madhva, Varuṇa transmitted both of them together.

9. B. N. Krishnamurti Sharma (1933). This paper, which has not been available to me, is referred to by A. Venkatasubbiah (1936-37: 12).

10. V. Bhattacharya (1943: xxxvii).

11. P. Deussen (1906: 30); A. Venkatasubbiah (1933: 181-193); (1935: 783-790); (1936-37: 1: 7-18; 2: 1-12).

12. V. Bhattacharya (1943: xxxviii-xlvii); also (1925: 119-125, 295-302).

13. BV III.8.26, p. 1294:

eṣo 'ntaryāmy-eṣa yoniḥ sarvasya prabhavāpyayau
māṇḍūkeya-śruti-vaca iti spaṣṭam adhīyate

This crucial passage, and its relevance to the controversy concerning the Māṇḍūkya and the Gauḍapādīya-kārikās, was first noted by Y. Subrahmaniya Sarma (1933: 196-204).

It should also be noted that it is virtually certain that Śaṃkara himself was acquainted with the Māṇḍūkya (though he does not cite it or name it), for in his *bhāṣya* on Bṛhad-āraṇyakopaniṣad 4.2.3 he uses the term "*vaiśvānara*" for the waking state and "*taijasa*" for the dreaming state. The Māṇḍūkya is the earliest known text in which these terms appear in this sense.

14. No doubt the TI interpretation is implicit in Śaṃkara's teachings, for (as I pointed out in the Introduction) the Śaṃkara school's separation of *brahman* from *īśvara* entails that *īśvara* must be assigned to the third, or sleeping state of the Self. What I mean here more specifically is that there are no extant writings of the Śaṃkara school which show that Śaṃkara or any of his immediate disciples wrote commentaries which *explicitly* applied the views of the Māyāvāda to the Māṇḍūkya. In particular, I will argue that Śaṃkara was not the author of the Āgama-śāstra-vivaraṇa, the oldest commentary on the Māṇḍūkya that unequivocally endorses the TI interpretation of the Māṇḍūkya.

CHAPTER II

1. Much more research and analysis needs to be devoted to these texts, whose influence on later Indian religion and culture has been enormous.

2. In order to follow the textual details involved in the discussion in this section the reader may find it helpful to refer to the

Sanskrit text of the Māṇḍūkya which is given in the Appendix (p. 165).

3. Thus the text has "*.....eṣa sarveśvara eṣa sarvajña eṣo 'ntaryāmy-eṣa yoniḥ sarvasya prabhavāpyayau hi bhūtānāṃ nāntaḥprajñaṃ na bahiḥprajñaṃ nobhayataḥprajñaṃ na prajñaṃ...*" etc., i.e. without any interruption between the end of Māṇḍ. 6 and the beginning of Māṇḍ. 7.

4. A. Weber's 1865 edition of the NPTU, incidentally, does not help us to decide between the TI and IC interpretations of the Māṇḍūkya.

At the point in NPTU 4 where the text cites the Māṇḍūkya, Weber's edition says: "4-10. om ity etad aksharam u.s.w., wie Māṇḍūkyop. 1.2." His comment then has the following footnote: "resp. in Rāmatāp. 2,3,2-8 und mit mehrfachen Differenzen unten im uttaratāp. 1,2.5-9.12 wiederkehrend."

Weber's edition of the Ramottara-tāpanīyopaniṣad, in turn, cites the Māṇḍūkya in the same way it is found as an independent text, except that the first *mantra* runs continuously through "*ayam ātmā brahma*" and "*so 'yam ātmā catuṣpāt*" is given as a separate *mantra*. There is therefore nothing in Weber's editions of these two later Upaniṣads which helps us decide between the IC and TI interpretations of the Māṇḍūkya.

5. G. A. Jacob (1886) carefully compared six different manuscripts of the Nṛsiṃha-tāpanīyopaniṣad. His results give an indication of some of the possibilities for this kind of research. Jacob wrote then (ibid., 70, fn. 28): "It is impossible to collate the existing printed texts of the Upanishads with the manuscripts which of late years have come to light, without seeing how much yet remains to be done in this department of Sanskrit literature." No doubt the same remains true today.

CHAPTER III

1. Mysore Hiriyanna (1923-24); S. Kuppuswami Sastri (1936-37) and Brahma-siddhi (1984: Introduction, pp. xxiv-lvii).

2. Brahma-siddhi, S. Kuppuswami Sastri (1984: 127).

3. Chānd. 7.26.2; Chānd. 8.7.1; Chānd. 7.25.2.

4. Although this does not appear to be Maṇḍana's own favored interpretation, he does not reject it either; it is, in a sense,

an *ekadeśa-siddhānta* (i.e. a view opposed to the *pūrvapakṣa* but not the favored formulation of the *siddhānta* either).

5. Chānd. 8.7.1; Chānd. 7.25.2.

6. Bṛhad. 3.9.28(7); Bṛhad. 3.723; Bṛhad. 4.3.32; Bṛhad. 5.6.1; Bṛhad. 3.8.9.

7. Kaṭha 5.15; Bṛhad. 3.7.23.

8. Bṛhad. 4.4.22; Kauṣ. 3.8.

9. I think it is advisable to use the Āgama-śāstra-vivaraṇa as the criterion for dating the introduction of the TI interpretation of the Māṇḍūkya into the Vedānta, for the ĀŚV is the oldest extant *commentary* on the Māṇḍūkya which explicitly endorses this interpretation. Although the above passage in the Brahma-siddhi indicates that Maṇḍanamiśra may have had such an interpretation in mind, this is not absolutely certain, and in any case his remarks are very brief. (Note, for example, that he does not, at least in this passage, explicitly associate *īśvara* with the state of deep sleep — an essential feature of the TI interpretation of the Māṇḍūkya.) I think, therefore, that it is accurate to say that the TI interpretation of the Māṇḍūkya is a post-Śaṃkara phenomenon, for, as I shall argue in later chapters, I do not believe that Ādi Śaṃkara was the author of the ĀŚV.

10. Monier-Williams (1970).

11. Ed. V. N. Krishnamacharya (ASS 62, 1912-13).

12. *evaṃ rūpa-trayaṃ nirūpya caturthaṃ pādaṃ nāntaḥprajñam-ity-ādinā nirūpayiṣyan-vaiśvānarādi-rūpānām-ukta-sthāna-vyaparādy-artheṣu ślokān-vivakṣur-madhye vakṣyamāna-caturtha-rūpeṇa saha caturṇāṃ rūpānāṃ mahimānam-āha*

13. Cited by T. M. P. Mahadevan (1975: 40-41).

14. T. M. P. Mahadevan (ibid: 41).

CHAPTER IV

1. For example, according to S. Radhakrishnan (1974: 456) the passage means that "when a person here sleeps, as it is called, then, my dear, he has reached pure being." Hume (1983: 244) also translates the expression "*saṃpanno bhavati*" as "he has reached pure being."

CHAPTER V

1. Bhattacharya (1943), "The Bṛhadāraṇyaka Upaniṣad as the Main Upaniṣadic Source of the Āgamaśāstra," p. lxxxxiii - ciii; Mahadevan (1975), "The Bṛhadāraṇyaka as the Main Source of Gauḍapāda's Thought," p. 65-73.

2. Literally, "Where, on being released from here, will you go?" (*vimucyamānaḥ kva gamiṣyasīti*).

Note that although the Bṛhad-āraṇyaka describes the states of sleeping and dreaming in considerable detail, these descriptions are not the main point of the dialogue. The real purpose is to describe what happens to the Self at death, and the states of dreaming and sleeping are regarded as important only because they are similar in certain respects to the postmortem state. They can be used to *point* to the state of final release from the body, but certainly cannot be identified with that state.

3. One of the most interesting correspondences between the Chāndogya and the Bṛhad-āraṇyaka is that both of them either associate or identify the state of dreamless sleep with the state of "weakness" which is the prelude to death.

4. This *mahāvākya* (*ayam ātmā brahma*) is cited in Māṇḍ. 2.

5. Of the two passages under consideration — BU 4.4.6- 4.4.25 and Chānd. 8.12 — it was clearly the Bṛhad-āraṇyaka that inspired the unknown author or authors of the Māṇḍūkya.

CHAPTER VII

1. The first scholar to question the traditional (i.e. Śaṃkara school) interpretation of the ALP was apparently the Buddhist scholar de La Vallée Poussin (1910). V. Bhattacharya followed up on Poussin's article in a number of publications: (1925), (1938) and (1943).

The question of the historical relationship between the ALP and Buddhism is also discussed by H. Jacobi (1913); S. N. Dasgupta (1922), vol. I, pp. 424-428; B. A. N. Roy (1938); T. M. P. Mahadevan (1975); S. Mayeda (1967-68); P. Hacker (1972); and R. D. Karmarkar (1953). See also T. R. V. Murti (1955: 115).

2. The *maṅgalācaraṇa* says:

> I pay homage to the best of bipeds (*dvipadāṃ varam*), who, through knowledge (*jñāna*) like the sky (*ākāśa-kalpa*), and not different from what is known, has fully realized (*saṃbuddha*) the *dharmas* resembling the sky (*gagana-upama*).

The following are some of the terms found in the ALP which one would expect to find in Buddhist works and which are undoubtedly derived primarily from the Buddhist tradition: *dvipadāṃ varam*, *saṃbuddha*, *dharma*, *paratantra*, *prajñapti*, *viparyāsa*, *saṃvṛti*, *ye dharmāḥ*, *kalpita saṃvṛti*, *paramārtha*, *paratantra-abhisaṃvṛti*, *paratantra-abhiniṣpatti*, *anutpatti*, *viṣayo buddhānām*, *dharmo dhātu-svabhāva*, *koṭyaś catasra*, *dvayaṃ laukika* and *śuddhaṃ laukika*, *lokottara*, *agrayāṇa* (=*agrayāna*), *ādibuddha*, *ādiśānta*, *anutpanna*, *viśārada* and *vaiśāradya*, *prakṛti-nirmala* and *tāyin buddha*. Furthermore, the *prakaraṇa* consistently uses the terms *dvaya* and *advaya* for "dual" and "nondual," rather than *dvaita* and *advaita*, as is more usual in Vedāntic texts. The word *buddha* is found, either by itself or in a compound word, eight times in the ALP.

3. See V. Bhattacharya (1943); T. R. V. Murti (1955: 115); S. Mayeda (1967-68: 87). S. Dasgupta (1922, Vol. I) was somewhat more cautious, but seems to have held essentially the same view. In his *History of Indian Philosophy* he said:

> I believe that there is sufficient evidence in (Gauḍapāda's) kārikās for thinking that he was possibly himself a Buddhist, and considered that the teachings of the Upaniṣads tallied with those of the Buddha. (p. 423)

And after summarizing the Alāta-śānti-prakaraṇa, he concluded:

> It is so obvious that these doctrines are borrowed from the Mādhyamika doctrines, as found in the Nāgārjuna's kārikās and the Vijñānavāda doctrines, as found in the Laṅkāvatāra, that it is needless to attempt to prove it. Gauḍapāda assimilated all the Buddhist Śūnyavāda and Vijñānavāda teachings, and thought that these held good of the ultimate truth preached by the Upaniṣads. It is immaterial whether he was a Hindu or a Buddhist, so long as we are sure that he had the highest respect

> for the Buddha and for the teachings which he believed to be his. (p. 429)

4. T. M. P. Mahadevan (1975); R. D. Karmarkar (1953). These scholars frequently agree with the ĀŚV in interpreting some very Buddhist-sounding terms in a Vedāntic sense. I shall not go into the details here.

5. I shall not attempt to defend this characterization of the classical Upaniṣads at any length here, partly because its truth seems to me to be self-evident. Here I shall only note the significant fact that one can find unmistakable support for this interpretation in a number of places in the Brahma-sūtras, among them I.1.2, *janmādy asya yataḥ*; II.1.33, *lokavat tu līlā kaivalyam*; and I.4.23-27: *prakṛtiś ca pratijña-dṛṣṭāntānuparodhāt / abhidhyopadeśāc-ca / sākṣāc cobhayāmnāyāt / ātmakṛteḥ pariṇāmāt / yoniś ca hi gīyate*). See also V. S. Ghate (1926). Besides this, there is, of course, the testimony of the Upaniṣads themselves.

6. The doctrine of absolute voidness is presented in a particularly severe and uncompromising way in Candrakīrti's Mūlamadhyamaka-kārikā-vṛtti (Prasannapadā). However, the doctrine of absolute voidness can be traced back at least as far as the Aṣṭasāhasrikā-prajñā-pāramitā, where, e.g., the statement that all *dharmas* are signless, wishless, unaffected, unproduced, unoriginated and *non-existent* (*abhāva*) appears as a leitmotif at least six different times. See Conze (1973: 177, 190, 209, 226, 249, and 278); Rajendralal Mitra, ed., Aṣṭa-sāhasrikā-prajñā-pāramitā-sūtra (*BI* 110, 1888: 273, 298, 341, 379-380, 424, 482).

7. In Majjhima-nikāya I.326, No. 49, the following opinion of Baka the Brahmā, is declared to be "pernicious" (*pāpakam*):

> It is permanent. It is eternal. It is always existent. It is independent existence. It has the *dharma* of non-perishing. Truly it is not born, does not become old, does not die, does not disappear, and is not born again. Further, no liberation superior to it exists elsewhere.

> *idaṃ niccaṃ idaṃ dhuvaṃ idaṃ sassataṃ idaṃ kevalam idaṃ acavanadhammaṃ, idaṃ hi na jāyati na jīyati na mīyati na cavati na upapajjati, ito ca pan 'aññaṃ uttariṃ nissaraṇaṃ natthīti*

Similarly, MN I.329, No. 49 proscribes the following view:

> There is a consciousness which the eye does not see, which does not have boundaries, and which shines in all places. It cannot be perceived even as the earthiness of the earth cannot be perceived even as the wateriness of the water.
>
> *viññānaṃ anidassanaṃ anantaṃ sabbatopabhaṃ taṃ paṭhaviya paṭhavattena ananūbhutaṃ, āpassa āpattena ananubhūtaṃ.*

Cited from H. Nakamura (1983: 138).

8. The second half of ALP 7 is also found at ADP 21cd and ALP 29cd.

9. V. Bhattacharya (1943: 109, 140).

10. There is further evidence for this statement in the fact that the ALP never uses the terms "empty" (*śūnya*) or "no self-nature" (*niḥsvabhāva*) to characterize the ultimate reality. Indeed, these concepts, which are absolutely fundamental to Nāgārjuna's dialectic, could not have been incorporated into the ALP's doctrines, for the ALP wants to argue that pure mind or consciousness, which is the substratum of the unreal *dharmas*, is real and unchanging. This was certainly not Nāgārjuna's view.

In Nāgārjuna, there is an essential logical connection between the statement that there can be no change of nature (*prakṛter-anyathābhāvo* etc.) and the doctrine of the emptiness or lack of self nature of all *dharmas*. This connection may be summarized by the following short argument: If entities were real, they could not change, for no entity can change its nature (*prakṛti*) or essence (*svabhāva*); but of course things *do* change; hence all *dharmas* are unreal, void (*śūnya*) etc.

11. T. M. P. Mahadevan (1975: 221).

12. According to the second interpretation of the ALP, we must interpret "*naitad buddhena bhāṣitam*" to mean that the doctrine that all *dharmas* are knowledge was not a Buddhist doctrine. However, this interpretation must be rejected, because the doctrine that all *dharmas* are knowledge was in fact a Mahāyāna doctrine. In Śāntideva's Śikṣā-samuccaya we find the following passage:

> All *dharmas* are the reality limit, without an end, without veiling, without a basis etc. All dharmas, O Bhagavan, are knowledge (*bodhi*), and it is to be recognized that they lack self-nature. Even the five mortal sins are *bodhi*. Why is this? Because, O Bhagavan, *bodhi* is characterized by a lack of nature (*aprakṛtika*), and the same is true of the five mortal sins. That is why it is said that the five mortal sins are *bodhi*.
>
> *sarva-dharmā bhūtakoṭir-antakoṭir-anāvaraṇakoṭir-apratiṣṭhita-koṭir-ity-ādi // sarva-dharmā bhagavan bodhi-svabhāva-virahitā boddhavyāḥ // antaśa ānantaryāṇy-api bodhiḥ // tat-kasya hetoḥ? aprakṛtikā hi bhagavan bodhiḥ aprakṛtikāni ca pañcānantaryāṇi / tenocyate ānantaryāṇi bodhir-iti*

Śikṣā-samuccayaḥ, ed. by P. L. Vaidya (1961: 137).

13. It was the Buddhist scholar de La Vallée Poussin (1910: 140) who first identified this meaning of ALP 99.

Cf. MMK 25.24:

> All things which are grasped and all things which are described by words are by nature quiescent and auspicious. No *dharma* was taught anywhere, to anyone, at any time, by the Buddha.
>
> *sarvopalambhopaśamaḥ prapañcopaśamaḥ śivaḥ*
> *na kvacit kasyacit kaścid dharmo buddhena deśitaḥ*

See also Bhattacharya (1943: 212-217), who cites this as well as sixteen other passages from the Buddhist works.

14. This doctrine raises the question: Whose mind or consciousness is the world in? There is a systematic evasion or ambiguity in the last three *prakaraṇas* of the ĀŚ on this question. Note that the *kārikā-kāra* cannot say that the *prapañca* exists in an absolute or universal mind (i.e., of *īśvara*, *brahman*, or *paramātman*), because the Buddha never recognized such a thing. There is no way that the *kārikā-kāra* could have attributed such a view to the Buddha and still be taken seriously. But the view that the world is in *my* mind does not make any sense. Whose mind, then, is the world in?

15. Udāna VIII, (ix) describes *nibbāna* as follows:

> The body is broken, perceiving is dissolved, all feelings are quiescent, component parts have ceased, and consciousness has reached its end.

The cessation of *vijñāna* in *nirvāṇa* is a fundamental teaching in Buddhism, and many other passages like this one could be cited.

CHAPTER VIII

1. E.g., T. M. P. Mahadevan (1975); R. D. Karmarkar (1953).

2. There is still a great deal of controversy about the dates of Śaṃkara and Gauḍapāda. Beginning with Max Müller, the most common scholarly dating of Śaṃkara has been 788-820 C.E., though there is a tendency in recent scholarship to move this up to the first part of the 8th century. Some have placed him as early as the first half of the 7th century.

In any case, the point to be made here is that the ĀŚV's interpretation of ALP 1 would have been regarded as highly implausible at any of these dates for Śaṃkara, for in these centuries Buddhism was a major challenge to the Vedic tradition and was being fought tooth and nail. (There is more discussion of this point in chapter 13.)

Gauḍapāda, incidentally, is sometimes placed much earlier than the usual dating for Śaṃkara — perhaps as early as the first half of of the 6th century. It should be noted that the usual dating of Śaṃkara (anywhere from 710 to 820 C.E.) and an early dating of Gauḍapāda (e.g. 510 C.E.) would be incompatible with the traditional account, according to which Gauḍapāda was Śaṃkara's *parama-guru*.

3. The charge of crypto-Buddhism was levelled against Śaṃkara's doctrines at a very early date. Bhāskara, for example, who was either a contemporary or near-contemporary of Śaṃkara, derides Śaṃkara's interpretation of the Vedānta as "this despicable, broken down *māyāvāda* that has been chanted by Mahāyāna Buddhists." (This quotation is taken from the paper by D. H. H. Ingalls (1967: 65), who cites Bhāskara's Brahma-sūtra-bhāsya 1.4.25.) H. Nakamura (1983: 120-122), has collated a long list of such charges.

CHAPTER IX

1. In the title pages and introductory and closing colophons of the Sanskrit texts, the commentary I have been calling the Āgama-śāstra-vivaraṇa is also referred to as the Śāṃkara-bhāṣya, the Gauḍapādīya-kārikā-sahita-māṇḍūkyopaniṣad-bhāṣya, the Gauḍapādīyāgama-śāstra-bhāṣya, and the Gauḍapādīya-bhāṣya āgama-śāstra-vivaraṇa. I shall refer to the commentary either as the *vivaraṇa* or as the *bhāṣya*, and its author (whoever he was) as the *bhāṣya-kāra*.

2. "*Prakaraṇa-catuṣṭaya*" is a genitive *tat-puruṣa* compound. If the *bhāṣya-kāra* had meant that the work on which he was commenting was a "four-chaptered work," he would presumably have used an entirely different expression.

The difference can be brought out by comparing the ĀŚV's introductory remarks with the introductions to the commentaries on the Bhagavad-gītā, the Bṛhad-āraṇyakopaniṣad and the Chāndogyopaniṣad which have been attributed to Śaṃkara:

Bhagavad-gītā, consisting of 700 *ślokas*:

> "This *dharma* was taught by the Lord, and the omniscient and adorable Veda-vyāsa embodied it in the seven hundred *ślokas* called the Gītā. This Gītā-śāstra is an epitome of the essence of the entire Vedānta, and its meaning is hard to grasp.
>
> *taṃ dharmaṃ bhagavatā yathopadiṣṭaṃ vedavyāsaḥ sarvajño bhagavān gītākhyaiḥ saptabhiḥ śloka-śatair-upanibabandha / tad-idaṃ gītā-śāstraṃ samaṣṭa-vedārtha-sāra-saṃgraha-bhūtaṃ dur-vijñeyārtham.*

Chāndogyopaniṣad, consisting of eight chapters (*adhyāyas*):

> "*Om ity etad akṣaram*" etc. is the eight-chaptered Chāndogyopaniṣad. On it this small work is commenced in the desire to make known its meaning briefly.

Om-ity-etad-akṣaram-ity-ādy-aṣṭādhyāyī chāndogyopaniṣat / tasyāḥ saṃkṣepato 'rtha jijñāsubhya ṛju-vivaraṇam-alpa-grantham-idam-ārabhyate

Bṛhad-āraṇyakopaniṣad, consisting of six chapters (*adhyāyas*):

"With the words 'The head of the sacrificial horse is, indeed, the dawn' is begun the Vājasaneyi Upaniṣad (i.e. the Bṛhad-āraṇyaka). Now there begins this small book which comments on it...This work consisting of six chapters is called '*āraṇyaka*' because it was taught in the forest. And because it is large it is called 'Bṛhad-āraṇyaka.'

uṣā vā aśvasya ity-evam-ādyā vājasaneyi-brāhmaṇopaniṣat / tasyā iyam-alpa-granthā vṛttiḥ ārabhyate / ... seyaṃ ṣaḍ-adhyāyī araṇye 'nūcyamānatvād-āraṇyakaṃ bṛhattvāt-parimānato bṛhad-āraṇyakam

Note that Śaṃkara gives the *title* or *name* of the works on which he is commenting. Note also that he calls the Chāndogya a work having eight chapters (*aṣṭādhyāyin*), and not an octet of treatises, and that he calls the Bṛhad-āraṇyaka a work having six chapters (*ṣaḍ-adhyāyin*), and not a sextet of treatises.

3. It should be mentioned that the body of the text confirms what we learn from the Introduction to the ĀŚV. There are cross-references in the work itself to passages in earlier and later *prakaraṇas*. (An example will be cited later, where the *bhāṣya-kāra* in his commentary on ĀP 6 says: "Thus it is said later" and then cites ADP 3.28cd.) But in no case does the *bhāṣya-kāra* refer to these passages as having been written by a *single author*. He obviously thinks that his *prakaraṇa-catuṣṭaya* can be usefully regarded *as if* it were a single treatise, but that is all that can reasonably be inferred from the text itself.

4. Bhattacharya (1943: xlvii-lvii).

5. Bhattacharya, ibid., xlviii.

It should also be mentioned that Bhattacharya doubted that this commentator — whom he calls Śaṃkara — was identical with Ādi Śaṃkara (Śaṃkara-bhagavat-pādācārya). Ibid, fn. 3, p. xxxiii.

6. A. Venkatasubbiah, "On Gauḍapāda's Āgamaśāstra," (1935: 783).

7. Sarma (1933). I have not had an opportunity to see this paper.

8. A. Venkatasubbiah (1933: 188). In this paper, Subbiah cited p. 1054 of MS 1556 from the Catalogue of Sanskrit MSS in the Tanjore Sarasvatī Mahal Library, No. 1556, p. 1054 as follows:

> *om-ity-etad-akṣaram-idaṃ-sarvam-ity-ādyā māṇḍūkyopanisac catuḥ-khaṇḍā / tāṃ khaṇḍaśaḥ paṭhitva 'traite ślokā bhavantīti catuḥ-paryāyair gauḍapādācāryā nārāyaṇānugraheṇa śloka-racanayā vyācacakṣire / tena śruti-tad-vyākhyā-ghaṭitaṃ prathamaṃ prakaraṇaṃ śruti-prāyam eveti tatra chāndasānām upaniṣad-vyavahāraḥ pravṛttaḥ / evaṃ tad-vicārātmaka-prakaraṇa-traye 'pi / vedāntārtha-sāra-saṃgraha-bhūtam idaṃ prakaraṇa-catuṣṭayam / ata eva na pṛthak saṃbandhābhidheya-prayojanāni vaktavyāni*

9. As I have argued already in chapter 1, the fact that the Āgama-prakaraṇa gives separate commentaries on Māṇḍ. 6 and Māṇḍ. 7 does not mean that Māṇḍ. 6 and 7 refer to two different states of the Self.

CHAPTER X

1. Brahma-siddhi, Foreword by P. P. Subrahmanya Sastri (1984: vi, fn. 2).

It is of interest that Maṇḍanamiśra, unlike Śaṃkara, was sympathetic to the *sphoṭa-vāda*. In his Sphoṭa-siddhi, Maṇḍanamiśra equates the noumenal substratum of the phenomenal world of speech (*śabda-brahman*) with the pure *brahman* (*śuddha-brahman*) forming the noumenal substratum of the phenomenal world of objects signified by speech. (See S. Kuppuswami's discussion in his introduction to the Brahma-siddhi, ibid., pp. xxvi-xxvii, and also pp. 16-18 of the Brahma-siddhi itself.) It is possible that the *bhāṣya-kāra* was a later commentator who followed Maṇḍanamiśra on this point rather than Śaṃkara.

2. Cf. Śaṃkara's discussion of the *sphoṭa-vāda* in BSB 1.3.28. The ĀŚV's interpretation of the meaning of *Aum* is also difficult to reconcile with BSB 1.3.10.

3. *yathā rajjvāṃ prāk-sarpotpatter rajjvātmanā sarpaḥ san-nevā" sīt / evaṃ sarva-bhāvānām-utpatteḥ prāk-prāṇa-bījātmanaiva sattvam.*

4. Note that the "*a-*" of "*asaṃbhūti*" has been elided through the *saṃdhi*. Without the *saṃdhi*, 12ab would read: *andhaṃ tamaḥ praviśanti ye asaṃbhūtim upāsate.*

5. Vasubandhu's Viṃśatikā begins: "In the Mahāyāna it has been established that the three worlds are nothing but representations of consciousness (*mahāyāne traidhātukaṃ vijñapti-mātraṃ vyavasthāpyate*)...Here the terms *citta*, *manas*, *vijñāna* and *vijñapti* [the latter term denoting ideas, representations, percepts etc.] are synonymous." S. Lévi, Vijñapti-mātratā-siddhi (1925: 3).

6. Śaṃkara begins his Brahma-sūtra-bhāṣya with this theme of the illusory superimposition of the qualities of the object on that of the subject: "The sense-object and the subject (lit. the 'You' and the 'I') which are within the denotation of the words '*asmat*' and '*yuṣmat*,' and which have natures as different as that of darkness and light" etc. (*yuṣmad-asmat-pratyaya-gocarayor-viṣaya-viṣayiṇoḥ tamaḥ-prakāśavad-viruddha-svabhāvayor...*).

7. At the end of the commentary on BS 2.2.31, the views of the Mādhyamikas or Śūnyavādins are dismissed in a mere two sentences as being contradicted by all of our means of knowledge (*sarva-pramāṇa-vipratiṣiddha*).

8. *nābhāva upalabdheḥ*

9. *vaidharmyāc-ca na svapnādivat*

10. Cf. Brahma-sūtra 1.1.2: *janmādy asya yataḥ* and Brahma-sūtra 1.4.26: *ātmakṛteḥ pariṇāmāt.*

11. Critics of Śaṃkara have argued that BS 2.2.28-29 also contradict Śaṃkara's own Māyāvāda interpretation of the Vedānta, according to which the world is unreal, though for different reasons than the ones given by the Buddhist idealists. (Rāmānuja says in his Śrībhāṣya, for example, that the *sūtras* refute the Vedavādins who are crypto-Buddhists (*pracanna-bauddha*) as well as the Buddhist Vijñānavādins.) No doubt these critics are right: the plain meaning of the *sūtras* would appear to exclude the Māyāvāda formulation as well as that of the Vijñānavādins.

12. *yad-antarjñeya-rūpaṃ tad-bahirvad-abhāsate.* This is a quotation of the first half of the sixth verse of Dignāga's Ālambana-

parīkṣā. (Ālambana-parīkṣā and Vṛtti, ed. N. Aiyaswami Sastri (1942: 2).)

13. P. Hacker (1972: 132).

14. S. Mayeda (1967-68: 90-93).

15. Hermann Jacobi (1933: 52, fn. 2) was inclined to think that the author of the commentary on VP 4 could not have been Śaṃkara because Śaṃkara would not have presented an *anumāna* of this sort. This contention has been criticized by T. R. Chintāmani (1924: 421).

16. Cf. Brahma-sūtra-bhāṣya 2.2.29: *mithyā jāgaritopalabdhir-upalabdhitvāt-svapnopalabdhivad-iti*, which Śaṃkara repudiates.

17. I do not know of any Vijñānavāda work which makes such an assertion or which presents such an argument, but the very same view can be found in the Prasannapadā, a commentary by the Mādhyamika Candrakīrti on the Mūla-madhayamaka-kārikās of Nāgārjuna.

The first *kārikā* of Nāgārjuna's work says:

> No entities exist at any time or at any place, (for) they do not originate from themselves, from others, from both self and others, or from a lack of causes.

In commenting on this verse, Candrakīrti tries to meet the objection that this view is untenable because origination is established by our own experience (*anubhava*). Candrakīrti says that this objection is untenable (*ayukta*), and he does so on the grounds that experience is false *because* it is experience, as in the experience of two moons seen by the victim of an ophthalmological defect (*yasmād anubhava eṣa mṛṣā anubhavatvāt taimirika-dvicandra-ādi-anubhavavad-iti*), and because experience itself must be justified (*tataś cānubhavasyāpi sādhya-samatvāt tena pratyavasthānaṃ na yuktam iti*).

CHAPTER XI

1. Brahma-siddhi, p. 150.

2. BV 1.4.712, p. 576 (Ānandāśrama ed.) has "*buddhau*" rather than "*baddhau*" and "*tu*" rather than "*tau*":

kārya-kāraṇa-buddhau tāv-iṣyete viśva-taijasau
prājñaḥ kāraṇa-baddhas-tu dvau tu turye na sidhyataḥ.

If this is not just a MS. error, it means: *Viśva* and *taijasa* are the discrimination (*buddhi*) of cause and effect, and *prājña* is bound by cause (alone), but neither the discrimination of cause and effect nor the bondage of the cause is present in *turya*.

3. B. N. K. Sharma (1931-33), in papers which have not been available to me, has suggested that ĀP 9 is also cited by Śaṃkara in BSB 2.1.33. This suggestion was discussed — and criticized — by A. Venkatasubbiah (1936-37: 9, 14-15), who showed, it seems to me, that Sharma's suggestion is probably untenable.

Brahma-sūtra 2.1.33 declares that *brahman* creates the world merely out of sport (*lokavat-tu līlā-kaivalyam*). In his commentary on this *sūtra*, Śaṃkara says that the activity of the Lord in manifesting the world is just part of his nature (*svabhāvādeva kevalaṃ līlā-rūpā*); although the creation of the world may appear to us to be a weighty thing, it would be a mere play to *parameśvara*, whose powers (*śakti*) are unlimited. Not even a subtle purpose could ever be detected in the Lord's creative activity, he says, because *śruti* tells us that he has all his desires fulfilled (*āpta-kāma-śruteḥ*).

Sharma has suggested that the phrase "*āpta-kāma-śruteḥ*" in the above passage must refer to ĀP 9cd, which says: "What desire could there be for the one who has attained all desires (*āpta-kāma*)?"

There are two problems with this suggestion. First, it would entail that Śaṃkara regarded ĀP 9 as *śruti*, but it is clear from Śaṃkara's citation of ĀP 16 and ADP 15 that he did not regard ĀP 16 and ĀDP 15 as *śruti*. (He refers them to those who know the Vedāntic tradition etc., and this implies that they had a human author, whereas *śruti* by definition has no human author.) Secondly, there is no need to suppose that Śaṃkara was referring to ĀP 9 in BSB 2.1.33. For the term "*āpta-kāma*" also occurs in BU 4.4.6, where the person who has no desires, who has attained all desires (*āpta-kāma*) and for whom the Self is his only desire, is said to become *brahman*, since he is *brahman*.

4. See BU 4.4.6-4.4.22 and the discussion above in chapter 5 on the Bṛhad-āraṇyakopaniṣad.

5. Cf. also BSB 2.1.14, where Śaṃkara says:

> There is non-difference of cause and effect (*kārya-kāraṇayor-ananyatvam*). The effect is this manifold world (*bahu-prapañcaṃ jagat*) consisting of *ākāśa* etc.; the cause is the highest *brahman*. Therefore, in reality the effect is identical with the cause because it has no existence apart from it (*tasmāt kāraṇāt paramārthato 'nanyatvaṃ vyatirekeṇa-abhāvaḥ kāryasya*).

And later in the same passage he says:

> Just as the spaces (*ākāśa*) inside jars and water-pots are not different from universal space (*mahākāśa*), or just as the water of a mirage etc. is not different from the sandy plain, because its nature is to be seen and (then) not seen and is therefore inexplicable, so also this manifold world consisting of enjoyers and objects of enjoyment has no existence apart from *brahman* (*brahma-vyatirekeṇa-abhāva*).

6. One of the things that makes dreaming paradoxical is that in our dreams we apparently frighten (and otherwise deceive) *ourselves*.

7. *suṣuptākhyaṃ tamo 'jñānaṃ bījaṃ svapna-prabodhayoḥ*
svātma-bodha-pradagdhaṃ syāḍ-bījaṃ dagdhaṃ yathā 'bhāvam

Upadeśa-sāhasrī, ed./tr. Swāmi Jagadānanda (1961: 17.26, p. 199). NS 4.43 has "*ātma-bodha*" rather than "*svātama-bodha*."

8. M. Walleser (1910: 2 ff).

9. According to Ānandagiri's commentary on BV 4.4.886, at least one of the "others" who are referred to in BV 4.4.886 is Veda-vyāsa. However, it is unlikely that Sureśvara thought that Gauḍapāda could actually be compared with the legendary and quasi-divine Veda-vyāsa. It is likely that Ānandagiri, a much later writer, was simply trying to explain away the fact that Sureśvara mentions Gauḍapāda as only *one* of many teachers who taught the true doctrine of the Vedānta.

CHAPTER XII

1. T. M. P. Mahadevan (1975: 6); A. Venкatasubbiah (1933: 184). However, on p. 16 (ibid.) Mahadevan shows that he is not so sure of this identification.

2. One cannot dismiss the possibility that the tradition that Gauḍapāda was the grand-teacher of Śaṃkara arose when later followers of the Śaṃkara school misinterpreted the term "*parama-guru*" of this verse to mean "grand-teacher" rather than "great teacher." This is not an intrinsically implausible suggestion. No doubt much stranger things have happened in the formation of the traditional *guru-paramparā* lists of the schools in India.

3. T. M. P. Mahadevan (1975: 2).

4. Noted by Venkatasubbiah (1933: 84, fn. 12). Another anachronism in the later traditions about these early teachers should also be mentioned.

In the Jagad-guru-ratna-mālā-stava of Sadāśivabrahmendra (fl. 1720), there is a verse, the second half of which runs:

atha gauḍapādān phanīśa-bhāṣya-prathamācāryāka-paṇḍitān.

"*Phaṇīśa*" means "lord of the serpents," and is an epithet of Patañjali, the author of the Mahābhāṣya on the Aṣṭādhyāyī of Pāṇini. Hence the verse means:

> "I resort to Gauḍapāda, the first of the learned teachers of the Mahābhāṣya of Patañjali.

(This verse is discussed by M. Hiriyanna (1926); Bhattacharya (1943: lxii-lxxiv); and T. M. P. Mahadevan (1975: 9-13).)

This tradition is, of course, unhistorical. No work on the Mahābhāṣya attributed to Gauḍapāda has come down to us, and the claim that Gauḍapāda was the first *ācārya* of the Mahābhāṣya is itself an anachronism. Furthermore, whereas the Śaṃkara-dig-vijaya treats Govinda as Patañjali, Sadāśivabrahmendra's Stava regards Gauḍapāda (the reputed teacher of Govinda) as the first of the teachers of the Mahābhāṣya.

5. E.g. Potter (1981: 103); Pandey (1974: 30).

6. Cf. Monier-Williams (1970: 359b, 348c). This — by far the most common meaning of "*garīyas*" in Sanskrit — is exemplified by BG 11.37b: "greater than Brahmā even" (*garīyase brahmaṇo 'pi*) and BG 11.43b: "thou art the revered *guru* of the world" (*tvam asya pūjyaś-ca gurur garīyān*).

7. *tasmād-idaṃ tyakta-sarva-bāhyaiṣaṇair-ananya-śaraṇaiḥ paramahaṃsa-parivrājakair-ity-āśramibhir-vedānta-vijñāna-parair-eva vedanīyaṃ pūjya-tamaiḥ prājāpatyaṃ cemaṃ saṃpradāyam-anusaradbhir-upanibaddhaṃ prakaraṇa-catuṣṭayena / tathā 'nuśāsaty-ady-āpi ta eva nānya iti.*

8. Monier-Williams (1970) gives "treatment," "discussion," "explanation," "subject," "topic," "question," "matter" and "occasion" as possible meanings of "*prakaraṇa*."

9. The context of Sureśvara's citation of the Māṇḍūkya should also be noted. The citation occurs in the chapter of the Vārttika which comments on BU 3.8. In this passage of the Vārttika, Sureśvara is principally interested in showing that the universe does not exist apart from the Self — a point which is quite compatible with the IC interpretation of the Māṇḍūkya. Sureśvara's position diverges from the IC interpretation, however, in that he believes that the *sarveśvara*, *sarvāntaryāmin* etc. is the Self as it is reflected in the primordial *avidyā*.

Sureśvara himself clearly linked *īśvara* with the state of deep sleep. This linkage appears most clearly, perhaps, in BV 4.3.1051 (p. 1566):

> *asti bhogaḥ suṣupte 'pi tathā-cā ''nanda-bhuṅ-mataḥ*
> *aiśvaro vā ''tra bhogo 'sti sarva-sthānābhimānataḥ*

> The enjoyment in sleep is said to be the enjoyment of bliss. Or else the bliss there is lordly (*aiśvara*) because there all the states are related to the self.

The question, however, is whether this linkage was the accepted Vedāntic interpretation of the Māṇḍūkya at the time that Sureśvara wrote. I believe that it was not.

10. The *kārikās* of the ĀP are introduced on each occasion with the words "Here there are the verses" (*atraite ślokā bhavanti*). These words must be a part of the ĀP, for the author of the ĀŚV

comments on them. For example, after Māṇḍ. 6 the ĀP says "*atraite ślokā bhavanti,*" and at this point the *bhāṣya-kāra* says "*atraitasmin-yathokte 'rtha ete ślokā bhavanti.*" This does not preclude the possibility, however, that he also added some verses of his own. As I have argued in chapter 9, the *bhāṣya-kāra* was not above taking certain liberties with texts.

CHAPTER XIII

1. There is, incidentally, internal evidence in the Āgama-śāstra that the redactors of the text were reluctant to ascribe the ALP to Gauḍapāda, for while the colophons at the beginning and end of the first three *prakaraṇas* mention Gauḍapāda, the introductory colophon for the ALP does not.

Thus, at the conclusion of the Āgama-prakaraṇa, the colophon reads "Thus the first *prakaraṇa*, the Āgama-prakaraṇa, consisting of the *gauḍapādīya-kārikās* which comment on the Māṇḍūkyopaniṣat" (*iti māṇḍūkyopaniṣad-arthāviṣkaraṇa-parāyāṃ-gauḍapādīya-kārikāyāṃ prathamam-āgama-prakaraṇam*). At the beginning and at the end of the Vaitathya-prakaraṇa there is the following colophon: "Here is the second *prakaraṇa*, called the Vaitathya, of the *gauḍapādīya-kārikās*." Similarly, the third *prakaraṇa* begins and ends with the colophon: "Thus the third *prakaraṇa*, called the Advaita Prakaraṇa, of the *gauḍapādīya-kārikās*." The fourth *prakaraṇa*, on the other hand, is introduced with a colophon which does not mention Gauḍapāda at all. It simply says: "Here is the fourth *prakaraṇa*, called the Alāta-śānti." (Ānandāśrama edition.)

It is true that the fourth *prakaraṇa* is apparently included in the closing colophon for the entire work, which says: "Here the *kārikās* on the Māṇḍūkyopaniṣad by Gauḍapādācārya are complete." However, this colophon is also strange, for the last three *prakaraṇas* are in no sense direct commentaries (*bhāṣyas*) on the Māṇḍūkya.

2. The fact that the ĀŚV is not mentioned by another writer until ca. 1300 C.E. is in fact a very good reason for thinking that the ĀŚV was not written by Ādi Śaṃkara. The definitive and well-authenticated works of Śaṃkara, like the Brahma-sūtra-bhāṣya and the Bṛhad-āraṇyakopaniṣad-bhāṣya, had commentaries written on them by very early writers.

Furthermore, it is particularly surprising that early writers do not mention the ĀŚV, for it teaches very radical doctrines. One would have expected the other writers of the Śaṃkara school to comment on it or at least to allude to it, and critics of the Māyāvāda to have chosen it as a special object of attack and criticism.

Since Ānandagiri is apparently the first writer to ascribe the ĀŚV to Ādi Śaṃkara, it is worth noting that he was not a particularly reliable guide to what is authentic in the many works which have been ascribed to Śaṃkarācārya. Ānandagiri wrote commentaries on the following works which are of doubtful authenticity: Ātma-jñānopadeśa, Dakṣiṇāmūrti-stotra, Hari-stuti, Pañcī-karaṇa, Śata-ślokī, Śvetāśvataropaniṣad-bhāṣya, Dṛg-dṛśya-viveka and the Vākya-vṛtti (Potter (1983: 127-158, 288-290); Potter (1981: 18-19)). Potter, incidentally, is dubious about the authenticity of the ĀŚV, too, but he follows the prevailing scholarly opinion and classifies it as an authentic work (Potter (1981: 104)).

3. I think it would be fair to say that there is about as much Buddhist influence on Śaṃkara's definitive works as there is of Vedāntist influence on the Tathāgata-garbha texts of Buddhism. Works like the Śrīmālā-devī-siṃha-nāda-sūtra, the Ratna-gotra-mahāvibhāga-śāstra, the Treatise on the Awakening of Faith in the Mahāyāna (Mahāyāna-śraddhotpāda-śāstra) and the Laṅkāvatāra-sūtra may be said to flirt with the conception of a Vedāntic Absolute, but they never fully embrace it; and I think that this is analogous to the Māyāvādins' treatment of certain Buddhist notions.

The reader who is interested in the Tathāgata-garbha texts may be referred to Ruegg (1969), who analyzes in detail the equivocations and ambivalences shown in these texts towards the Vedāntic doctrine of the Absolute.

4. M. Walleser (1910), V. Bhattacharya (1943) and H. Nakamura (1983) have drawn attention to two works in the Tibetan Bstan-'gyur which describe (and criticize) the Vedānta system. These are the Madhyamaka-hṛdaya-kārikā (with the autocommentary Tarka-jvālā) by Bhāvaviveka (ca. 550 C.E.); the other is the Madhyamakālaṅkāra-kārikā of Śāntarakṣita (ca. 750 C.E.) (with the commentary by Kamalaśīla called the Pañjikā). (These works exist only in the Tibetan; translations of the relevant portions of the Bhāvaviveka text may be found in Nakamura (1983: 219).) It has

been suggested that these works show that some of Gauḍapāda's *kārikās*, or at any rate views very similar to them, were prevalent in the Vedānta at the comparatively early time that Bhāvaviveka, Śāntarakṣita and Kamalaśīla wrote.

It would take us too far out of the way to discuss these works in detail. I will only say here that it seems to me (to judge from the available translations from the Tibetan) that there is very little, if anything, of Śaṃkarite or Māyāvādin views in the very early work by Bhāvaviveka, and no more in the later works by Śāntarakṣita and Kamalaśīla (who may have been contemporaries of Ādi Śaṃkara) than there is in Śaṃkara's definitive works. The same is true, it seems to me, of the *puruṣa-parīkṣā* and *ātma-parīkṣā* of the Tattva-saṃgraha-(pañjikā). [The TS(P) exists in both Tibetan and Sanskrit; the two *parīkṣās* mentioned above have been discussed by Nakamura (1983: 221-257).]

For one thing, the Vedāntins discussed by all these Buddhist writers adhered to the *pariṇāma-vāda*. Furthermore, although these early works contain some verses which are either identical with, or very similar to, verses in the first three *prakaraṇas* of the Āgama-śāstra, there are none which look as if they had been taken from the ALP or any work like it. This in itself is a very striking fact, for all three of these Buddhist writers are describing and criticizing Vedāntist views from a Buddhist perspective. If there had been a school of the Vedānta in their time that held that Buddhism and the Vedānta taught the *same* doctrine under the guise of different terminologies, it is very strange that these Buddhist authors fail to mention it. This is especially true of Śāntarakṣita, because Śāntarakṣita, like Gauḍapāda, may have come from Bengal (*gauḍa-deśa*).

This point seems to have been generally overlooked, perhaps because it is almost invariably assumed that the four *prakaraṇas* of the Āgama-śāstra form a single work. An interesting recent example of this is Lindtner (1982).

Walleser's original list of Gauḍapādīya-kārikās cited by Buddhist writers (1910: 18-20) included III.5 (by Bhāvaviveka in his Tarka-jvālā), and II.17-20 and III.4, 6, 8 and 30 from Śāntarakṣita's autocommentary on *śloka* 93 of his Madhyamakālaṅkāra. According to Lindtner (1982: 280), this list is incomplete. To Walleser's original list he adds II.31-32, 35 and III.31-32. We also learn from

Lindtner that in citing II.31-32, 35 Śāntarakṣita exclaims: "What they state has already been said by the Tathāgata!" (*de dag gis gaṅ brjod pa de ni bde bar gśegs pas gsuṅs pa*).

Śāntarakṣita's reaction is interesting, but not as interesting, it seems to me, as the fact that he merely cites Vedāntist verses which express views which are (at least superficially) identical with Mahāyānist views, rather than any verses which actually *assert* that what the Vedānta taught and what the Buddha taught were *identical*. (Note also that the Buddhist writers do not cite any verses from the ĀŚ which support the *ajātivāda* through a critique of the notion of causality.) This raises the following question: if the ALP existed in Śāntarakṣita's day, why didn't Śāntarakṣita make the point he makes in the Madhyamakālaṅkāra(-vṛtti) much more forcefully by citing ALP 1 (which clearly praises the Buddha himself) — or for that matter, many other *kārikās* in the ALP where the Buddhist terminology is even more specific and explicit than it is in the verses cited in the Madhyamakālaṅkāra? Consider, for example, the following list:

IV.1 *jñānenā "kāśakalpena dharmān-yo gaganopamān /*
jñeyābhinnena saṃbuddhas-tāṃ vande dvipadāṃ varam //

IV.10 *...sarve dharmāḥ...*

IV.19 *...buddhair...*

IV.24 *...saṃkleśasyopalabdheś-ca paratantrāstitā mātā //*

IV.42 *...buddhair...*

IV.53 *...dravyatvam-anyabhāvo vā dharmāṇāṃ nopapadyate //*

IV.57 *...śāśvata/uccheda...*

IV.58 *ye dharmāḥ...*

IV.59 *...nāsau nityo na cocchedī tatvād-dharmeṣu yojanā //*

IV.60 *nājeṣu sarva-dharmeṣu śāśvatāśāśvatābhidhā /*

IV.73 *yo 'sti kalpita-saṃvṛtyā paramārthena nāsty-asau /*
paratantrābhisaṃvṛtyā syān-nāsti paramārthataḥ //

IV.74 *ajaḥ kalpita-saṃvṛtyā paramārthena nāpy-ajaḥ* /

IV.80 *...viṣayaḥ sa hi buddhānāṃ...*

IV.81 *...dharmo dhātu-svabhāvataḥ (= dharma-dhātu-svabhāvataḥ)* //

IV.84 *koṭyaś catasra...*

IV.87 *...dvayaṃ laukikam / śuddhaṃ laukikam...*

IV.88 *...lokottaram ... buddhaiḥ...*

IV.90 *...agrayāṇataḥ (=agrayānataḥ)* /

IV.91 *...sarve dharmā anādayaḥ* /

IV.92 *ādibuddhāḥ prakṛtyaiva sarve dharmāḥ suniścitāḥ* /

IV.98 *alabdhāvaranāḥ sarve dharmāḥ prakṛti-nirmalāḥ* /
ādau buddhās-tathā muktā budhyanta iti nāyakāḥ //

IV.99 *kramate na hi buddhasya jñānaṃ dharmeṣu tāyinaḥ* /
sarve dharmās-tathā jñānaṃ naitad-buddhena bhāṣitam //

It is universally acknowledged that the most Buddhist-sounding verses of the Āgama-śāstra are in the Alāta-śānti-prakaraṇa, and no explanation of the Āgama-śāstra can be accounted wholly adequate which fails to explain the fact that the ALP — by far the most interesting and distinctive of all the four *prakaraṇas* — is cited neither by the old Advaita texts (which cite only verses from the first three *prakaraṇas*) nor by the Buddhist texts (which cite only verses from the second and third).

For all these reasons I do not regard the Buddhist works as providing any evidence against my thesis that the ALP was a post-Śaṃkara work. On the contrary, they provide, if anything, strong evidence that the ALP *was* a post-Śaṃkara work.

5. The interpretation of the crucial verse in the Gīta-govinda which describes the Buddha-*avatāra* appears to be somewhat controversial. The interested reader may wish to consult Lee Siegel (1978: 243, 288).

6. According to the hypothesis I am advancing, both the ĀŚ and its individual *prakaraṇas* are composite works. Such composite

works were undoubtedly very common in ancient and medieval India, as the Indian scholastics took a more impersonal view of philosophical and religious works than is the case in the present age, where a great deal of emphasis is placed on the individuality and personality of an author.

One passage can be cited which, it seems to me, shows almost certainly that the "ĀŚ" is a composite work. As was noted in footnote 4, Bhāvaviveka (ca. 550 C.E.) cites ADP 5 in a chapter of his MHK(V). Does this mean that the whole of the "ĀŚ" existed at the time that Bhāvaviveka wrote? Either answer to this question raises problems for the traditional view, according to which the ĀŚ was written as a single work in four chapters by Gauḍapāda, the *parama-guru* of Śaṃkarācārya.

On the one hand, if it is claimed that the ĀŚ did exist in its entirety ca. 550 C.E., it becomes virtually impossible to explain why Bhāvaviveka failed to mention other *kārikās* in the ĀŚ which come much closer to Mahāyānist views than the one he does cite. Since Bhavya was specifically concerned in the chapter of the work in question with comparing and contrasting Vedāntic views with his own Buddhist views, one would have expected him to cite the verses that Śāntarakṣita exclaimed about two centuries later — not to mention the even more startling verses (mentioned in footnote 4) which even Śāntarakṣita fails to cite.

On the other hand, if the work we now know as the "Āgama-śāstra" did *not* exist in Bhavya's time, then we must conclude that the ADP, at any rate, is a composite work, for if we are to assume that the saying which is now embodied in ADP 5 existed before verses like ĀP 3, ĀP 11, ĀP 14, ĀP 15, ĀP 16, VP 17, VP 38, ADP 15 and ADP 46 (which *were* written by Gauḍapāda) then ADP 5 must have been attributed to Gauḍapāda at a later date through its incorporation in the larger work which was also attributed to him.

My suggestion is that what happened to Gauḍapāda was similar to what happened to the unknown author of ADP 5. Gauḍapāda's genuine *kārikās* (of which only a few are cited by early Advaitin writers) were included with passages from other (and no doubt later writers) in the work now known as the "Āgama-śāstra." Even the spurious *kārikās* were later attributed to Gauḍapāda when the Śaṃkara school attempted to trace its interpretation of the Upaniṣads past Śaṃkara to Patañjali, Śuka and Vyāsa and ultimately to a divine source, i.e., Nārāyaṇa. In this way, the Advaitin thinker Gauḍapāda, who was mentioned by Sureśvara occasionally in his NKS and BV, came to play a crucial role in an historical reconstruction.

CHAPTER XIV

1. This point is emphasized by ĀP 12, which says:

> Neither the self, nor others, nor truth nor even untruth: the sleeping state knows nothing. *Turya* is always all-seeing.

This, of course, only restates the classical Upaniṣadic teaching of the sleeping state which can be found in Chānd. 8.7.

2. ĀP 23 may seem to suggest on a superficial reading that deep sleep (*prājña*) is closer to the ultimate state (*turya*) than the waking state is, but in fact ĀP 23 will not support this kind of interpretation. ĀP 23 says:

> The letter *a* leads (*nayate*) to the waking state;the letter *u*, as well, leads to the dreaming state; the letter *m*, again, leads to the state of deep sleep. There is no goal (*gati*) in what has no element.

It is easy to read this to mean that meditation on the waking state leads to the dreaming state, that meditation on the dreaming state leads to the sleeping state, and that meditation on the sleeping state leads to the *turīya*. But ĀP 23 does not say this. It simply says that meditation on each of these letters leads to the state with which it has been correlated for the purposes of meditation. ĀP 23 certainly does not mean that there is a progression — even for the purposes of meditation — from the waking state to the *turīya* through the intermediate states of dreaming and sleeping.

3. The great saying (*mahāvākya*) "This Self is *brahman*" (*ayam ātmā brahma*) is cited in Māṇḍ. 2.

4. It is sometimes useful to think of these *dharmas* as qualities (which is what the term "*dharma*" often means in Sanskrit), though this is not quite accurate, since qualities are properties of substances, and Mahāyānist philosophy explicitly rejected the notion of substance (*dharmin*). Hence it would be more accurate to think of

the *dharmas* of some of the later Buddhist scholastics as what qualities become when they are not ascribed to any underlying substance. In the later Buddhist writings the *dharmas* are thought of as "point instants."

5. Cf. Saṃyutta-nikāya XII, 3. ¶21:

> So 'this' being, 'that' becomes; from the arising of this that arises; this not being, that becomes not; from the ceasing of this, that ceases. That is to say, conditioned by ignorance (come) activities, conditioned by activities consciousness, ... name-and-shape, sense, contact, feeling, craving etc....

6. It may not be wholly irrelevant to point out here that the notion of a "state" or a "property" is fundamental to science, and that there is no apparent contradiction involved in saying of some entity x that in one set of conditions x has the set of properties $\{P\}$ and that at a later time (in another set of conditions) x has the set of properties $\{P'\}$.

Quantum mechanics is stated in terms of such "state-descriptions." Indeed, physicists maintain that all physical changes of state — like the transformation of water into ice or milk into curds — are deducible (at least in principle) from the Schrödinger equation.

7. This passage is probably inspired by BU 4.5.15.

8. Note the distinction that is expressed here between mind and *dharmas*. So far as I know, this distinction cannot be found in any orthodox Buddhist school.

9. The view that the world and *my* consciousness of it are one and the same thing is the view of subjective idealism or solipsism. There is every reason to think that this is not a meaningful or coherent doctrine.

Bertrand Russell once received a letter from a solipsist who said that she was surprised that more people were not solipsists like herself. Russell thought that her position was frivolous and insincere, and with good reason: for if the woman really were a solipsist, she could not speak of "others" at all. The logician who wrote this letter to Russell did not appreciate how radical the doctrine of solipsism is *when it is internally consistent*. As Russell showed, the more consistent the formulation of solipsism is, the more implausible the doctrine becomes. (Russell (1948: 175-181.))

10. Śvetāśvataropaniṣad 4.3 is even more striking:

> You are a woman. You are a man. You are the youth and the maiden, too. You, as an old man, dodder along with a staff. Being born you come to face in all directions.
>
> *tvaṃ strī tvaṃ pumān asi tvaṃ kumāra uta vā kumārī; tvaṃ jīrṇo daṇḍena vañcasi tvaṃ jāto bhavasi viśvatomukhaḥ*

11. The doctrine of Maitrī 7.11.7-8, according to which the three empirical conditions of waking, dreaming and sleeping comprise only a fourth part of *brahman*, whereas the transcendent *turya* comprises three-quarters of it, can be traced to Ṛgveda 10.90.3,4.

GLOSSARY

GLOSSARY

Abhidharma — Buddhist metaphysics; a theory or classification of the *dharmas*

advaita — nondual

advaitin — a nondualist

advaya — nondual

āgama — a traditional doctrine or precept; sacred writing or scripture; sometimes used to refer to the Vedas

agni — fire; the deity of fire

ajāti — birthlessness

akṣara — imperishable

antaryāmin — inner controller

apauruṣeya — having no human author

āpta-kāma — satisfied

apūrva — moral retribution; *karma*

ātman — the Self

avatāra — incarnation of God

bauddha — Buddhist

bhāva — being; entity

bhāṣya — commentary

bīja — seed; cause

brahman — the Absolute

brāhmaṇas — the second part of the Vedic literature

caturtha — the fourth, absolute state of the Self

caitanya — consciousness

citta — mind

deva	a god or effulgent being; God
dharma	religion, religious duty, teaching; in later Buddhism the term also refers to a quality, regarded as a substanceless, purely phenomenal "point instant"
dravya	substance
dvaita	duality
dvaitin	dualist
guru	teacher
hetu	cause; reason
īśvara	God
jāgarita(-sthāna)	the waking state (Māṇḍūkya)
jīva	individual, conditioned, finite self; sentient being
jñāna	knowledge; wisdom
-kāra	author, creator, maker; as in *kārikā-kāra*, the author of a verse, or *bhāṣya-kāra*, the author of a commentary
kāraṇa	cause
kārikā	verse
karma	action, activity; moral retribution
kārya	effect
krīḍā	play, sport
līlā	play, sport
Madhyamaka	another name for the Śūnyavāda of the Mahāyāna
manas	mind
mantra	prose sentence; mystic saying
mātrā	element; phoneme; letter; sound

māyā	illusion
mokṣa	liberation; *nirvāṇa*
nyāya	maxim; reasoning
para-brahman	*brahman*; "great *brahman*"
parama-guru	supreme *guru*; the *guru* of one's *guru*
paramātman	the supreme Self; God
parameśvara	the supreme god; God
pariṇāma-vāda	the doctrine that the effect is merely a transformation or modification of the underlying cause
phala	effect
pradhāna	the subtle matter of the Sāṃkhya system
prājña	the sleeping state (ĀP)
prakaraṇa	treatise, chapter
prakṛti	nature
pralaya	cosmic dissolution
prāṇa	breath; the vital force
praṇava	the mystic syllable *Aum*
prapañca	phenomenal world
prapañcopaśama	the cessation or quiescence of the phenomenal world
pratītya-samutpāda	the Buddhist doctrine of dependent co-origination
purāṇas	a body of literature consisting of myths, legends and history
pūrvapakṣin	philosophical opponent
śabda-brahman	*brahman* as the essence of sound or speech
sādhya	the proposition to be proven

śakti	power, force, energy
samādhi	state of realization
saṃhitās	the first part of the Vedic literature, consisting of hymns
saṃpradāya	school, tradition, lineage of teachers
saṃsāra	the world of birth and death; suffering; rebirth
sarveśvara	the lord of all; God
śāśvata	eternal
satkārya-vāda	the doctrine that the cause is the effect (see *pariṇāma-vāda*)
siddhānta	the correct view or doctrine; the view to be defended or established
skandha	heap, set, aggregate; in Buddhism a set or aggregate of *dharmas*
śloka	verse
smṛtis	authoritative religious writings; unlike *śruti*, it is held to have a human author
śruti	scripture; divine revelation
Śuddhādvaita	the "pure nondualism" (Vallabhācārya) school of the Vedānta
śūnya	empty
śūnyatā	emptiness
suṣupta(-sthāna)	the deep sleep state (Māṇḍūkya)
sūtra	an aphoristic statement of doctrine in religious, philosophical, and scientific literature
svabhāva	self-nature
svapna	dream; sometimes sleep generally
svapna(-sthāna)	the dreaming state (Māṇḍūkya)

svarūpa	essence, self-nature
taijasa	brilliant; the dreaming state (ĀP)
tattva	reality; category
tṛtīya	the third, or deep sleep, state of the Self (Māṇḍūkya)
turīya, turya	fourth state of the Self (ĀŚ)
uccheda	annihilation; annihilationist
vāda	doctrine, as in *māyā-vāda*, *śūnya-vāda*
-vādin	holder of a doctrine, as in *māyā-vādin*, *śūnya-vādin*
Vaiṣṇava	a devotee of the god Viṣṇu
vaiśvānara	waking state (Māṇḍ.)
vastu	entity, thing, object
vijñāna	mind
vijñāna-vāda	the idealist school of Mahāyāna Buddhism
vijñapti-mātratā	the Buddhist doctrine of mind- or consciousness-only
vikalpa	imagination
viparyāsa	error
Viśiṣṭādvaita	the Vedantic school of qualified nondualism
virāj	the universal, all-pervading Self; the world-soul
viśva	the world; the waking state (ĀP)
vivarta-vāda	the doctrine that the effect is an illusory superimposition on the cause

BIBLIOGRAPHY

ABBREVIATIONS

ABORI	*Annals of the Bhandarkar Oriental Research Institute*
AL(B)	*Adyar Library (Bulletin)*
ASS	*Ānandāśrama Sanskrit Series*
BEHE	*Bibliothèque de l'École des Hautes Études*
BI	*Bibliotheca Indica*
BORI	*Bhandarkar Oriental Research Institute*
BSPS	*Bombay Sanskrit and Prakrit Series*
BST	*Buddhist Sanskrit Texts*
CSS	*Chowkhambā Sanskrit Series*
EIP	*Encyclopedia of Indian Philosophies*
GOS	*Gaekwad's Oriental Series*
IHQ	*Indian Historical Quarterly*
IA	*Indian Antiquary*
IIJ	*Indo-Iranian Journal*
IS	*Indische Studien*
ISt	*Indiske Studier*
JAOS	*Journal of the American Oriental Society*
JIH	*Journal of Indian History*
JIP	*Journal of Indian Philosophy*
JRAS	*Journal of the Royal Asiatic Society*
NIA	*New Indian Antiquary*
PAIOC	*Proceedings of the All-India Oriental Conference*
PEW	*Philosophy East and West*
PO	*Poona Orientalist*
RPR	*Review of Philosophy and Religion*
SBH	*Sacred Books of the Hindus*

ZDMG	*Zeitschrift der Deutschen Morgenländischen Gesellschaft*
WZKSOA	*Wiener Zeitschrift für die Kunde Süd- und Ostasiens*

BIBLIOGRAPHY

Sagauḍapādīyakārikātharvavedīyamāṇḍūkyopaniṣat, ānandagirikṛtaṭīkāsaṃvalita śāṃkarabhāṣyasametā. A. Kathavate, ed. (*ASS* 10, 1977)

***

Aṣṭasāhasrikāprajñāpāramitāsūtra. Rajendralal Mitra, ed. *BI* 110, 1888. Abbreviated English translation in E. Conze, *The Perfection of Wisdom in Eight Thousand Lines and Its Verse Summary*. (San Francisco, 1973)

Saddharmalaṅkāvatārasūtram. P. L. Vaidya, ed. (*BST*, Darbhanga, 1963)

Nṛsiṃhatāpanīyopaniṣat (Pūrva and Uttara) with the Bhāṣya by Śaṃkarācārya and the Dīpikā of Vidyāraṇya on the Uttara Tāpanīya. (*ASS* 30, 1895)

***

Aiyar, K. Nārāyaṇasvāmī (1980), tr. *Thirty Minor Upanishads*. (El Reno, Oklahoma)

Balasubramaniam, R. (1962). "Identity of Maṇḍanamiśra." *JAOS* 82: 522-532.

Bhāskara. Brahmasūtrabhāṣya. V. P. Dvivedin, ed. (*CSS* 1915, Nos. 70, 185, 209)

Bhattacharya, V.

(1925) "The Māṇḍūkya Upaniṣad and the Gauḍapāda Kārikās." *IHQ* 1: 119-125, 295-302.

(1938) "Gauḍapāda." *IHQ* 14: 392-397.

(1943) *The Āgamaśāstra of Gauḍapāda*. (Calcutta)

Biderman, Shlomo (1978). "Śaṅkara and the Buddhists." *JIP* 6: 405-414.

Burridge, L. (1973). "A Discrepancy between a Bibliotheca Indica Edition and Its Manuscript." *ABORI* 54: 248-249.

Cardona, George (1976). *Pāṇini: A Survey of Research*. (The Hague-Paris)

Chintāmani, T. R. (1924). "Śaṅkara — The Commentator on the Māṇḍūkya Kārikās." *PAIOC* 3: 419-425.

Conio, Caterina (1971). *The Philosophy of Māṇḍūkya Kārikā*. (Vārāṇasī)

de La Vallée Poussin, L. (1910). "Vedanta and Buddhism." *JRAS*: 129-140.

Dasgupta, Surendranath (1922). Vol I. *A History of Indian Philosophy*. (Cambridge)

Deussen, P.

(1906) *The Philosophy of the Upanishads*. (Edinburgh)

(1963) *Sechzig Upanishaden des Veda* (Darmstadt). English translation in *Sixty Upanishads of the Veda*, trans. by V. M. Bedekar and G. B. Palsule (Delhi, 1980).

Dignāga. Ālambanaparīkṣā and Vṛtti, with the commentary of Dharmapāla and copious notes from Vinītadeva's commentary. N. Aiyaswami Sastri, ed/tr. (Adyar, 1942)

Ensinck, J. and P. Gaeffke, eds. (1972). *India maior: Congratulatory volume presented to J. Gonda*. (Leiden)

Ghate, V. S. (1926). *The Vedānta*. (*BORI*, Poona)

Gokhale, V. V.

(1958) "The Vedānta-Philosophy Described by Bhavya in His *Madhyamakahṛdaya*." *IIJ* 2: 165-80.

(1962) "Masters of Buddhism Adore the Brahman through Non-Adoration" (Bhavya, *Madhyamakahṛdaya*, III). *IIJ* 5: 271-275.

Hacker, Paul

(1947) "Śaṅkarācārya and Śaṅkarabhagavatpāda." *NIA* 9: 175-186.

(1951) "Eigentümlichkeiten der Lehre und Terminologie Śaṅkaras: Avidyā, Nāmarūpa, Māyā, Īśvara." *ZDMG* 100: 246-286.

(1968-69) "Śaṃkara der Yogin und Śaṃkara der Advaitin. Einige Beobachtungen." *WZKSOA* 12-13: 119-148.

(1972) "Notes on the Māṇḍūkyopaniṣad and Śaṅkara's Āgamaśāstravivaraṇa." In *India Maior*, edited by J. Ensink and P. Gaeffke, pp. 115-132.

Hakeda, Y. S. (1967). *The Awakening of Faith*. (New York)

Hiriyanna, M.

(1923-24) "Sureśvara and Maṇḍanamiśra." *JRAS* (1923) 259-263; (1924) 96-97.

(1926) "The First Commentary on the Mahābhāṣya." IHQ: 415-416.

Hume, R. E., tr. (1983). *The Thirteen Principal Upanishads*. Second edition, revised. (Delhi)

Ingalls, Daniel H. H.

(1952) "The Study of Śaṃkarācārya." *ABORI* 23: 1-14.

(1953) "Śaṃkara on the Question: Whose is *avidyā*?" *PEW* 3: 69-72.

(1954) "Śaṃkara's Arguments Against the Buddhists." *PEW*: 291-306.

(1967) "Bhāskara the Vedāntin." *PEW* 17: 61-88.

Jacob, G. A. (1886). "The Nrsimhatapaniya-Upanishad." *IA* 15: 69-74.

Jacobi, H. (1913). "On *Māyāvāda*." *JAOS* 33: 51-54.

Joshi, R. B. (1959). "The origin of *māyā* in Śaṃkara's philosophy." *JIH* 37: 179-200, 289-311.

Kaplan, Stephen (1983). "A Critique of an Ontological Approach to Gauḍapāda's Māṇḍūkya Kārikās." *JIP* 11: 339-355.

Karmarkar, R. D. (1953). *Gauḍapāda-Kārikā*. (*BORI*, Poona)

Kūranārāyaṇa. Māṇḍūkyopaniṣadprakāśikā. V. N. Krishnamacharya, ed. (*ASS* 62, 1912-13)

Lindtner, C. (1982). *Nagarjuniana*. *ISt* IV. (Copenhagen)

Mādhava-Vidyāraṇya. Śrīvidyāraṇya-viracitaḥ śrīmac-chaṃkara-dig-vijayaḥ. (*ASS* 22: 1915)

Madhva. Māṇḍuka Upaniṣad Bhāṣya. S. C. Vasu, tr. (*SBH* 1, Allahabad, 1909)

Mahadevan, T. M. P. (1975). *Gauḍapāda: A Study in Early Advaita*. (Madras)

Maṇḍanamiśra. Brahmasiddhi with Śaṅkhapāṇi's Vyākhyā. S. Kuppuswami Sastri, ed., with a Foreword by P. P. Subrahmanya Sastri. (Delhi, 1984)

Mayeda, S. (1967-68). "On the Author of the *Māṇḍūkyopaniṣad*- and the *Gauḍapādīya-bhāṣya*." *ALB* 31-32: 73-94.

Monier-Williams (1970). *A Sanskrit-English Dictionary*. (Delhi)

Murti, T. R. V. (1955). *The Central Philosophy of Buddhism*. (London)

Nāgārjuna. Madhyamakaśāstram with the Prasannapadā of Candrakīrti. Dvārikādāsa Śāstrī, ed. (Vārāṇasī, 1983)

Nakamura, H. (1983). *A History of Early Vedānta Philosophy*. Part I. (Delhi)

Nikhilānanda, Swāmī, tr. *The Māṇḍūkyopaniṣad with Gauḍapāda's Kārikā and Śaṅkara's Commentary*. (Mysore, 1974)

Pandey, S. L. (1974). *Pre-Śaṃkara Advaita Philosophy*. (Allahabad)

Pansikar, Wasudev Laxman Shastri, ed. (1913). *One Hundred and Eight Upanishads*. (Bombay)

Potter, Karl

(1980) "Was Gauḍapāda an Idealist?" in M. Nagatomi, B. K. Matilal, J. M. Masson, and E. Dimock (eds.), *Sanskrit and Indian Studies*. (Boston)

(1981) "Gauḍapāda." In *EIP: Advaita Vedānta up to Śaṃkara and His Pupils*, ed. by Karl H. Potter. (Princeton)

(1983) *EIP*, Vol. I, *Bibliography* (Revised Edition), ed. by Karl H. Potter. (Delhi)

Radhakrishnan, S.

(1960) *The Brahma Sūtra*. (London)

(1974) The *Principal Upanishads*. (London)

Rāmānuja. Srībhāṣyam. U.Vīrarāghavācārya, ed. (Madras, 1963)

Ranade, R. D. (1926). *A Constructive Survey of Upanishadic Philosophy*. (Poona)

Ray, Amarnath (1931). "A Note on Sureśvara and Maṇḍana Misra." *IHQ* 7: 632.

Roy, B. A. N. (1938). "The Māṇḍūkya Upaniṣad and the *kārikās* of Gauḍapāda." *IHQ* 14: 564-569.

Ruegg, D. S. (1969). *La theorie du tathāgatagarbha et du gotra*. (Paris)

Russell, Bertrand (1948). *Human Knowledge: Its Scope and Limits*. (New York)

Śaṃkara

Bṛhadāraṇyakopaniṣadbhāṣya with Ānandagiri's Ṭīkā (*ASS* 15, 1902)

Brahmasūtrabhāṣya with Ānandagiri's Nyāyanirṇaya. H. N. Apte, ed. (*ASS* 21, 1903)

Bhagavadgītābhāṣya, with Ānandagiri's Vivaraṇa. K. S. Agase, ed. (*ASS* 34: 1908)

Chāndogyopaniṣadbhāṣya with Ānandagiri's Ṭīkā (*ASS* 14, 1913). English translation by Ganganatha Jha (Poona, Madras, 1899).

Nṛsinha Tāpanī with the commentary of Śankara Āchārya. Rāmamaya Tarkaratna, ed. (*BI* 70, 1871)

Upadeśasāhasrī. Swāmī Jagadānanda, ed/tr. (Madras, 1979)

Śāntarakṣita. Tattvasaṃgraha with the Pañjikā of Kamalaśīla. E. Krishnamacharya, ed. (*GOS* 30-31, 1926)

Śāntideva. Śikṣāsamuccaya. P. L. Vaidya, ed. (Darbhanga, 1961)

Sarma, Y. Subrahmanya (1933). "The Upaniṣadic Theory of the Gauḍapāda-kārikās." *RPR* 4.2: 196-204.

Sastri, S. Kuppuswami (1936-37). "Maṇḍana-Sureśvara equation in the history of Advaita." *ABORI* 18: 121-157.

Sharma, B. N. K.

(1931-33) "New light on the Gauḍapāda *kārikās*." *RPR* 2.1 (1931): 35-36; 3.1 (1932): 45-55; 4.2 (1933): 174-195.

(1933) "Still further light on the Gauḍapāda-*kārikās*." *RPR* 4.2: 1-22.

(1936-37) "The Upaniṣadic Theory of the Gauḍapāda *Kārikās* —A Rejoinder." *PO* 1.2: 27-38.

(1937-38) "Are the Gauḍapāda Kārikās *śruti* — A Rejoinder." *PO* 2.1: 20-30.

Shastri, J. L., ed. (1970). *Upaniṣatsaṃgraha*. (Delhi)

Siegel, Lee (1978). *Sacred and Profane Dimensions of Love in Indian Traditions as Exemplified in the* Gītagovinda *of Jayadeva*. (Delhi)

Sureśvara

Bṛhadāraṇyakopaniṣadbhāṣyavārtikam with Ānandagiri's Śāstraprakāśikā. K. S. Agase, ed. (*ASS* 16, 1892)

Naiṣkarmyasiddhi with Jñānottama's Candrikā. Revised edition by M. Hiriyanna. (*BSPS* 38, 1980, Fourth Edition)

Takasaki, J. (1966). *A Study on the Ratnagotravibhāga*. (*SOR* 33)

Upaniṣadbrahmayogin. Nṛsiṃhapūrvatāpinyupaniṣad, with the commentary of Śrī Upaniṣadbrahmayogin. Vaiṣṇava-upaniṣads. (Madras, 1923)

Vasubandhu. Vijñaptimātratāsiddhi: Viṃśatikā et Triṃśikā. S. Lévi, ed. (*BEHE*, 1925)

Venkatasubbiah, A.

(1933) "The Māṇḍūkyopaniṣad and Gauḍapāda." *IA* 62: 181-193.

(1935) "On Gauḍapāda's Āgamaśāstra." *IHQ* 11: 783-790.

(1936-37) "Are the Gauḍapāda-Kārikās *śruti*?" *PO* 1.1: 7-18; 2: 2-12.

Vetter, Tilmann

(1968-69) "Zur Bedeutung des Illusionismus bei Śaṅkara." *WZKSOA* 12-13: 407-423.

(1978) "Die Gauḍapādīya-kārikās: Zur Entstehung und zur Bedeutung von (A)dvaita." *WZKSOA* 22: 95-131.

(1979) *Studien zur Lehre und Entwicklung Śaṅkaras*. (Wien)

Walleser, M. (1910). *Der ältere Vedānta*. (Heidelberg)

Wayman, Alex and Hideko, trs. (1974). *The Lion's Roar of Queen Śrīmālā*. (Śrīmālādevīsūtra) (New York)

Weber, A.

(1864) *Die Rāma-Tāpanīya-Upaniṣad.* (Berlin)

(1865) "Analyse der in Anquetil du Perron's Uebersetzung enthaltenen Upanishad. (Fortsetzung und Schlufs.) Vom Herausgeber." Nṛisiṅha-Tāpanīya-Upanishad, pp. 53-173. *IS* 9.

Whaling, Frank (1979). "Śaṃkara and Buddhism." *JIP* 7: 1-42.

INDEX